ACCLAIM FOR BODIE AND BROCK THOENE

"Jesus is refreshingly portrayed as divine yet human, making him accessible on a personal level that will leave him on readers' minds long after the book is closed."

—*ROMANTIC TIMES*, 4-STAR REVIEW OF *TAKE THIS CUP*

"A gentle, message-driven story of Jesus' final days."

—*BOOKLIST* REVIEW OF *TAKE THIS CUP*

"The Thoenes begin their Jerusalem Chronicles rooted in the secrets of the Old Testament. Readers will have a better understanding of the Bible and why Jesus did what he did."

—*ROMANTIC TIMES*, 4-STAR REVIEW OF *WHEN JESUS WEPT*

"These authors bring the scriptures to life with true-to-life character-izations, dialogue, and settings that enable readers to visualize and feel connected to distant times, peoples, and events. It's not a book to miss. If you aren't already fans of the Thoenes' writings you will be after reading this book and will understand why they have earned eight ECPA Gold Medallion Awards."

—*EXAMINER.COM* REVIEW OF *WHEN JESUS WEPT*

"Page-turning . . . Set against the political and religious turmoil of the times, the Thoenes' story vividly reimagines the evolving friendship between Jesus and Lazarus."

—*PUBLISHERS WEEKLY* ON *WHEN JESUS WEPT*

Behold the Man

BODIE & BROCK THOENE

Behold the Man

Jerusalem Chronicles, Book Three

ZONDERVAN

Behold the Man
Copyright © 2015 by Bodie Thoene and Brock Thoene

This title is also available as a Zondervan ebook.
Visit www.zondervan.com/ebooks.

This title is also available in a Zondervan audio edition.
Visit www.zondervan.fm.

Requests for information should be addressed to:

Zondervan, *Grand Rapids, Michigan 49530*

ISBN: 978-0-310-33604-4 (Library Edition)

Library of Congress Cataloging-in-Publication Data

Names: Thoene, Bodie, 1951- | Thoene, Brock, 1952- author.
Title: Behold the man / Bodie and Brock Thoene.
Description: Nashville : Zondervan, 2016. | Series: The Jerusalem chronicles
; 3
Identifiers: LCCN 2015036778 | ISBN 9780310336044 (hardcover)
Subjects: LCSH: Jesus Christ--Fiction. | Pilate, Pontius, active 1st
century--Fiction. | Procula, Claudia--Fiction. | Bible. New
Testament--History of Biblical events--Fiction. | GSAFD: Christian
fiction. | Historical fiction. | Bible fiction.
Classification: LCC PS3570.H46 B44 2016 | DDC 813/.54--dc23 LC record available at http://
lccn.loc.gov/2015036778

All Scripture quotations, unless otherwise indicated, are taken from the Holy Bible, New
International Version®, NIV®. Copyright © 1973, 1978, 1984, 2011 by Biblica, Inc.™ Used by
permission of Zondervan. All rights reserved worldwide. www.zondervan.com. The "NIV"and
"New International Version" are trademarks registered in the United States Patent and
Trademark Office by Biblica, Inc.™

Scripture quotations marked KJV are taken from the King James Version of the Bible.

Scripture quotations marked NASB are taken from the New American Standard Bible®,
Copyright © 1960, 1962, 1963, 1968, 1971, 1972, 1973, 1975, 1977, 1995 by The Lockman
Foundation. Used by permission. (www.Lockman.org)

Scripture quotations marked NKJV are taken from the New King James Version®. Copyright ©
1982 by Thomas Nelson. Used by permission. All rights reserved.

Note: The format and spellings of some Scripture passages have been changed for general
consistency.

Any Internet addresses (websites, blogs, etc.) and telephone numbers printed in this book are
offered as a resource. They are not intended in any way to be or imply an endorsement by
Zondervan, nor does Zondervan vouch for the content of these sites and numbers for the life of
this book.

Cover design: Kirk DouPonce
Cover illustration: Robin Hanley
Interior illustration: Ruth Pettis
Interior design: Katherine Lloyd, The DESK
Editing: Ramona Cramer Tucker, Amanda Bostic

Printed in the United States of America

HB 12.21.2017

For my parents, Tom and Bettie Turner, who truly modeled their faith and love and righteous joy in the Lord, for my life. Psalm 91!

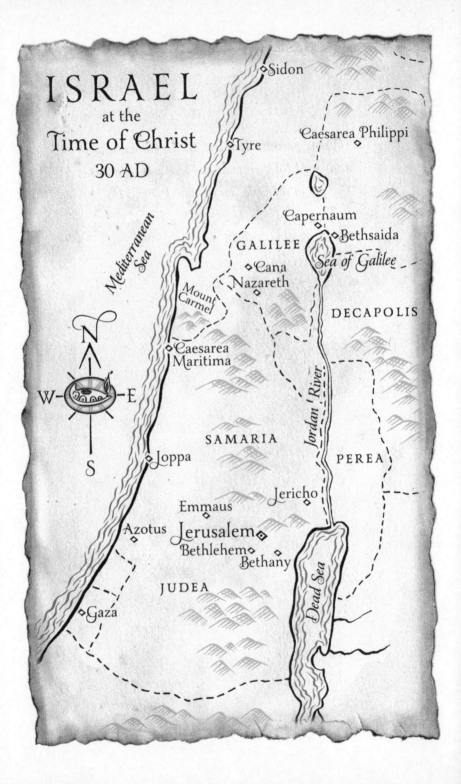

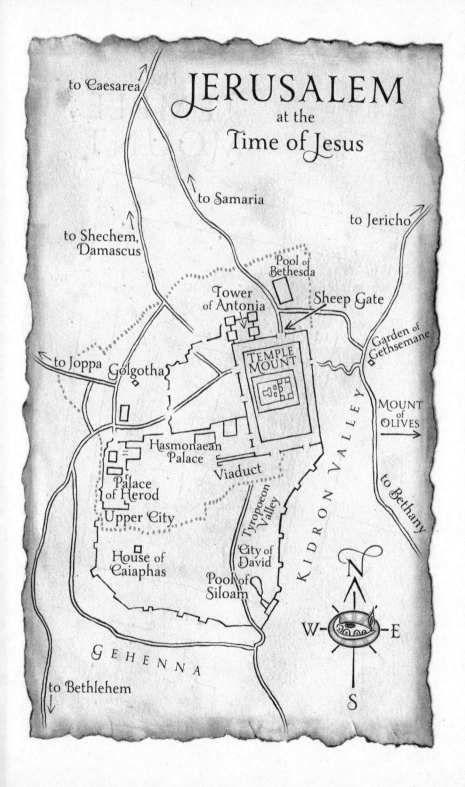

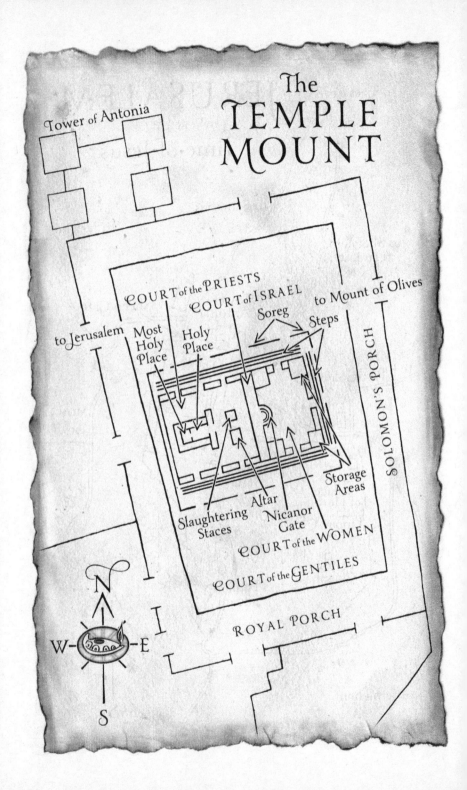

The TEMPLE MOUNT

Tower of Antonia

to Jerusalem

COURT of the PRIESTS

COURT of ISRAEL

to Mount of Olives

Soreg

Steps

Most Holy Place

Holy Place

SOLOMON'S PORCH

Slaughtering Staces

Altar

Nicanor Gate

Storage Areas

COURT of the WOMEN

COURT of the GENTILES

ROYAL PORCH

N
W — E
S

Part One

Where then is my hope—who can see any hope for me?

JOB 17:15

Chapter 1

*I*t was market day in the open square beneath the Roman Senate and the temples of the gods. The stalls and shops of the Forum Romanum were packed with citizens of Rome. Clothed in hues of yellow, blue, and rusty red, the buyers and sellers seemed to be a human flower garden swaying in the wind.

The crippled eight-year-old boy, wooden sword in his belt, bobbed above the crowd as he rode high upon the shoulders of the Ethiopian slave named Jono. Small hands were clasped on the ebony giant's forehead.

The boy drew his sword and raised it to point at arches, porticos, and pillars. "Jono, my trusty warhorse, we must be ready to fight! Cherusci warriors hide among the trees!"

The child's name was Philo, which meant "love." He was the grandson of Tiberius Caesar by his illegitimate daughter Claudia. So Philo was descended from a shopgirl and the emperor of Rome. His roots had sprung from the common folk. Because of this, the boy captured the people's interest and affection.

Philo was also much beloved by his mother. Claudia, a

red-haired beauty, had the cheerful humor of her mother and the education of her royal father. It was whispered among the nobles that Claudia was the only worthwhile thing to come forth from the corrupt tyrant.

At the age of eighteen, Claudia had fallen in love with a commoner and thought to run away with him . . . far away. They would live a peasant's life in Gaul, perhaps. But Caesar had discovered her plot and married her off to Pontius Pilate, an ambitious member of the equestrian class. Philo's birth had followed soon thereafter.

This afternoon, shoppers waved at Philo as the cavalcade passed. Heads tipped together. Lips murmured inside cupped hands. Curious eyes followed as the tale of the common-born mistress and the illegitimate daughter was repeated. Old scandal became the new entertainment of the day.

Claudia peered out at her son through the curtains of her sedan chair.

Jono hefted Philo higher upon broad shoulders as Claudia's retinue of porters and bodyguards wove through the crush.

As they neared the seller of spices, she called, "Come, Philo, ride inside with me, where it's safe."

Philo surveyed the temples and bustling market stalls. "Please, Mother! Soldiers do not ride in sedan chairs. Father is at the wars fighting. I want to ride my horse too." He patted Jono's head. "Steady, Jono, old boy. There are Cherusci bandits lurking in the wood."

Jono grinned and obligingly pranced and whinnied.

Claudia asked, "Is he all right up there, Jono?"

In a deep, rumbling voice, Jono answered, "Yes, my lady. I am too large a horse for any barbarians to attack. Philo is well out of reach from harm." Kind brown eyes gazed at her. "It is a good thing for the young master to ride upon his horse and guard his mother."

Philo had been born with a clubfoot. The midwives suggested to Pilate such an embarrassment could be easily snuffed out. Claudia heard their whispered conspiracy and, like a lioness, rose up from her bed and fought for her baby's life.

Though Pilate was ashamed of his son, Claudia became Philo's champion. He had the best tutors. He could read both Latin and Greek. Mathematics came easily to him. Daily classes included art and music.

Twice Philo had played his lute for his aging grand-father. Caesar pronounced his grandson clever and talented, though he could not walk without crutches.

All Philo wanted, truly, was to be a soldier like his father. Now that Pilate had gone north to conquer the last wild enemies of Rome, Philo considered himself Claudia's protector.

The great capital of the Empire was a pit of violence, corruption, and political intrigue. Claudia wanted only to raise her son in the vineyard country house of her husband's Ponti estate.

She did not look forward to this unexpected meeting with her father.

Black-cloaked Praetorian guards surrounded the palace.

A centurion met Claudia and escorted her in. The window-less great hall was as dark as a cavern. Without being told that his noisy play must cease, Philo shivered, tucked away his weapon, and clung even more tightly to Jono's neck.

Lucius Sejanus, head of the Imperial guard, emerged from an inner recess. The smile he offered never reached his eyes. "Ah, Lady Claudia. Prompt as always, I see. Your father is waiting for you."

Two steps forward and Sejanus held up his hand. "Let the slave and the boy remain here." It was an order.

Claudia got a quick, fearful nod of agreement from her son.

Sejanus led her to the door, flung it aside, and remained outside as she entered. The door slammed shut behind her. She was alone with the great man.

The office chamber occupied by Tiberius was filled with maps. A mahogany table in the center of the room spilled parchments etched with mountain ranges, rivers, and forests onto the marble floor. The Roman emperor, a tall, gray-haired man with a hawk-like nose and piercing gray eyes, raised his head and peered nearsightedly as if he did not recognize his daughter.

Tiberius let his gaze remain too long on her face. He drank her in. "So . . . you. In the flesh, still beautiful . . . more beautiful than before."

Claudia lowered her gaze. "My father."

He frowned. "Ah, yes. Claudia. Her daughter. You are so like her. For a moment I thought your mother had returned from the grave."

"If only she would."

"I dreamed of her last night. Your mother . . . my Sarah of the wine merchant. My first love. My beautiful Sarah, my Hebrew mistress . . ." His eyes again grew misty.

"She came to you in a dream?"

"And across a wide gulf she commanded that I bring you and the boy here to the palace."

"Did she give a reason?"

"No. I thought perhaps her Jewish God had revealed something . . . regarding me. Or regarding you. Or your husband. Or the child. But she did not tell me why she came. Only commanded that I remember in all that you are my daughter."

Claudia stood in silence. The fact of Tiberius's paternity brought her no joy. In a world where politics was the true religion of the Empire, there was always danger in this relationship, no matter how distant she was from court.

"So here you are."

"Was she . . . happy, Father?"

"Your mother, long dead to me and to you, seems to have found some other kingdom to dwell in. And she is concerned that you and the boy are safe. Protected from my disapproval." Tiberius shrugged. "I will not argue with the dead."

"Disapproval? Of what?"

Summoning her forward, Tiberius impatiently swept aside a heap of charts, then jabbed his thumb downward at the one he sought. "There. Latest news. A decisive battle is expected there soon. Your husband"—Tiberius spat the word with some disdain—"has been given an important task. He may attain some glory from it, or he may get killed. Either way, your lot will improve." Tiberius shrugged again. "You know how Rome is. Thought you should be warned so you don't hear it first from a fishmonger."

"Yes, thank you." Claudia dipped her head.

"He hasn't been much of a husband, but then he isn't much of a man, either." Softening his voice only slightly, the emperor offered, "Want to move into the palace? You and the boy? If things go badly, there may be riots."

"I . . . no . . . thank you. We are fine at home." Life in the palace in Rome was not as depraved as when the emperor vacationed on Capri, but she would never willingly bring Philo into the court.

"Well enough." Tiberius's finger started to trace a wavy blue line on the parchment, and his attention followed. "Let Sejanus know if you need anything."

Claudia shivered when the Praetorian commander's eyes lingered on her as she exited the office chamber. She was grateful when she, Philo, and Jono were once more in the bright sunshine. Even then they were halfway home before she felt warm again.

∽◌∾

The world was mottled in shades of dark green and drab brown. Overhead, sunlight flickered through the leafy canopy, but none of it reached the roots of the massive trees. The forest the Cherusci called home lay shrouded in darkness, even at midday.

Here on the far northern boundary of the Roman Empire, it was late autumn. Unseen, robins called to each other in muted song. A black woodpecker hammered out a rhythmic clatter, then fell silent.

More silent than the birds, silent as the shadows, a hundred Cherusci warriors lurked unseen beside a narrow trail. Their hair was wild and matted. Twigs and leaves stuck from wiry beards until the fighters appeared no more than spindly bushes . . . armed with axes, bows, and spears.

They waited for the right moment to spring their trap for the next Roman intruders.

∽◦∾

Pontius Pilate, seated on a gray horse, glanced up as a pair of starlings flitted back and forth across the muddy track. The sable-colored birds did not brighten the somber scene.

The distant echoing thump of drums pulsed in unison with the hobnailed tread of a Roman legion. Pilate's Roman cavalry troopers awaited orders. "Come on, then," Pilate urged. "Don't you hear it? The army is already on the march."

"Your pardon, Tribune," the returning scout cautioned. "The storm, sir. A tree down. The path of the stream altered, washing out the road."

"The route is . . ."

"Blocked, sir," the scout reported.

"Then we go around!" Pilate gestured with a silver-handled whip. "That is another trail, yes?"

A Praetorian officer, the leader of Pilate's bodyguard,

spoke up. "Tribune Pilate, General Severus ordered us to avoid Cherusci territory. No skirmishes that would delay our mission."

"We must not be delayed, sir," a second Praetorian emphasized. "Centurion Marcus Longinus and our brothers hold the front line. Alone."

"We backtrack to the planned alternate route," the first suggested.

Pilate protested, "When the main battle is about to be joined? When an hour could decide everything? Remember, without blood there is no glory."

A grizzled trooper several yards away muttered to his comrade, "As always, our blood, his glory," but Pilate decided to ignore the treasonous words . . . for now. Greater events were in play.

"The shorter route," Pilate commanded. "Now." Then in a concession to caution, he grudgingly added, "Send out four scouts. We'll move carefully, but with speed!"

The subordinate officers exchanged grim looks but thumped their chests in salute. There could be no other response to a command from Caesar's son-in-law.

The chosen path was only barely shoulder-width across. The column of four changed to single file. The distance between the mounted men increased when Pilate impatiently trotted ahead of the rest.

The trail dwindled further. At first aiming northeast, it doubled back on itself, then ascended a rocky knoll. Underfoot the surface changed from clay to gravel. As it grew steeper, hooves scrabbled for purchase. Heavily armed troopers leaned forward over the withers of their mounts. A towering oak on the crest of the hill was home to a flock of croaking ravens. Past the tree the road's direction changed again, dipping into a narrow defile.

"Where are those scouts?" Pilate scowled. "They should have reported in by now."

Two miles into the scarcely passable forest, the column was strung out over a half mile of narrow gorge. With barely room to turn, each man could view his comrades immediately before and behind, but no others. A pair of ravens rasped at each other from opposite sides of the ravine.

Just as the last trooper passed the summit of the knoll, the oak shuddered and toppled sideways. Gaining momentum and noise, the giant tree crashed into and crushed three more trees as it thundered across the trail, blocking it completely.

The echoes of the shattering oak had not died away before being replaced with the whistle of slingstones. Faces streaked with black grease and eyes wide with murderous intent, Cherusci warriors appeared from behind every boulder and stump, like demons emerging from the pit itself.

A dozen Romans, struck by that many fist-sized rocks apiece, toppled from their saddles. Cherusci axes chopped down screaming men and horses alike.

A black-fletched arrow zipped within an inch of Pilate's nose. Struck on the haunch by a stone, his horse reared and plunged, threatening to unseat him.

"Turn! Turn and fight!" he ordered. But how? Short

swords and lances were of no use against arrows and rocks that buzzed like angry hornets.

"Flee, Tribune," the chief bodyguard shouted. "Ride for your life!"

Confronted by an ax-wielding giant of a barbarian, Pilate's gray stallion launched into parade ground canter. Front hooves churned with fury, and the horse knocked the Cherusci warrior aside.

A stone from a sling grazed Pilate's forehead, bloodying him. Another struck squarely in the back of his helmet. The protective gear saved his life, but the blow left him dazed while the horse carried him out of the battle.

An arrow struck and lodged in the mount's right hind leg. A Cherusci spear, flung from atop a fallen tree, wounded the horse near the same spot. Bleeding profusely, the gray never slowed until facing the climb up another hill. There it pulled up lame.

Looking over his shoulder in terror, Pilate beat the horse with his braided whip, demanding, "Keep going! Go!"

Behind him the noises of battle still raged. Shrieks of pain from barbarian throats proved the legionaries were giving a good account of themselves. Pilate dismissed the thought he should return to the fight.

At the top of the next hill, where the path at last snaked out of the canyon, loomed a pair of standing stones. They flanked the trail like a triumphal arch honoring his escape. Pilate once more demanded the horse continue moving and, haltingly, it obliged.

Coming abreast of the boulders, Pilate congratulated

himself on pushing through to safety. He was relaxed in the saddle when another pair of warriors leapt at him from either side and brought him crashing heavily to the ground.

Hands tied behind his back, Pilate was led with a noose around his neck to the Cherusci chieftain.

"Can we kill him now?" one of the young warriors inquired.

"Cut his throat?" the other suggested.

The chieftain backhanded one, and the other ducked out of reach. "This one's worth more alive. See the silver buckles on his uniform? Ransom we'll get for such a one."

"That's right, ransom," Pilate hurriedly agreed.

The barbarian cuffed Pilate into silence. Peering more closely, he roughly wiped the blood from Pilate's face. "I know this man. Kin to Caesar himself. Take him to my tent and tie him up."

Chapter 2

*I*t was near dusk. A vast, undulating cloud of starlings swept across the skies above the Ponti vineyards. The flock emitted high-pitched screeches like the ungreased wheels of a line of carts.

Claudia and Philo sat together on the balcony and watched the millions fly in perfect formation, creating rapidly shifting patterns of spirals and whorls.

"Look, Mother, there is a helix! How do starlings know geometry?"

"The superstitious believe the birds are messengers flying with news of the wars to Rome. The priests and oracles of the Roman gods claim the starlings are inscribing prophecy in the skies."

"And they know Greek." Philo pointed upward. "Look, Mother—the letter Omega."

The dusky ghost of the symbol for infinity formed for an instant against the sky, then shattered.

"Tonight Caesar will gather all his prophets at the palace to recite what omen the starlings have brought to him."

"Omens only for Tiberius, Mother? Or for Rome?"

She sighed. "For good or ill, your grandfather is Rome. Caesar believes his gods will send no word to anyone that is more important than what the starlings write to Rome."

A black spiral rose like a whirlwind, then collapsed in on itself, reappearing as a wineskin turned inside out.

"What do you think it means?" the boy pondered. Two clouds of winged creatures merged and mingled before separating again, like the flames of twin wicks dancing in a breeze. "It is as though they battle to conquer the sky."

Claudia shielded her eyes as a ray of sunlight pierced the dark mass like a roaring flame. She did not speak, but her imagination flew to a battlefield . . .

∽∾∾

Spiraling smoke from the watch fires drifted up into the autumn sky. Riding the same currents, vultures completed lazy circles, drawing Centurion Marcus Longinus's attention down toward the unburied corpses littering the battlefield. Rows of sharpened stakes patrolled by watchful sentries kept the Cherusci at bay . . . so far. Supplies, especially water, were low. Now they awaited the arrival of Pontius Pilate and his troops to join them in the task of holding the front lines.

Marcus made his circuit of the camp. Clapping one legionary on the shoulder, he inquired, "That son of yours, Philip? He must be, what—five years old now?"

"Six, Commander." The soldier continued whetting the edge of his sword. "See him again soon, I expect."

"That's the spirit," Marcus praised. Rubbing his crooked wrestler's nose that matched his stocky wrestler's build, the centurion passed on in his inspection.

Two wounded men, one with an arrowhead in his guts and the other with a crushed skull, would not see tomorrow morning. Others, trying to get some sleep before their turn on guard, coughed fitfully. The nights were damp in this cursed forest and growing colder with every passing day.

Cassius, the second-in-command, walked one pace behind.

Clustered around another small fire was a knot of men playing dice. As Marcus watched, a soldier hesitated before a throw, then pushed all his coins into the wager.

"How's the game going?" Marcus inquired.

The trooper gave a wry grin. "Badly, sir. But what have I got to lose? Can't spend any hereabouts, can I?"

Out of reach of being overheard, Cassius said, "If reinforcements don't come by morning . . ."

"The legion won't fail us," Marcus returned. "Pilate must be nearly here. Then we'll teach these brutes a few things. Just like we did ten years ago, eh?"

As if to mock his words, a file of Cherusci warriors appeared at the bottom of the hill. Chanting and laughing, they mocked the encircled Romans. All of the Cherusci were adorned with bits of mismatched Roman armor. One wore a captured breastplate that he thumped proudly. Another's waist was encircled by an empty sword belt that he wagged, provoking the mirth of his comrades.

The Romans stopped their activities and stood to watch. Even the sentries at the rear barricade turned.

Cassius snarled, "Back to your posts! I'll flay the hide off any man who doesn't mind his duty!"

A Cherusci chief, half a head taller and broader than the others, stepped forward. He wore a Roman helmet, its scarlet plume shorn off close to the crest. Nodding to either side, he ordered two warriors forward, each carrying covered wicker baskets.

Marcus frowned and dropped his chin. He knew what was coming.

The chief impulsively knocked the covers off both containers. Lifting a pair of severed legionary heads, he shook them aloft by their hair. "Romans," he called derisively, "I bring greetings from those you await to rescue you. Can you hear them?" Playfully he brought blood-smeared lips close to his ear. "What's that? Louder, please. What's that, you say? Not coming? Not coming at all?"

Quintus, Marcus's grim-faced guard sergeant who was old enough to be his father, said wryly, "I know one of those two legionaries. Dio Fortis. Furioso, we called him. Great fighter, lousy gambler. Owed me money, he did." In a softer tone Quintus added, "Pilate's men for certain."

The barbarian commander kicked one basket over, letting a dozen heads bump and rattle to the ground. "Romans," the chief taunted, "your brothers' bones are toys for Cherusci wolf cubs! Their eyes plucked out by vultures." He waved a head aloft. "Now we hold your tribune hostage. You know his name—Pilate of the family Ponti."

"Shut him up, Cassius," Marcus ordered.

"Only waiting the order. Now!" Cassius concluded sharply. Five Roman archers, concealed in trees within the compound, launched a volley of arrows down the slope. The Cherusci scattered, but the chief tripped over a fallen head and one of the missiles pierced his arm. He gave a shrill cry of pain as two of his warriors dragged him to safety.

The Romans cheered.

"Hope that was old Furioso who tripped him," Quintus remarked.

"So Pilate's been captured," Cassius observed.

Marcus exhaled heavily. "So it seems."

Cassius squinted at the horizon. "Sunset in less than an hour. Sick and wounded keep the fires as best they're able. Give the rest of us a fighting chance. Then it's every man for himself."

Marcus gnawed his lip. "How many can still hold a sword?"

"Less than four hundred," Cassius replied.

"Enough." Marcus nodded.

"Enough for what?" Cassius frowned. "Marcus . . . Centurion . . . there are seven thousand Cherusci encamped beyond that hill."

Marcus lifted his chin. "Gather the four hundred. You're right about the wounded tending the fires, but it's not every man for himself. Not yet."

Chapter 3

*T*he mood of Tiberius was black.

The sun had set, and the palace torches were lit long before the chatter of the starlings fell silent.

Tiberius barely touched his supper. He demanded that Sejanus, the commander of the Praetorian Guard, send for the temple augurs—priests skilled at the interpretation of the omens of bird flight.

By the flickering light, four diviners were ushered into Caesar's bedchamber.

One after another they foretold that disaster was at hand for the Roman Legion's conquest in the lands of the Cherusci.

Tiberius scowled as the bad news was laid before him.

A gray-bearded priest who had climbed the tower at Jupiter's temple declared, "Caesar, I saw clearly as the starlings flew over the north quarter. The flock took the shape of a battle-ax descending upon the neck of a great eagle." He bared one arm and made a chopping motion. "You see?"

Caesar turned toward the golden eagle standard on display beside him. "The Legion will be defeated, then?"

"And I saw the shape of a vulture feasting upon a fallen horse."

Tiberius sipped his wine. "The cavalry. That would be my son-in-law."

The priest nodded and spoke slowly. "The gods have spoken. The signs are clear. The Legion and Pilate of the Ponti, the husband of your daughter, will be slaughtered."

The youngest diviner confirmed, "Devastation and defeat for the army and the cavalry troops of Pilate."

Tiberius roared with anger and threw his cup. Furious color leapt into his sallow cheeks. The silver chalice clanged across the floor and rolled into a fireplace. "What? Is there never any good news from you? Augurs! You read the signs, and all is defeat in the north! Half the time your reports are wrong. What are the odds of you ever delivering truth to me? Where are auspices of good fortune?" He whirled and snatched up his sword. "I should kill you all myself and read the omens in your rotten guts!"

At this, three of the seers, eyes wide with terror since Tiberius was capable of fulfilling his threat, stepped back out of the light. No augur was needed to interpret the smell of their fear.

The eldest of the mystics, bald-headed and white-bearded, came forward with his hands raised. He smiled at the emperor and spoke to him as if he were a naughty child in the midst of a tantrum. "Tiberius, sit and calm yourself. All is not lost."

The emperor sank onto his chair. "Well, old deceiver, I am waiting. Rome is waiting. What good news, then?"

The old man gestured toward the west. "The starlings have flown south. As the sun was setting, I saw a golden portal opened in the clouds. Like a crown, it ringed the sun—a corona of such brightness and glory that one could not look upon it."

Cynically, Tiberius spat, "The sun sets every day. What of it? The temples and the Senate of Rome are now covered in stinking bird feces. It is not hard to discern from the smell alone what disrespect the gods have for us."

Pausing to smooth the folds of his robe, the augur advised, "Wait, my lord, before you believe judgment. The starlings are gone. Think of this . . . instead, a golden light, like the finger of Mars, lingered upon the Senate. Mars stooped and touched the white marble carving of one victorious soldier. A common man, his head crowned with the golden wreath of victory."

Tiberius leaned forward and growled, "Speak plainly, old man, or your head and the heads of these false prophets decorate the spikes at the city gates!"

The elder seemed unafraid. "The gods are saying one man will come forth and save the army from destruction. When all seems lost, there will arise a victory. The signs may be correct. But one must read each sign properly."

Tiberius sat back and considered the weathered priest's words. He stroked the blade of his weapon. "You have bought yourself and your cronies some time. It will take a while before the messengers come to us from the north. Then I will know if you speak the truth. You claim the signs declare victory snatched from the jaws of the lion—one man saving the Legion. So I will sheathe my sword and spare you execution for now. We shall wait and see."

❧

"Do you hear it, Jono?" Philo called through the dark hall to the cot of the slave.

The chirping of a single bird outside the window had persisted for hours. It was not the pleasant singing of a night bird, but the measured *kak-kak-kak* of distress.

Jono's shadow loomed in the doorway. "Did you call me, young master?"

"Listen," Philo instructed. "The bird."

Jono was ever on call to protect the young master, to carry him to the latrine, or to bring him whatever he needed. But to be wakened from a deep sleep and asked to listen to a croaking bird clearly grated on the giant's patience.

"Shall I carry you to the latrine? Have you had an evil dream?"

"No!" Philo pointed to the window, where a cloud slid across the face of the quarter moon. "Listen, I say, Jono. There is a bird out there. Knocking."

Jono cocked his head and lowered his chin. He listened as Philo commanded. "Yes. A starling, no doubt, left behind by the flock. Wounded, perhaps. I shall go outside and kill it."

"Noooooo!" Philo wailed. "She is calling for help. The owls or the cats will find her and kill her if we do not rescue her. Can you not hear her terror? She is pleading for help!"

"As you say, young master. Yes. It must be the case. But it is late, and the moon is sliding down the sky in the west. We must sleep, or tomorrow we will see the sun and long for nightfall."

Philo sat up and swung his legs over the edge of his bed. "Take me out before the moon sets. We will find Starling, bring her in the house, and save her from the prowling cats."

Jono hefted the child in his arms and slid him up onto his shoulder. Following the clacking cry of the bird, they emerged into the moonlight and crept down the stone steps into the garden.

An owl on the hunt hooted from the sycamore tree.

"We must hurry!" Philo urged.

The shape of man and boy created a shadowed form like a giant bear. Philo inhaled the fragrance of the rosebushes. Jono paused. They listened together. Water splashed in the stone fountain.

"She's over there," Philo whispered.

"Yes. Beside the fountain. Hush now. She could die of fright." Jono tiptoed along the stone path. He crouched lower to examine the shadows.

The starling's cry quickened.

Philo pointed to the tiny black form huddled at the base of a statue. Jono nodded. They stooped.

Starling fell silent. One wing drooped low, feather tips touching the stone.

"See there," Jono murmured. "Her wing must have been broken in the great dance of her flock today."

"Will she live?"

"Who can say? She may grieve so much for her family, who have all flown south by now, that her heart may break like her wing. There is no mending a broken heart."

"Mother will fix her wing. I will tend her heart . . . feed her and sing to her."

"If a wild bird can be healed, then I suppose Starling tumbled from the sky and landed in the right place. The magic of your mother can do it."

"How shall we carry her inside?"

"I cup my left hand thus." Jono demonstrated, reaching down to lift the tiny creature. "See here . . . I scoop her up, and you will carry her in, and we shall put her in a basket lined with linen." The white teeth of the giant flashed in a grin as he placed the bird into Philo's hands. "Mind the wind . . . and there she is. Safe from whatever evil lurks in the sycamore tree."

The starling's trembling feathers were soft in Philo's palm. Philo held her close to his lips and breathed warmth on her back. He whispered the command, "Live, little bird."

Starling's heart fluttered in fear.

"Don't be afraid," Philo told her. "You are safe now from talons of owls and fangs of cats."

◦◦◦◦◦

Cool night air touched Claudia's face like a silk scarf. She smiled as Philo's midnight drama played out in the garden below. Philo was a kind child with a tender heart.

A sleek golden cat crouched low, flicked its tail, and

crept across the paving stones toward the bird. At the whiff of man and boy, the hunter halted midstride. Too late to catch an easy meal, the cat sat and licked its paws.

By moonlight from her balcony, Claudia observed the nonchalant disappointment of the hungry feline. It lay down and watched the progress of Philo and the slave as they carried the broken bird into the house. The rescue was a success.

Claudia knew it would only be a short while before Philo called for her to come and see what they had found. She returned to her bedchamber and closed the shutters. Except for the gently splashing fountain, the night was quiet again.

She sat at her dressing table and brushed her hair by the flickering candle flame. Catching a glimpse of her reflection in the glass, she paused. The golden eyes looking back at her were filled with loneliness.

What would life have been like if she had been able to marry for love? If she were in the arms of the man she longed for?

Eight years of marriage to Pilate had not dulled the knife of her desire for another. She had prayed for a sign, for a way out. The absence of Pilate was a reprieve for her.

Claudia wondered what was in store for her husband and those who fought with him on far-off battlefields.

She thought of Pilate and then of Marcus. Two soldiers. Once friends, raised on the same vineyard estate. They loved the same woman. They fought the same Cherusci enemy. And the two soldiers now warred against one another.

How would Caesar's soothsayers have interpreted the fallen bird and the cat? she wondered. *The priests of Jupiter would read some personal prophecy into the behaviors of animals and humans.*

Claudia's mother had taught her that even small portents were harbingers of something greater. The starling and the cat surely were a prophecy of danger.

Claudia was certain that the diviners of Caesar's court were hard at work deciphering the future of Rome and Tiberius Caesar by the patterns of the starlings.

But what did the omen of one bird crying outside the house of Ponti mean to her future?

In the tragic drama of Claudia and Pontius Pilate, it was clear who the wounded starling was . . . and who was the prowling cat.

Was there a champion who would rescue her in the nick of time, like Philo and Jono had rescued the starling?

Claudia rubbed her aching forehead.

A knock sounded on her door.

"Mother," Philo cried, "come quickly! See what Jono and I found in the garden . . . the beautiful bird we have rescued!"

Chapter 4

The night closed in like the lid of a stone coffin. The watch fires of the hilltop refuge flickered low. There were plenty of rocks, but little brush and few remaining limbs on the trees. These were rapidly butchered to use for fuel, and that very sparingly. By Marcus Longinus's express order, no one lit the tar-soaked torches each man carried tied to his pack.

"The scouts are back," Quintus reported. "There is a gully to the west we can use. I'll post a handful of healthy men to remain here and keep the fires going. Perhaps the gods will smile on us. If not . . ." He shrugged.

"Thank you, Sergeant. We will use the gully. And there"—he indicated the glow of many fires only a couple of miles away—"is the main Cherusci camp. If Pilate and any of his men remain alive, that is where they are held."

"A couple hundred of us against that many thousand?"

Laughing, the centurion corrected, "Quintus, I've seen you wager a month's pay on worse odds than that!" Then he added, "Besides, it is not a move our enemy expects."

"You are right about that," Quintus agreed drily.

"The wounded and one man out of each company of fifty are to remain behind and tend the fires. Let them make as much noise as they wish—to convince the Cherusci we are all still here. If our men have received no further order beforehand, at dawn they may make whatever escape they can."

Well past midnight the Roman troops slipped down the slope, across the creek, and up to the outskirts of the Cherusci encampment. A lone Cherusci guard rose up out of the darkness and offered a guttural challenge. But before he raised an alarm, two Romans seized him, clamped his mouth shut, and silenced him permanently.

Marcus formed his men into an arc to the northwest of the enemy camp. Lying prone, he, Cassius, and Quintus surveyed the position from a ridgeline screened with holly bushes, while his men waited behind the brow of the hill.

Quintus whispered hoarsely, "I was wrong. We're not outnumbered ten to one. It's more like a hundred to one."

"Courage leads to honor," Marcus said.

"Courage leads to honor," the guard sergeant repeated. Then, anticipating the next query, he replied, "All the captains know what to do."

Two Cherusci sentries were plainly dozing. Two more leaned sleepily on the staffs of their spears. Seeing only one pacing his post, his tread slow, the centurion judged the time to be right.

"Now!" he shouted, jumping upright. Placing a trumpet

to his lips, he gave a blast that shattered the night. To the left and right other hunting horns repeated the call, the way tribesmen warriors drive wild hogs into a waiting trap of spearmen.

Every tenth Roman carried a gourd. Rather than transporting water, the hollow containers held embers from the fire. In seconds new life was breathed into the concealed coals, and the torches blazed.

"Courage and honor!" Marcus called.

Four hundred voices echoed, "Courage and honor!"

The near side of the Cherusci camp awoke first, stumbling out of their tents and blundering about. One running guard, likely mistaken for an assassin, was skewered by a friend's spear. Two of his comrades must have believed their enemies were already in the camp, for they hacked and hewed at each other.

Dazed men, bumbling about without any orders, pointed toward the legionaries and cried with alarm. The enemy that appeared out of nowhere, with torches blazing and trumpets blaring, seemed to be a force of thousands surrounding them.

"Drive them! Drive them now!" Marcus bellowed.

Like fire falling from heaven, wave upon wave of flaming brands poured down the slope. The Romans yelled and flailed their arms like demonic attackers dancing between the flames. A forest of javelins arched out of the darkness, piercing some where they slept.

Remembering the heads of their butchered comrades, the Roman troopers needed no encouragement. They swept into the Cherusci camp, overwhelming the first resistance. More and more combat broke out amongst the Cherusci, and between them and their allies, as friend fought friend.

By Marcus's command, every tent they passed was set afire, adding to the panic and confusion. The Cherusci made no attempt to form lines. Single combats dissolved into flight.

As the Romans approached the center of the camp, Marcus spotted a captured Roman standard propped outside a burning tent. "There!" he yelled to Quintus. "Follow me!"

Slashing his way past two defenders, he ducked his head and entered amid smoke and flames. Pontius Pilate was tied to a pole, but his guards had run away. Cutting him free, Marcus tossed him a sword. The three emerged from the pavilion just as it erupted entirely into flames, falling in on itself with a roar. It exhaled smoke and belched fire.

Pilate and Marcus fought back to back. The Cherusci regrouped and returned to the battle, so the two Romans faced off against eight of the enemy.

Pontius Pilate was headstrong, arrogant, and ambitious, but also an excellent swordsman. When cornered, he fought ferociously, swiftly dispatching two of his opponents before taking on the remaining enemies.

The four who surrounded the centurion tried to close in but got in each other's way. None had room enough for a full swing of an ax or a decent thrust with a sword.

Marcus used this situation to his advantage, lunging at one man who already looked fearful. The opponent leapt back just as one of his comrades swung a blow, but the slash landed across the Cherusci's own hand.

Dueling with his remaining adversaries, Pilate remarked to Marcus, "You still fight like a farm boy playing with sticks."

Parrying an ax cut with his blade while giving back a pace, Marcus let his assailant's blow overbalance him. The attacker's chest fell on the point of the Roman's sword; then Marcus kicked him loose. One of the other Cherusci stumbled over the wounded man, and both tumbled to earth.

"You're welcome," Marcus said to Pilate. "Should I have let you roast?"

Three more Cherusci rushed up to attack.

"Is this"—Pilate panted as his blow disarmed another man—"your idea of a rescue?"

Quintus appeared at exactly the right moment. Catching two enemies from behind, he cracked their heads together, then flung them onto another Cherusci swordsman.

More trumpets rang out, this time from off to the east, in the direction of the marshy plain.

"You may be right," Marcus admitted to Pilate, wondering if he was about to join Pilate as a captive.

"No," Quintus corrected as he chopped the legs out from under another assailant. "Those are Roman trumpets. General Severus has seen the flames and is attacking."

∼∞∼

On the morning following the battle, the plain between the central hill and the river was torn and scored, as if a monstrous yoke of oxen had plowed it in every direction. Heaps of dead bodies were mounded into artificial hills in front of the Roman camp. Piles of discarded or captured Cherusci weapons formed others.

The four hundred soldiers with Marcus had scattered seven thousand Cherusci. The panic that followed the night assault not only saved Pontius Pilate but decided the battle in favor of the Romans.

Weary Roman troops and their tribal allies drew themselves up in ragged lines, facing a hastily constructed platform. On it stood General Severus, his key officers, and Marcus.

"Victors and heroes of Rome!" Severus shouted.

This opening provoked a cheer from the men.

The general motioned for Marcus to come to his side, then flourished a bronzed crown woven of spiked leaves above the centurion's head. "This is the *corona obsidionalis*. It is always woven from whatever grows on the field of battle. It is only awarded when someone performs a heroic action that saves an army from destruction. Ten years ago it was won by Centurion Marcus Longinus at the Battle of Idistaviso and presented to him from the hands of General Germanicus himself. The centurion has once again proven his worth to Rome. Victors!" he repeated to louder cheering. "I give you the Hero of Idistaviso and Scourge of the Cherusci, Centurion Marcus Longinus. Courage and honor!" With that he placed the crown of thorns atop Marcus's head.

Thousands of hoarse throats bellowed, "Longinus! Courage and honor."

Severus continued. "Hail, Rome. Hail, Tiberius Caesar. Courage and honor. Hail, Marcus Longinus!"

"Rome! Caesar!" the men cheered. Then, "Longinus! Longinus! Longinus!"

Marcus saw only one sour face in the crowd that day. Standing below the front of the platform, his face still streaked with blood and soot, his uniform torn and muddy, was Pontius Pilate. Instead of cheering, Pilate sulked. He stared at the ground and dug into the mire with the toe of his boot.

∾∾∾

After the ceremony concluded, the Roman army went back to licking their wounds. General Severus announced to much cheering that most of the legions were going home. One unit would remain posted on this northern frontier to keep the peace.

Severus summoned Marcus into his tent, dismissed his servants and his lieutenants, and invited the centurion to sit. "I have decided to keep your unit here."

Marcus nodded.

"But not you," Severus added. "You are detached from your troop and coming back to Rome with me."

A tall silver flagon stood on a table beside the general, flanked by a pair of onyx chalices worked in a vine leaf pattern. Severus poured two cups of wine and handed one to Marcus. With his free hand he indicated the holly wreath that ringed the top of Marcus's head. Marcus glanced up past his bushy brows at the overhanging circlet of spiked leaves. His face reddened with embarrassment as he removed the corona.

Severus revolved it slowly in his hands before placing it on the table beside the jug of wine. Turning to a discussion of the nighttime battle, the general praised, "Brilliant strategy, Centurion. How did you come up with it?"

"Necessity, sir. Not original with me, either. Written in the book of Jewish wars. A general named Gideon."

Severus nodded. "I shall remember that, if ever I fight the Jews." Drawing his chair closer and leaning forward, he asked, "As a child, you were taken captive by Rome, were you not? And also from Britannia?"

"Very young, yes, sir. I remember very little."

In the latter Marcus was lying. He remembered well his mother and the aching grief that haunted him for years as he grew up apart from her. She was a princess of the Catuvellauni and so a more valuable prisoner than Marcus.

"Yet you fight for Rome . . . you serve Rome?"

The centurion answered with the response he had rehearsed many years before. "I serve Rome because Rome is ultimate power. Power is the only god any rational man can serve."

Severus nodded. "And you were raised as a fosterling alongside Pontius Pilate?"

Where was this conversation leading? Because of Pilate's connection to the household of Tiberius, the general knew all the correct replies without having to ask.

Cautiously, Marcus replied, "Rome has no better servant than Pontius Pilate."

Severus raised his brows. "But Pilate's ego and ambition led to a costly gamble . . . a gamble that cost the lives of nearly all his men, and almost his own. I do not say your actions saved the army as at Idistaviso, but it seems you have saved Pilate and his honor."

Spreading his hands, Marcus said, "I did my duty as a soldier, sir. Pilate would have done the same . . ."

Waving dismissively, Severus interrupted. "Pilate is your friend, I understand that." There was a long pause while the general stared into Marcus's eyes. "Is he also a friend of Caesar?"

"Sir? He is married to Caesar's daughter."

"Claudia. Caesar's beautiful, illegitimate daughter." There was another searching inspection of the centurion's carefully guarded expression. "Did you not also seek her hand? With, it is said, her encouragement?"

Marcus brushed his calloused hands over his stained tunic. "She is the daughter of the emperor, and I am a common man."

"But an uncommon soldier."

"Claudia is well loved by her father. Pilate is of the equestrian class. The match is suitable. And they have a child . . . Tiberius's grandson."

"Pilate's boy . . . Philo, yes? . . . is a cripple." Severus drained his cup of wine.

Marcus took advantage of the interruption imposed by his swallows to argue, "Claudia loves her son, and Tiberius loves his daughter. Sir, it is not for me to have an opinion about these things, much less meddle in them. Pilate is a brave man. It takes great courage to throw the dice when so much is at stake." Lowering his chin, the centurion stared into the red wine, tightened his jaw, and said nothing further. His words sounded false even to his own ears.

"But thanks to you," Severus continued, "Pilate did not die, and Tiberius has another victory to celebrate. I find your friend vain, proud, tedious, and foolish. But at your recommendation, Pilate is spared the consequences of his incompetence. I am sending both of you back to Rome. Caesar can deal with his own household in his own way."

"General." Marcus stood and saluted with his arm across his chest. "I hope you will consider taking me with you on your next campaign. It would be my honor to serve with you again."

Severus returned the gesture, but his thoughts already seemed far away.

❧

The triumph decreed by Tiberius Caesar to celebrate Severus's victory over the Cherusci was set for a day in late spring.

"A most auspicious day," the emperor's astrologer decreed. "The anniversary of the founding of Rome." His casting of Caesar's horoscope was confirmed by a favorable reading of the entrails of a goat. "Very auspicious indeed."

"Very good for the emperor," Severus remarked as he and Marcus Longinus waited in the predawn mist hovering above the Campus Martius for the parade to begin. "Once more a little victory and he proclaims we have peace throughout the Empire." The broad sweep of his arms took in the gathering crowds, the rising clouds of incense, the hawkers of sausages, and the purveyors of sprigs of laurel. Severus pointed toward the mobs lining the rooftop parapets, waving handkerchiefs and branches and shouting, "Triumph! Triumph!"

"Very different from the thick German woods," the general added. "No arrows being launched, nor spears, but never doubt the dangers here are just as real, if less obvious."

In honor of the festivities, Marcus was clad in his best armor, burnished for the occasion, and a new red, ankle-length cloak. In contrast, the general wore a purple toga bordered in gold and red boots, matching the way the god Jupiter was portrayed in the temple that was their destination.

Marcus remained silent, uncomfortable at the criticism of Caesar his commander was implying and fearful of the consequences should he be overheard.

Severus accepted two cups of honeyed wine, handed one to Marcus, then waved away the slave before continuing. "You have already proven your loyalty, Centurion. There is no one else to whom I can speak my mind." Lifting the silver chalice toward the bronzed corona of holly perched above Marcus's brow, he muttered, "Consider it a duty that goes with that honor. Think of it: No peace treaty has been concluded, yet to please the people, Caesar calls it 'peace.' He summons me back here for a 'triumph,' reduces the size of the army, and pretends that all is well, while Praetorian Commander Sejanus grows ever more ambitious and powerful. Sometimes I think he's cast a spell on Tiberius Caesar."

Marcus, the Hero of Idistaviso and Scourge of the Cherusci, stood with his chin tucked in and his head bowed.

"Centurion," Severus added, "I'd ten times rather face howling tribesmen screaming out of the woods waving axes than brave the politics here in Rome. Ten times? A thousand! But Caesar will turn our victory . . . your victory," he corrected himself, "to his advantage."

Though it was barely daylight, the lines were forming. Excited throngs mobbed the streets. Only twenty-five stadia in length—a distance any Roman soldier could march in half an hour—nevertheless, the triumph's winding route would take several hours to traverse.

A cadre of priests of Jove arrived, leading a pair of snow-white oxen garlanded with flowers. These would precede Severus to the temple and there be sacrificed in his honor.

"Walk beside my chariot," Severus insisted as he stepped up, indicating a place for Marcus at the right of the silver-and-gold embossed rig drawn by four white horses. Leaning down, he offered one last observation. "By rights you should ride here beside me. But for your sake, I think it's better this way. I speak plainly. What you have done has already made enemies for you. There are those who are consumed with envy. Pilate has truly poisoned himself with jealousy while wishing for your death."

The goal of the cavalcade was the Temple of Capitoline Jupiter, but Severus's chariot halted before it had moved more than three hundred yards. Once across the Tiber, just through a newly raised triumphal arch, was the sacred boundary of the city. They were met there by the city prefect, accompanied by a pair of senators.

Waving for silence, the prefect intoned in an obnoxiously nasal but piercing voice, "General Severus, do you come in peace?"

"I come in peace," Severus agreed.

"Do you voluntarily surrender command of your army?"

"I do."

"Then in the names of the senate and the people of Rome, I welcome you. Let the triumph begin!"

After the general ceremonially handed over his sword, the procession continued. Riding behind Severus in the chariot was a slave, holding a laurel wreath signifying victory over his head. Throughout the parade Marcus heard the slave whisper, "Remember, you are only a man. *Sic transit gloria mundi*. All earthly glory is fleeting."

Many in the crowd shouted for Severus.

Some peered toward Marcus and loudly inquired, "Who's that?"

Then a voice the centurion would have recognized anywhere called his name. "Marcus! Marcus Longinus!"

Leaning over the balustrade of a rooftop was Claudia. The triumph was for Severus, but the smile on Claudia's heart-shaped face was for Marcus. The sunlight glinting on her coppery hair warmed him. At every wave of her slender, graceful arms his emotions leaped, though he had steeled himself to feel nothing for her at all.

Impossible command.

Forcing himself to look away, he could not help but glance back. Each time he found her still gazing at him. Was that wistful longing he saw there, or did he only imagine it?

Chapter 5

A t her first glimpse of Marcus striding beside the chariot of Severus, Claudia gasped and leaned against the balustrade. Centurion Marcus Longinus, the commoner, and Hero of Idistaviso, was again being acclaimed by Rome. Word had swept through Rome's halls of power like a wind, clearing away the dusty self-aggrandizement from the nobility.

The starling, Claudia's good omen of rescue, peered out from the bars of a small cage on the table.

Claudia felt a surge of pride. Tears welled in her eyes. The sunlight glinted on his armor. And then, as if by a miracle, his face turned again toward her. This time she was certain he saw her. She raised her hand slightly as if to say, "Yes, I am here. Yes. I see you, my dearest."

Then the forward motion of the procession carried Marcus from her sight.

Far behind Marcus pranced the horse ridden by Pontius Pilate. Proud and arrogant in his blue cloak and plumed helmet, Pilate curled his lip as he glanced at her. She winced instinctively. It would be he who would enter her bedchamber and lay claim to her body, like the spoils of war, tonight—not the one man she truly loved.

Claudia remembered her desperate thoughts the night of the bird's rescue. Who was the starling, and who was the cat? Once again, her heart pattered like a frightened bird's in need of rescue.

Philo, resting in the arms of Jono, peered over the railing. "Oh, Mother, so many soldiers! Is my father among them?"

She did not answer for a moment. It had been two years since Pilate had been sent to serve the legions in the north. Philo did not remember him.

Jono leaned close to the boy. "See there, young master? Tribune Pontius Pilate rides the proud white horse all trimmed in blue. But this triumph is in honor of General Severus and the heroic centurion Marcus Longinus."

Philo pondered the scene a moment. "If the centurion is the real hero, why does he not ride in a chariot? Or have a white horse like my father?"

Claudia answered, "He is humble."

"What is 'humble,' Mother?"

"It means . . . recognizing that we are not on earth to show others how important we are, but to make a difference in the lives of others."

"The centurion needs no chariot," Jono murmured. "He wears the corona of courage upon his head. There are many who know the meaning of his crown."

"Do you know him, Jono?" Philo turned in the giant's arms to gaze into his face.

"Yes. I fought against him in my own country as a

champion to decide the last battle. He broke my arm, and I fell. My nation was defeated. My family dead. I did not care if I lived or died. The crowd cried that he should slit my throat in the arena. Instead he kept my life, and I am a slave. After your birth, he brought me here as a gift to serve you and your mother."

The boy beamed in wonder. "A new story, Jono! You were like our starling. A broken wing, but now you sing for us."

The giant laughed. "He could have plucked my head off. I would have welcomed it. But now I rejoice. Yes. I owe him everything."

Philo gazed down at the parade, straining for another glimpse of the centurion. "I would like to meet a true hero, Mother. Will I get to meet him, do you think?"

Claudia nodded. "Your father would approve such a meeting I am sure."

∼∾∽

The looping, wandering course the procession followed caused the pageant to double back on itself several times. At some points Marcus saw the leading edge of the spectacle from his place near its middle. The first such occasion was when they circled the Circus Flaminius.

There, at the head of the column, was a captured Cherusci mother and young son—the living emblem of their defeated nation. Chained by the ankles, she struggled to keep her chin aloft, staring back at the jeering mob. The boy, no more than four or five years old, was plainly terrified. It was a pitiful sight.

These were followed by Cherusci chieftains, dragging even heavier chains and forced to pull carts loaded with captured weapons. In the yellow, hazy light of a Roman morning, the blunted axes and notched swords did not look remotely frightening. The onlookers shook their fists and taunted the prisoners.

Still, when Marcus remembered his fallen comrades, slaughtered ten years ago in the Idistaviso woods and those recently mutilated by Cherusci savages, he clenched his jaw and set his face against any sign of pity. By the time they reached the place where the enemy tribal chiefs were to be executed, he was fully with the crowds in his emotions.

There was no gold and precious little glory returned to Rome in this triumph, no rich spices or ivory or new territory, but the citizens still cheered and capered as if Persia or India had fallen to the Empire's might. Mobs of bakers and cloth-dyers and wine merchants, who had never been nearer to any battle than hundreds of miles, chanted and sang as if they were personally responsible for the victory.

The procession halted every city block for each of the trade guilds to present their tokens of esteem to Severus— flowers and flowery words. Another loop of the route showed Marcus the soldiers and other officers of the legion, marching in procession.

As the pageant wound through the streets of Rome, Marcus became increasingly aware of Pilate's black mood. More morose and bitter appearing than Marcus had ever seen him, Pilate glared at the centurion with undisguised hatred.

Marcus felt a surge of irrational guilt, as if Pilate had somehow caught Claudia and Marcus in something improper in their staring at each other.

In that moment the winner of the corona recognized the truth of Severus's words: envy is a deadly poison, capable of killing twice. True, it may be used to destroy its intended victim, but it will then turn and devour the perpetrator as well.

Marcus shivered at the premonition.

Chapter 6

*T*here was a royal reception for the returning officers after the victory parade. Though Claudia was invited and expected, she begged off, claiming a headache.

Now, alone in her chamber with the starling, she wished she had gone. It might have been easier to greet her husband for the first time in two years while in a crowded room of strutting officers and plumed women.

It was near midnight. Pilate would soon come to her chamber. She sensed it with the same dread the starling felt at the approach of the cat.

The little cage was covered with a dark blue scarf. Starling was sleeping on her perch. Claudia imagined the tiny creature dreaming of soaring dances in the sky with a million others.

"I am like you, Little Starling." Claudia rested her chin in her hand. "We are captives. Longing for freedom but safe behind our bars."

Claudia wished she had been attuned to the shifting of seasons the way the birds knew when to fly south. She had fallen deeply in love one summer but had waited too long to flee.

The cold winter of Caesar's political necessity had doomed her to a marriage of loveless servitude.

Even when the lamps were out, Claudia could not close her eyes and simply imagine Pilate loved her. She was merely a convenient means for his physical gratification. She meant no more to him than the ritual prostitutes in the temple of Venus.

For a time she had hoped Caesar had chosen her husband because of some sentimental reason. Claudia's mother had been a shopgirl from a family of Jewish wine merchants, and the estates of Ponti owned the vineyards in the north.

Like those who wait for winter to pass, she had waited for the curtain of her life to be pulled back to reveal color, light, and joy. But spring had never come to her heart. The curtains opened, and all was leafless desolation.

As long as Pilate was in Rome, his ambition forced her to live in the metropolis. How she detested the intrigue, clamor, and brutality of this wicked place.

Two years of Pilate's absence when she and Philo lived in the vineyards had been heaven. Now the landowner was back. He was coming for her tonight.

She groaned and, needing air, stepped out onto the balcony of the Ponti townhouse. The breeze carried on it the stench of sewage.

She whispered the song her mother had sung. "If only I had the wings of a dove, then I would fly away."

In the street below, the clip-clop of shod hooves sounded on the cobblestones.

"Oh, God of all the gods, God of my mother . . . help me. He is coming."

Claudia turned in panic and entered her chamber. She hovered above Starling's cage, remembering the cat.

"He is coming."

⌁

Five deep bruises formed the print of a man's hand on Claudia's arm. Her back carried the black mark of Pilate's fist.

"I was drunk." He smirked.

"I am the daughter of Tiberius."

"In the dark, how could I tell who or what you are? The way you howled, I thought you were a Cherusci peasant's wife." He laughed and took another sip of wine.

Claudia did not look at him. She brushed her hair angrily. "If you ever lay a hand on me again, I will—"

Pilate leapt to his feet and threw his cup against the wall. "You will what?" He rushed toward her and grabbed her hair at the base of her neck.

"Stop!" she said through gritted teeth.

He planted his lips against her cheek. "Do you know I once saw a legionary bite the nose off a captive woman before he raped her?"

She grabbed his wrists with both hands. "Pilate! The boy will hear you. Please, stop!"

He shoved her down and glowered over her. "And don't think I am unaware who you prayed for to your gods!"

"You are mad!" She cowered, expecting a kick, but it did not come.

He hesitated. Clenching his fists, he stepped back. "That father of yours. Placed both your lover and your husband together on the front lines. Well, we both lived, Claudia. I know that disappoints you and your father as well. But at least my spies tell me you had no other men to bed while I was gone." He nudged her with his toe.

"I can't go to the banquet tonight," she stammered, unmoving on the floor.

"You WILL GO!" he roared.

"My father will see the marks. He will know."

"I am careful not to beat your pretty face. And if Tiberius did see, do you think he would care? He would simply think it was the sport of a soldier bedding his woman after two years apart."

"All right, Pilate. Yes. Yes." She prayed that he would leave her.

Silence. He glared at her, then spat. "Get up. Get dressed. You will be the most beautiful woman at the banquet tonight. And every man . . . *every man* . . . will look at you and know I own you."

Chapter 7

*A*fter the battlefield shelters Marcus had endured in the
service of Rome, the buildings of the capital were
like another world. Marching from his temporary quarters
in the Praetorian Guard barracks, marble columns closed
in like the forests of the north. Much about Rome made
Marcus uneasy. At least in Germania the enemies were
recognizable by their weapons and actions. Here an enemy
might smile while fingering an unseen dagger or a vial of
poison.

A century of Praetorian soldiers, acting as the emper-
or's bodyguards, were stationed within the colonnade
surrounding the Imperial dining hall. They were easily
recognized by their black-and-white dress uniforms, their
distinctive oval-shaped shields, and their perpetually arrogant sneers. However, at the sight of the bronzed leaves on
Marcus's head, each trooper offered a proper salute as he
approached.

When the bronze doors were opened to admit the centurion, the lilting music of harps and soft mewing of flutes
poured out. A low hum of conversation and the aromas

of wine and flowers added another octave to the note of welcome.

This evening was partly in his honor. Why then was Marcus still so suspicious and doubtful of his safety?

The center portion of the room was occupied by a triclinium—three tables set in a U-shape, all furnished with silver and gold platters and goblets. Each table was provided with three couches on which the high-ranking guests would recline . . . nine places of special honor in all.

The rest of the room was filled with additional tables and couches so that the number in attendance would exceed two hundred, waited on by twice that number of servants.

The tables were already occupied when Marcus entered. At his appearance there was a brief lull in the conversations between senators and favored officials. The chatter amongst Imperial praetors and aediles, as well as their wives, quickly resumed.

He was escorted to a place at the foot of one leg of the horseshoe. By Marcus's request, his armor-bearer, Carta, was present to serve the centurion. From a curved-necked pitcher of ruby red wine, the teenager filled a silver cup depicting a stag-hunting scene, handed it to his master, then stepped back.

∞⌒∞

The steward announced Pilate and Claudia and led them to their seats at Tiberius Caesar's table. In a gown of gold and cream, Claudia's beauty rivaled that of any woman at the feast. She let a lock of her thick red hair tumble over her bare shoulder. Full lips were fixed in a smile that did not betray the secret of bruises and body aches inflicted by Pilate.

Heads turned as she passed.

A few moments later the glory of Caesar's banqueting room blurred as Claudia raised her eyes and saw Marcus at the opposite side of the room from her. Music, the clatter of dishes, and the chatter of voices became dull.

Eight years had come and gone since they pledged their love and laid their plans of escape. Her mind flicked back over the scene, tenderly treasuring the memories of a time when she had truly been loved.

They met beneath the oak tree beside the vineyard of his Ponti benefactor . . .

Marcus promised her, "There is a stone house in southern Gaul. The land, much like this. We will plant vineyards and raise a crop of children. Rome will drink wine from our vineyards but shall not remember us, Claudia."

"When? When shall we go?" she had asked eagerly.

"Tomorrow night at midnight. Leave through the palace kitchen. Dress as a scullery maid. I will come in a cart, and no one will notice you are gone until they come to wake you in the morning."

A day of breathless anticipation and joy was followed by disaster. Marcus had confided their plans in his best friend, Pontius Pilate, son of the vineyard owner.

Arrested at the palace gates, Marcus was thrown in prison. His release was negotiated by the elder Ponti on condition Marcus either join the army or be exiled from

Rome forever. Claudia was married off to Pilate as a reward for his service to Tiberius.

And so Claudia's hope for happiness ended. She became a political commodity to be joined to Pilate, the son of a rich merchant, who was promised a military rank far out of reach of Marcus Longinus.

Claudia mused at how much had changed since then. The honor now belonged to Marcus. Pilate, though a member of Caesar's extended family, was a disgrace . . . and in disgrace.

Would Marcus have achieved greatness if he had succeeded in running away with Claudia? She sipped her wine and looked at her reflection in the silver cup. Perhaps if she and Marcus had succeeded, it would have been wine from their vineyards being poured tonight. And in that happy little stone house, how many children would they have had around their table?

She had called out Marcus's name in the moment of Philo's birth.

How she longed for the boy to meet Marcus. But how could such a thing be arranged?

Tonight she prayed only that Marcus would look at her, truly see her. She desired him to know that her heart had never left him. Never. Not in her loveless marriage. Not in Marcus's banishment.

However, Marcus did not permit his gaze to linger on her more than an instant. Perhaps he sensed, as she did, that the seating arrangement had been some cruel joke of Caesar to torment them. Or perhaps it was a trap set by Sejanus to lure Marcus to his death through an accusation of adultery with Claudia.

Eight years of heartache must now be governed by self-preservation. Claudia supposed that if all the moments of wanting him had been counted, they would almost equal the sum of her waking hours.

Soon Marcus would be posted to a faraway land. He would become only a distant dream again. But on this night, Claudia's old longing was real . . . and dangerous.

Chapter 8

It was only after Carta poured the wine that Marcus noticed who was seated on the other side of the open space of the triclinium, directly across from him—Pilate and Claudia. His eyes had met Claudia's, but they both swiftly looked away.

Unfortunately, in doing so, his gaze collided with Pilate's. The hatred glimpsed during the triumph procession still smoldered, now like a banked fire instead of a blaze. With seeming good humor and manifest respect, Pilate lifted a cup toward his thin, tightly pressed lips, received Marcus's acknowledgment, then drained the goblet without ever taking his stare from the centurion's face.

Either by some trick of the vaulting or because Pilate wanted Marcus to overhear, he had no difficulty catching the sneering observation offered to Claudia. "Our friend wears his honor like an unbroken colt under saddle for the first time. He looks ready to bolt and flee at any moment."

Claudia's reply was not audible, but it must have stung her husband, for Pilate slammed the cup savagely onto the table and retorted loudly, "Would you have preferred me dead?"

Claudia applied a cautioning hand to Pilate's arm and whispered a word in his ear, and Pilate subsided. They were joined at their table by an elderly senator. Pilate forcibly cut off any further retort and clamped his jaw shut.

Another patrician and his wife reclined next to Marcus.

Tiberius Caesar swept into the room with a fanfare of trumpets and all present hastily stood. Praetorian Prefect Sejanus was on his left and Severus on his right. A bevy of slaves scurried after Caesar and one thrust a cup into his outstretched hand.

"An evening of honor," Caesar announced in his habitually hoarse roar. "We honor the return of our much-loved General Severus, and we name him Hero of the North. Once again Rome is safe from the Cherusci barbarians. We drink to Severus!"

"To Severus!" the room echoed.

Across the room Pilate's eyes darted toward the general and then to Marcus before he drowned his bitter stare in the wine. He muttered something into his cup, quickly shushed by Claudia.

Pilate seemed envious not only of Marcus but of Severus as well. The centurion was confused. He and Pilate had been boys together, and their rivalry was understandable on many levels. But to envy and resent a Roman general made no sense to the common soldier. Did Pilate's insane ambition rise to an absurd height? Did he think he could be Caesar's successor?

Tiberius spoke again: "And honor to another hero of the hour—a true Roman, though not born of Rome, and once again a true servant of the Empire. Centurion Marcus Longinus: Honor and long life."

"Honor and long life!" replied the political power of Rome.

Pilate had waved his cup under his nose but neither echoed the sentiment nor drank.

The emperor continued, "Longinus, they tell me you are uncomfortable wearing your crown in public."

"A helmet suits a soldier better, sire. The crown of Rome's honor is for you to wear," Marcus responded, having been warned in advance to have a comment prepared.

The wavering light of the torches in the wall sconces made the black panther on the mural behind Caesar writhe as if alive and stalking the guests.

"Don't be so modest," Caesar scolded.

Supper proceeded through fourteen courses. Despite the rumors about Caesar's extravagance, the dishes were all recognizable—meats, heavily spiced, in thick sauces. The guest on Marcus's right whispered, "Caesar economizes on state occasions. He saves the truly lavish displays for dining with his close friends."

There was more music and a display of acrobatics by a troupe of Nubian gymnasts. A magician was succeeded by a snake-charmer. This act was followed by an animal trainer with a pack of dancing monkeys costumed as recognizable Roman senators. The man beside Marcus laughed a trifle uncomfortably, the centurion thought.

Severus was encouraged to describe the battle. He did so, giving Marcus much of the credit and thereby giving Pilate additional incentive to hate the centurion.

Supper concluded, Caesar rose again and addressed the crowd. "Rome's honor is indeed mine to share with whomever I choose. And tonight I have additional honors to bestow."

The crowd waited expectantly.

A crooked smile turned up one corner of the emperor's mouth. "Such as, on my son-in-law."

A flush burst across Pilate's face. He never could hold his wine. Marcus prayed, for Claudia's sake, that tonight Pilate could hold his tongue.

"For Pontius Pilate," Caesar continued. "A fellow who thinks of himself . . . I mean to say, thinks *for* himself."

Pilate squirmed. Color leapt across the space between them, imprinting scarlet on Claudia's cheeks as well.

"Tribune Pilate, you are present tonight so I can honor you as well as General Severus and Centurion Longinus. Now that you have proven . . ." Caesar's next words were uttered singly and distinctly. Each hung in the air like the beat of a wave on a rocky shore. "What . . . metal . . . you . . . are . . . made . . . of."

There was a collective intake of breath at the threat hanging over Pilate's head, as if the entire audience sensed the panther about to spring. The emperor had once been a soldier—a good one, plainspoken and forthright. Since those days he had learned the ways of politics well. The assembled group, some showing signs of dread, awaited whatever doom followed this statement.

But an instant later Tiberius recovered his good humor. With a smile from the small mouth that competed for attention with his prominent nose, the emperor said, "We tested your military metal in the cold north, but in the east there is a hot land, requiring a different sort of alloy . . . a political metal. Two governors have failed in their duty to me. I hereby appoint you to the office of Prefect of Judea. We shall see how you distinguish yourself in governing the Jews."

The exaggerated color drained from Pilate's face. He became nearly as pale as the tile clouds surrounding the mosaic face of Augustus Caesar set into the ceiling.

Marcus saw Claudia bite her lip and give the smallest shake of her head.

Judea, where better men than Pontius Pilate had already tried to govern and failed. One had been too harsh, another too lax. Both men had succumbed to pressure in the form of Jewish letters of complaint addressed to Tiberius on two distinct themes.

The way this man acts, he is no friend of Caesar. His measures cause riots and interfere with the collection of taxes.

He is failing to control bandits, which interferes with the collection of taxes.

It was rightly said that Jews were a stiff-necked people, impossible to govern. Even though they were left alone to worship their invisible, unnamable deity, there seemed no pleasing them.

Marcus did not envy Pilate his task, but there was no refusing an Imperial offer. It was a command.

Tiberius rumbled, "Have you nothing to say to this

proclamation about the hot east? Are you . . . lukewarm . . . to this final honor?"

Most of the audience chuckled appreciatively at the humor contained in the word *lukewarm*. But there were some, including Marcus, who focused instead on the word *final*. To those who knew the tension between Caesar and his son-in-law, the threat was perfectly clear. This appointment was Pilate's last chance to make good.

Evidently recollecting that the emperor and all the guests were staring at him, Pilate stammered, "I-I am overwhelmed, sire. Overwhelmed with . . . gratitude."

"So, son-in-law," Tiberius resumed, running the flat of his hand over short, straight hair combed forward, "friend to Caesar that you are, there will be no difficulty taking up this post at once, eh? You have much to do, and your ship sails in thirty days. You must be ready."

Pilate gazed longingly at Claudia as if beseeching her to do something, to intercede with her father on his behalf. Claudia simply looked away.

"Ah, yes," Tiberius said, clearly noticing Pilate's mute appeal to his wife. "You're concerned about leaving your wife and son . . . separating again so soon after your return from the north. Very well, they shall go with you."

As if suddenly irritated with the political games and self-conscious revelry, Tiberius declared, "Enough! Severus, you and Sejanus, come with me."

Everyone jumped to their feet to salute the emperor's abrupt departure.

Just as Marcus was congratulating himself on escaping

unscathed to the barracks, back to life as a simple soldier, Tiberius turned again to the room. "Centurion, holder of the *corona obsidionalis*, come with us. This concerns you as well."

∽∾∽

The room into which Emperor Tiberius led Marcus and Severus was an audience chamber. It was the place where Caesar conferred with visiting foreign dignitaries, or delivered his orders to his highest military commanders. Stern-faced Praetorian guards occupied each of the corners.

The aroma of incense replaced the smells of the banquet. To Marcus it resembled more the inner sanctum of a temple than a government office. Everything Caesar did was deliberate, so this impression had to be also.

At one end of the apartment was a dais, flanked by two marble statues—the image of the god Jupiter as the patron of Rome and a bust of Augustus. Caesar's adoptive father, Augustus, was now also divine. It reinforced Tiberius's authority to be the son of a god.

The general and Marcus marched in unison, their feet echoing on the cold marble floor. The centurion used the time to look around him. The room was decorated with wall paintings. The largest depicted the river god Tiberinus, from whom the emperor took his name. The message of association was none too subtle. The god was painted as having the emperor's own craggy features.

Caesar went directly to the dais, ascended it, and sat on the carved ivory curule chair, the X-shaped seat from which official pronouncements were made. Sejanus, with his tightly curled dark hair and high cheekbones, positioned himself behind Caesar's right shoulder, though he looked more patrician than Caesar.

Marcus stood a pace behind Severus. Fingering the *corona obsidionalis* uneasily, he slipped it off and held it by his side, where his sword hilt should have been.

Caesar saw but did not approve. "Put it on," he snapped. "Or aren't you pleased with it, as Pilate is not pleased with the honor I gave him?"

The centurion quickly obeyed.

"Severus," Tiberius continued, "don't get too comfortable here in Rome. I am also sending you east . . . to Cappadocia. Like Germany, there are more rebels in need of lessons in proper respect for the Empire."

Marcus trusted his face was as unreadable as that of the general's. Safety lay in never letting Caesar know one's true thoughts. Even so, Marcus's hopes rose. He knew this new assignment was caused by Caesar's envy of Severus's popularity. Would being sent with Severus be Marcus's reward for saving Pilate's life? Going to Cappadocia to fight another war was preferable to the pain of anything to do with Claudia and Pilate.

An instant later Marcus's prospects fell and with them his emotions.

"So," Tiberius announced, "one solution raises another question. Who is capable of watching over the new Judean prefect and his family?" His query was directed not at Severus nor at Sejanus but at Marcus. "Pilate must have a wise friend at his side who can learn the ways of the Jews. Strong and resourceful without being headstrong and foolish."

Marcus stifled a sigh, then replied in the only way possible. "I live to serve you and the Empire."

Peering at the image of the god Tiberinus, Caesar rubbed his chin as if consulting a mirror about the need for a shave. Musing aloud, he said, "I'm told Herod Antipas has named a city after me . . . on the shore of the Lake of Galilee."

"Now Lake Tiberias," Sejanus corrected. "A beautiful place."

Caesar offered a negligent wave. "Herod's trying to impress me. I'm not entirely sure if it's an honor or an insult. They say he built the new city atop an old cemetery. The Jews were offended. They rioted and refuse to enter the city."

Leaning forward, Sejanus suggested, "There is little that does not offend the Jews. They are the most easily insulted of all peoples, while having the least reason for pride. What have they ever contributed of lasting value?" Sejanus's prejudice against Jews was well known. His persecutions had driven most of their race out of Rome or into hiding. It was said he would prefer to exterminate them altogether.

Studying Marcus from his deep-set eyes, Caesar asked, "You know Pilate as well as any man living. You were raised as a fosterling alongside him. You come from Britannia, a race of conquered people like the Jews. Tell me, what do you think of him as the new procurator of Judea?"

This was the moment Marcus had been dreading ever since being dragged into this consultation. Pilate, though in disfavor, was still Caesar's son-in-law. Neither Severus nor the crown of honor Marcus wore could protect him from falling if he put a foot wrong now.

To gain more time to think, he equivocated. "Is it your intention to make him responsible to the governor in Syria?"

Caesar snorted. "Of course! And the legions in Syria can put down a Jewish revolt, if it comes to that. But those legions won't save Pilate's neck if he's the cause of the rioting."

"The Jews are . . . difficult, Caesar," Severus said, coming to the aid of his subordinate. "They have holy men beloved by their people, while those same holy men are hated by Herod. He is not even Jewish, but Herod would like to be king of the Jews."

"And the Jews hate him for it," Sejanus added. "They even hate their own priests. Hardheaded and rebellious at all times."

"And ungrateful," Caesar added. "Don't forget that. I give them freedom to worship their own god. What else do they want?"

Silence hovered in the audience chamber. Then Tiberius Caesar, master of the world, shouted at Marcus, "Speak plainly, Centurion! One soldier to another. What do you think?"

"Here is what I have heard," Marcus offered in response to the direct command. "The Jewish high priest keeps his position by permission of Rome. His family receives part of every tithe and every sacrifice. The common people know this. And they know the high priest only survives because of Rome."

Laughing without real mirth, Caesar said, "And I hear the high priest is richer than I am. Sejanus, remind me to raise their taxes." He motioned for Marcus to continue his recitation.

"So, if this is true," the centurion resumed, "then the Jews despise the Jewish leaders almost as much as they hate the half-breed Herod and Rome. Anyone who represents the oppression of Rome inherits the whole load of their hatred."

As soon as the word *oppression* was out of his mouth, Marcus regretted it. Holding his breath, he wondered if he had gone too far, spoken too frankly. After years of guarding his emotions, had he allowed himself to think and speak as a Briton and not as a Roman officer?

"Oppression?" Caesar repeated in a disbelieving tone. "Have I not been merciful? Have I not offered the Jews Rome's protection? If they refuse to yield, then by the lash and the cross we will teach them the meaning of mercy!"

There was an awkward silence as all considered the lions' den into which Pilate was about to be thrust.

Severus cleared his throat, but it was Caesar who spoke again. "You, Longinus. You speak truth that no one else has dared whisper. I will send an edict with you to place in the hand of the high priest. Tell him Tiberius Caesar requires that the Jews make sacrifice every day to their god on my behalf. In this way I demonstrate my respect for their religion and their god."

Sejanus interrupted. "Respect! They don't deserve it. The last *Primus Pilus* of our legion there was kidnapped and murdered by Jewish rebels and left to be eaten by vultures."

Caesar turned toward his Praetorian prefect with narrowed eyes. Despite Marcus's dangerous words, Sejanus was closer to receiving a dose of Imperial rebuke.

Severus offered, "The Jews are an educated people, much in love with learning. They are a people of law, not like the barbarian Cherusci. Perhaps their leaders can be reasoned with? And the might of Rome always remains the final response to broken treaties."

Caesar nodded. "And so we are agreed. If Pilate is to have any chance to succeed with diplomacy, he must be supported by someone who understands the judicious application of force. You." He pulled up the sleeve of his toga and pointed a bony finger at Marcus's chest. "You, Centurion Marcus Longinus, are that man. You are hereby appointed the chief centurion, the *Primus Pilus* of Judea. You will leave tomorrow so that all is in readiness for Pilate's arrival."

Chapter 9

laudia sat on the edge of the bed beside her sleeping son. Jono, who often slept in a cubbyhole down the hall in order to be near the young master in the night, was not there now. He had been banished to the servants' quarters by Pilate.

Reaching out a tentative hand, Claudia brushed a lock of hair back from Philo's forehead. Her tender gesture uncovered one of his ears, revealing a familiar and much-loved distinctive earlobe. It was identical to . . .

Philo's eyelids fluttered to match Claudia's heartbeat. "Mama?" he asked drowsily. "Time to get up?"

"No, shh, baby. Sleep. Go back to sleep."

Philo grasped his mother's fingers, sighed deeply, and slipped back into sleep.

A noise from the hallway made her turn her head. Pilate stood there, glowering at the two of them with barely concealed hostility.

Claudia tucked the covers around Philo's shoulders. She got to her feet and, without hurrying, bent to kiss his cheek before exiting the room.

At a peremptory summons from her husband, Claudia followed Pilate back to his study. He walked ahead of her as if she were a slave, never speaking nor even looking to see if she obeyed.

Diamond-shaped shelving made of mahogany held hundreds of scrolls. Unread Greek philosophers jostled for space with unstudied legal codices. Ignored military histories shared cubbyholes with unopened genealogies.

The only parchment in view was spread across the claw-footed table in the center of the chamber. It was a map of the eastern reaches of the Roman Empire, displaying Syria, Egypt, Judea, and the border with Parthia.

Pilate circled the table and hunched over the map. His fists pressed into the work surface until his knuckles turned white. His mouth clamped into a humorless line. "Judea! We have a month . . . a month!" He spoke tersely, spitting out the words as if tasting acid.

Claudia regarded him coldly. "You heard Father. This is your last chance."

Slamming his fist into the middle of Jerusalem, Pilate demanded, "You can change his mind. You must! This is exile. Judea's a prison where everyone is doomed to failure."

Claudia shrugged. "Didn't you hear? I'm to share in this exile . . . this punishment. I can't change his mind. Don't you understand him at all? Prison? That will be the least of your worries. If you disobey, the next words out of his mouth will be to order your execution."

Pilate savagely jerked a chair away from the table. The brass feet screeched on the stone floor like a sacrificial rooster being slaughtered. He sank into the seat and pressed his hands into his temples. "He'll listen to you," he argued. "He always has. You have a month to soften him."

Claudia's head shook in denial of this assertion. "If even your friend Sejanus can't move him . . ."

Pilate whined, "There, in Germany, what I did, I did for friendship. I feared for Longinus's life. I wanted to keep him—" This was such a transparent falsehood that Pilate abandoned the excuse midsentence.

"Friendship," Claudia scoffed. "Ambition, you mean! You don't know the meaning of friendship. You and Sejanus have made certain Marcus Longinus never got any assignments except those no one else would tackle. You fear him. You fear how I feel about him."

"And still he won't die," Pilate lamented.

Disregarding the outburst of evil honesty, Claudia tugged her shawl more tightly around her shoulders. "Now it's all come back on your head. Judea! Judea, and Philo and I are condemned to go with you."

Lifting his gaze from staring at the wavy line of the Jordan River, Pilate retorted, "It's because Caesar wants you and that cripple out of his sight. Whose son is he anyway, Claudia? That cripple?"

Claudia charged around the table, clawing through the air toward Pilate's cheeks.

Roughly seizing her wrists, Pilate wrenched her hands away.

"Let go of me," Claudia demanded. "Don't touch me. You're hurting me."

Pilate thrust her aside. Claudia tripped over another chair and fell, cracking her head on the shelving.

As she lay sprawled on the floor, Pilate stalked past her and out of the room. Over his shoulder he added, "So . . . I have my answer."

⁘

Despite the late hour, Pilate found Sejanus wide awake. While Pilate waited, Sejanus dispatched messengers to the guard barracks and to the city prefect of Pompeii, and sent a letter to the commander of the garrison at Alexandria.

The home Sejanus occupied was modest, almost Spartan, in size and furnishings. As commander of the Imperial Guard, Sejanus had already aroused envy because of his close contact with Caesar. Because of this, he kept any display of wealth to a minimum.

For those who knew how to read such signs, though, it was the location of Sejanus's house that was most meaningful. No more than a minute's walk from Caesar's palace, it lay at the intersection of the Appian Way with the street leading directly to the Praetorian barracks. The former cavalry officer was at the nerve center of both political and military power.

Telling his servant he was not to be disturbed, Sejanus closed the door to his office. Motioning for Pilate to be seated, he tapped a forefinger on a document awaiting his signature. "Senator Paulus Hadrianus is guilty of *maiestas*. He is not properly respectful of the emperor's dignity, and he doesn't care who knows it."

Pilate frowned.

"He will die for it," Sejanus added. "The last words he will hear when the silk cord goes around his neck will be, 'You are no friend of Caesar.'"

"Hadrianus? That grumpy old man?" Pilate interjected. "He's no threat to Tiberius. He campaigned with Augustus!"

"Yes," Sejanus agreed with weary patience, "and he never stops making unfavorable comparisons between our present emperor and the last one. He will die for it." With two knife strokes of a pen, Sejanus signed the death warrant but left it in Pilate's view. "The world is divided into two camps. Between General Severus and me. Your rival, Marcus Longinus, stands with the general. And where do you stand?" Sejanus tilted his head, studying Pilate.

"Isn't that obvious?" Pilate retorted petulantly.

"I knew you'd come here tonight. At the Imperial supper you showed yourself angry, frustrated, and fearful. You will never make a successful politician unless you learn to control your face, Pilate. At the very least I hope you kept your mouth shut."

Pilate ground his teeth. "I should have left Longinus to die in the forest."

Sejanus snorted. "Don't forget who you're speaking to! You *did* leave him to die. I know the truth of it all. It is the centurion who could have let *you* be dismembered by the Cherusci after you disobeyed orders. Instead, at great risk to himself, Marcus rescued you from your foolish ambition. You tried to win glory for yourself . . . and you failed. And now your rival again wears the crown, while you are banished."

Spreading his hands in appeal, Pilate winced at the blunt reminder. "What am I to do?"

Musing aloud, Sejanus continued, "Severus and Longinus are connected, just as you and I are. The general opposes my route to the throne. He prays daily that you will fail again so I will be further humiliated."

The link between Pilate's shortcomings and Sejanus's disgrace made Pilate grimace again.

"There is no room for mistakes this time," Sejanus ordered. "Know this. If you do not rule the Jews well, I will not support you. I will not intercede for you. It was hard enough convincing Caesar to give you this posting."

"You did this?" Pilate uttered with astonishment. "You contrived to banish me to Judea? I thought you were my friend."

"I *am* your friend," Sejanus corrected. "Caesar was so upset with you he was ready to have you strangled for failing to follow orders and for getting ambushed. He already had a list of eligible suitors for your widow. It was all I could do to make Caesar talk himself into giving you one more chance."

Swallowing hard, Pilate lifted his chin and declared forcefully, "The Jews. I will crush them."

Sejanus shrugged, unimpressed with Pilate's display. "Caesar has given Marcus Longinus the post of *Primus Pilus* of Judea. You may have a month, but he sails at dawn. Never doubt he is there to look over your shoulder and report to Caesar. It's late. Go home. Keep your mouth shut. Stay out of trouble. Learn what you can about the ways of the Jews."

Walking Pilate to the chamber door, Sejanus added, "Tiberius is already weary of the affairs of state. He will soon sail for Capri and leave the government in my hands. I'll be free to weed out all who oppose us. You need a year without a disaster—a few years at most. You needn't be heroic, just competent. You'll be able to return here in honor with a great future ahead, only remember—" Sejanus clapped Pilate on the shoulder, then pointed at the newly signed order of execution. "He had a future once . . . but no longer."

Chapter 10

Marcus, accompanied by Carta, arrived at the seacoast at midday following the banquet. The centurion was struck by how rapidly the sweet and sour smells of the capital were replaced by the tangy salt and exotic scents of foreign travel.

Nineteen miles southwest of Rome, the bustling port city of Ostia provided Rome with access to all the riches of the Empire. Dates and figs and wine from Antioch were being unloaded, as were grain from Alexandria and pomegranates from Ephesus. The reach of Rome was wide, and had to be, in order to feed its insatiable appetite.

After arriving at his ship, Marcus worked nonstop. "Quintus," he ordered, "detail two men to see that my horse is properly stabled. Detail four more to load enough grain and hay for the trip."

"Right away."

Marcus's transport to his new assignment was not a warship but a commercial vessel. Using two masts for sails, as well as triple-banked oars, it was capable of carrying either fifty thousand measures of grain or seven thousand amphorae of wine.

Sailing eastward, it was bearing neither. A continuous cycle of slaves toted bags of rock dust down into the hold. Pulverized volcanic ash from Vesuvius, when mixed with lime and gravel, was capable of forming the strongest concrete, even setting under water and growing stronger as it aged.

"Cassius," Marcus said to his second-in-command, "have the men help with loading. And keep them moving."

Soon a double line of Roman legionaries trudged up and back down the gangplank, loaded with supplies and ballast. The constant loop turned the ship into an anthill of activity.

"Doesn't Judea have enough dust of its own?" Quintus groused.

The grit escaping from the sacks filled hair and eyes and mouths with bitter brown residue.

"Not for proper Roman engineering," Marcus corrected. "This dirt was used to create Herod's man-made harbor at Caesarea Maritima. Also much in demand for the aqueducts Rome wants to crisscross the land of the Jews."

∞

Before dawn, boy and bird sat together at the window and searched the empty sky above the majestic buildings of the Forum. A pair of doves soared over Palatine Hill.

Starling, her splinted wing decorated with yellow flower petals, perched on Philo's finger. She trilled.

"Jono says all your friends have flown south," Philo explained. "The flock lives out the winter near Jerusalem—the land where my father will govern and we will live. I will take you there, little friend, and perhaps you will find your mother and father."

Jono came to the door. "You are awake early, young master."

"Starling woke me up. She was calling for her family. I fed her bread crumbs, and she ate out of my hand."

Jono lowered his broad face. "I knew an old man who had a starling as a friend once. The bird learned to speak in human words. It sounded exactly like his wife, who was a shrew. When the woman died, the bird continued to scold and tell the man what a fool he was. And so the old fellow was never lonely."

Philo addressed Starling. "Little bird, you will only speak kind words . . . like my mother. Not like my father."

Jono's smile faded. He straightened and towered over the boy. "Your father rode out to tend to matters at the estate. I came to tell you I must be away today."

"Where?"

"I will accompany your mother on a day's journey to visit an old friend. Someone she knew when she was a girl."

"Can't I go too, Jono?"

"Not today."

"Who will be my legs?"

"Hyllie. A strong fellow."

Philo slumped. "But he has no tongue. He cannot speak even a word. I will spend a day without any conversation."

"The gods have given you Starling to talk to when you are alone. Teach her some good word . . . a word to speak to your heart. A simple word. Short. Something you want to remember if the days are long and dark and you are without company."

Philo tucked Starling under his chin and tried not to let his tears spill over. Jono covered Philo's head with his enormous hand as if to bless him.

The big man turned to go but then hesitated. He looked back. "You have not said. What is the first word you will teach your bird, young master?"

Philo pondered the golden eyes that blinked at the pale morning sky. "I think she is searching for those who left her behind." Starling ruffled her gleaming feathers and gripped Philo's finger with her claws.

A wistful half-smile returned to Jono's face. "How can such a tiny thing know of longing and family? It is a mystery."

"Mother says animals know such things as we know. I wish I could run like other boys. Starling wants to fly."

"She will fly again one day."

"And if only I could walk."

Jono nodded. "So, what word will you teach her?"

Philo placed his lips near Starling's head and whispered, "Hope."

Jono left the boy as the great city awakened. Farmers' carts trundled over the stone pavement toward the Forum. Bakers and fishmongers hawked their wares in the canyons of the streets.

By and by Philo spotted Jono alongside Claudia's sedan chair, weaving through the crowds and vanishing around the corner.

❧❧❧

The smell of fish penetrated the curtains that hid Claudia from the plebian rabble on the quay. Flies buzzed angrily, blending with the sounds of hawkers, sailors, and prostitutes milling nearby.

"Jono, come here," Claudia commanded. Her voice trembled.

The giant put his ear to the opening in the drape. "Yes, my lady?"

"I dare not get out. Dare not be seen in the open. Someone will surely report to my . . ." She covered her almost-slip swiftly. ". . . father that I was here."

"Yes, my lady. People are already staring at your chair and wondering who is behind the veil."

"Four hours to get here. Is his ship still moored? Are we too late?"

Jono straightened and was mute for a minute. She prayed that she was not too late and that there were no spies lurking.

At last Jono spoke. "I cannot tell, my lady, if he has sailed."

"Perhaps we should return to Rome, Jono. It was foolish of me."

"A few minutes more. The tide has not turned."

"I am sure I shall regret this. I regret it already."

"No, my lady. Wait here, and I shall see if I might find your dear old friend. Bring him back here to speak with you."

He did not wait for her to answer.

"Jono . . . Jono, wait," she called out to him, but he was gone.

There was nothing to do but wait.

◦◦◦

Tired from a sleepless night and hungry, Marcus was ready to pause for a meal when a tall, powerfully built black man with a regal bearing and a hoop of bronze around his neck approached him.

"It is good to see you again, sir. Marcus Longinus."

"Jono," Marcus greeted his old enemy. "You are well?"

Bowing deeply, Jono reported, "The lady wishes to speak with you."

"Where is she?" Marcus scanned the docks.

"If you would please follow me . . ."

Brushing rock dust from his uniform, Marcus accompanied the messenger a distance of two blocks by way of two turns.

As if sensing Marcus's impatience, Jono hastily noted, "She is just there, sir. You see?"

A sedan chair, completely enclosed by heavy drapes, was guarded by another quartet of Nubians. Jono called out, "He is here, madam," then he and the sentries stepped several paces aside.

The curtain parted. Claudia was framed in the opening.

The sudden shock of seeing her so near robbed Marcus of politeness.

"What are you doing here?" he demanded.

"I wanted to say . . . thank you."

"For what?"

Giving a long sigh, Claudia explained, "I know that, despite everything, you did all you could to defend him. You saved him, and you are still trying to protect him."

"You shouldn't be here," Marcus scolded. "Go home. Pilate is madly jealous. Use the month you have left to persuade your father against this. Pilate is neither a soldier nor a diplomat. Now it is you who must save your husband."

"Husband was not my choice," Claudia replied.

Marcus chose to ignore this argument. The circumstances of Claudia's marriage to Pilate were in the past. Too much had happened since. There was no going back. This was pain to no purpose.

He snapped at her, trying to sound as blunt and uncaring as he could. "Make him be a farmer. Take over the family's estates. Make wine and more babies."

"He is no kind of husband. Neither is he a father. He despises the child."

Turning one shoulder away from her, Marcus said, "I won't listen to this. I can't. He is the new governor of Judea and will be my superior."

Continuing as if she had not heard, Claudia leaned forward and seized his hand. "I can forgive him everything . . . even the worst that he has done to me, to Philo . . . but . . . Marcus, Philo is a good boy . . . a bright boy, a caring boy."

Marcus was stabbed in the heart by what might have been . . . what should have been. "It's too late, Claudia. Do what you can to change Caesar's mind. Stay out of Judea if possible." He added harshly, "It's too bad you weren't born a man. I believe you could have ruled the Jews. But if you come to Jerusalem now, I'll do what I can, but don't expect much."

Then, very much against his will and better judgment, he clasped her fingers in his. Lifting her hands to his lips, he kissed them, savoring once more the scent of the jasmine perfume she favored. She pressed his rough, soldier's hand to her cheek. Marcus felt a warm tear trickle down.

Abruptly, he let go. "I pray we don't meet again, Claudia. It would be better for us both."

With that he turned his back and strode away toward the ship.

Part Two

I am a foreigner and stranger among you.

GENESIS 23:4

Chapter 11

Marcus Longinus was ushered into the Jerusalem audience chamber chosen by Herod Antipas for state visits. The centurion, now *Primus Pilus* and the highest Roman officer in Judea, was left there to wait for almost an hour. He was convinced the act was merely to impress upon him their relative ranks.

The Hasmonean palace, while large and grand in its day, was old and drafty. The crumbling plaster on the walls meant that the wall paintings were disintegrating as well. It was not in the fashionable Upper City but just inside the northern city walls. It was further humbled by being placed below the Temple Mount and on the main caravan route into the city. It suffered from dust, flies, and the stench of camels and pilgrims.

Caesar allowed Herod the use of the place, which was more than a hundred years old. It was rumored, Marcus knew, that this slight was only one among a long list of grievances Herod felt he suffered at the hands of Rome. Herod's cherished ambition was to someday be acclaimed King of the Jews, as his father had been. To Herod it did not matter he was not Jewish. His mother had been a Samaritan and his father a half-breed Idumean, but this was politics, not race or religion as far as he was concerned.

Instead Rome provided Judea with a twenty-year-long series of prefects of whom Pontius Pilate would merely be the latest. Herod was called "tetrarch" and reduced to holding authority over only a fourth of his father's former kingdom. He ruled the region known as Galilee and a section of territory east of the Jordan called Perea, but not in Judea proper or in Jerusalem.

When Herod, enveloped in brocade robes, finally swept into the room, Marcus was struck by how similar his description might be to that of the old dwelling. Both were graying, sallow of complexion, greasy, and sagging.

Tetrarch Herod was not lodged in his father's much grander Jerusalem palace. That expansive mansion, built by the elder Herod, was furnished with marble halls, lush gardens, and spouting jets of water.

For two decades that magnificent structure had been the Jerusalem residence of the Roman prefect. It would now belong to Pontius Pilate.

If Herod resembled the pigs his subjects despised, his wife was more like a vixen. Thin where he was fat, Herodias had a pointed nose, sharp cheekbones, and coppery red hair. She also exuded aggressive sexuality.

Herodias's teenage daughter, Salome, stood behind her mother's shoulder. Both studied Marcus with frank, unblinking appraisal, while Herod's eyes darted around the room.

At his nod, Guard Sergeant Quintus, who waited with Marcus, produced a leather tube containing the Imperial dispatch. The container passed through the hands of three slaves before being opened by Herod's steward, Kuza. The document was in Latin, but Kuza translated as he whispered its contents to the tetrarch.

After listening with a lazy, unconcerned expression, Herod waved for the translation to stop. "So," he drawled in Greek, "my friend Tiberius is sending yet another caretaker."

Leaning forward, Herodias observed, "Pontius Pilate. I've heard of him. They say he's handsome." These words she spoke while staring at Marcus and darting sideways glances at her husband.

Salome studied the centurion with undisguised interest. To her mother she commented, "Not as handsome as this one, I wager."

This remark, deliberately made loudly enough for Marcus to overhear, caused him to unconsciously raise his hand to his thrice broken nose, then drop it quickly.

Salome smirked, pursing her lips as if blowing a kiss.

Doing his best to make his face expressionless, Marcus addressed his explanation to Herod. "Pilate has military experience, sire. The emperor assesses that such may be needed in the territory."

"And what of your own . . . experience?" Herodias asked.

Herod's flabby jowls quivered as he shook his head. Clearly he did not enjoy the teasing innuendo.

"You are the one who saved Pilate's neck in Germania, isn't that so, Centurion?" Herod offered the statement without any praise in his tone.

"You see," Herodias purred, "your reputation as a warrior goes before you."

Marcus paused. "Pilate and I were both in that battle, yes."

"I can see you both now," Herodias breathed. "Back to back, swords drawn. Cleaving the enemy. Now you're here. Exciting."

Herod sniffed. "The new governor may find this place more of a battle. The high priest slanders us. Religious fanatics stir up the people. A new battle every day." Gesturing toward a slave holding a jug, Herod accepted a filled cup of wine and drained it completely before continuing. "Depressing at best. Tiresome."

Trying his hand at diplomacy, Marcus noted, "Your friend Caesar wishes to lighten your burden."

Unimpressed, Herod snapped, "Then first he should silence the so-called prophets. Rome should permit us to share in the wealth extorted from the people by the high priest. By the gods, do you know what I could accomplish if my income was a tenth of what High Priest Caiaphas steals from pilgrims' pockets?"

"There is much to accomplish. Aqueducts. Road building. Peacekeeping. Governor Pilate's wife, Claudia . . . Caesar's daughter," Marcus stressed, "accompanies him here. Thus you know how much the emperor esteems you."

Salome clapped her hands. "Oh, Mother, we must have a banquet in their honor when they arrive." She wiggled sensuously for Marcus's benefit. "We'll hear all the news from Rome. Can't we?"

Moments later Marcus was dismissed with grudging thanks for bringing the news of yet another Roman governor.

After the two soldiers passed the gates of the palace and marched amid a squad of their own men, Quintus said wryly, "That pretty young thing has her eye on you."

"A younger version of the same breed of spider as her mother," Marcus shot back. "I plan to stay far away from all Herodian webs."

"Aye," Quintus agreed. "That sort of spider devours her mates."

∽∾∽

The bow of the ship rose and fell with the even cadence of a horse. Claudia smiled as salt spray sprinkled her cheeks. A sense of freedom washed over her like none she had ever felt.

"It's very good, isn't it, Mother?" Philo leaned his head against her. "We are like Starling, flying across the waves."

"Oh, look! Look!" Claudia laughed and pointed as a pod of dolphins raced beside them and played in the bow wave.

The prying eyes of Caesar's court receded. Fear had no power on this sea voyage. She had not imagined that leaving Rome would be so exhilarating.

"We should have been sailors, you and I," she answered her son.

Philo motioned toward the bird in her cage. "And look at her—she likes the wind. Yes, I will be captain of my own ship one day, and I will call it *Starling*."

At that instant Pilate puked over the rail of the ship nearby, then staggered off to disappear down the steps of the galley.

"But Father does not like the sea," the boy observed. "Nor does Jono. Jono is sleeping in the cargo hold and told me to wake him when we reach land."

"He will be sleeping several weeks if that's the case." Claudia gazed into the sparkling aqua water of the coastline.

Philo slipped his hand into hers. "Mother? I don't ever want to go back there."

She did not answer. Perhaps she did not need to reply. Were they not thinking the same thoughts? Feeling the same sense of light as the darkness of Rome fell away behind them?

The boy peered up at her. "Mother, our shadows. See? My hair and yours!"

Claudia's copper hair had tumbled loose in the sea breeze and gone wild with curls. "My mother had curly hair." She ran her fingers through the thick mane and tossed her head. "She told me once that there was a king in Jerusalem, King David, and he had curly red hair like hers . . . like yours and mine. Perhaps King David is our great-great-great-grandfather, and the closer we get to home, everything about us will become what we were meant to be."

"Do you think so, Mother? I feel like we are coming home."

She nodded and closed her eyes as the image of Marcus came to her. She thought of him riding through the city of her mother's ancestors. Would she see him there? Would they speak often and learn to smile at one another in spite of the heartache of never speaking about what they had once meant to one another?

No doubt Caesar had arranged this posting to mock Pilate and torment Claudia and Marcus with a love that could never be fulfilled. There was danger in Caesar's games, she knew.

Yet today, with the sun on her back and the wind in her hair, Claudia was unafraid. She licked the tangy kiss of salt spray from her lips and dreamed of Marcus.

∽⌀∾

The blocky fortress known as the Antonia loomed above the northwest corner of the Temple Mount the way Roman rule overshadowed local authority throughout the Empire. Besides being the barracks for the Roman soldiers in Jerusalem, it was also where the high priest's vestments were stored. Though the Jews were permitted to worship their strange god in their own strange ways, this bit of extortion was a constant reminder that such privileges could be revoked.

A simple wooden, cross-shaped frame stood in the corner of Marcus's room in the Antonia. From it hung his dress uniform—red tunic with gold embroidery and cuirass of polished, segmented metal punctuated with brass fittings.

Atop the upright was his helmet with its red transverse plume. Finally, resting like a bronze collar at the juncture of upright and crosspiece, was the *corona obsidionalis*.

Carta sat on the floor at the foot of the cross. He polished Marcus's greaves so that the embossed rampant brass bulls gleamed. The Roman legion assigned to patrol Judea, the Tenth, was actually in Caesarea Maritima, since that was the governor's official residence. Marcus had a small contingent of Roman troops permanently based in the Antonia, but most of the men under his command were auxiliary legionaries—Samaritans, along with Syrians, a few Greeks, and some Thracians.

The garrison in Jerusalem was enlarged as visiting dignitaries and turmoil in the streets dictated. The Temple officials had their own troops to patrol the sacred precincts. Herod Antipas also brought bodyguards with him to the Holy City.

Sometimes keeping the varying factions from slitting each other's throats was the greatest challenge. This would have been a constant struggle, were it not for the one thing that united them. They all hated Jews.

A couple hundred paces outside his window was a thick column of oily smoke from the evening sacrifice. A wind out of the north bent the pillar of black fumes just after it rose above the rooftops, carrying it away from Marcus and toward the Sinai.

"Smell that?" Quintus asked appreciatively, inhaling the scent of roasting meat. "Makes my mouth water. Wish the Jewish god wasn't so stingy."

"The priests of this unnamed being share it," Marcus corrected.

"Aye, but do they ever think to offer us a haunch of lamb? A little prime meat to supplement our rations would mend discord."

"You're dreaming." Marcus laughed, jamming a thumb out the window. "With every plume of smoke go prayers that we will choke on our rations. Why do you think they sell us the toughest, stringiest old mutton? Selfish, eh, Carta?"

The boy's head bobbed in agreement. "Selfish." Picking up his work, he moved to the window so the light would reveal any unpolished spots.

"And me such a cheerful fellow," Marcus teased, "for them to wish me dead."

"We've only been here a month," Quintus grumped. "How I hate the Jews."

Marcus grinned. "They return that investment with enthusiastic interest."

Carta turned toward Marcus. "Master, something is happening. Look." He pointed out the window.

Both Quintus and Marcus joined the boy at the casement. Following the line of his outstretched arm, Marcus witnessed a confrontation between a half dozen soldiers uniformed as auxiliary legionaries and a dozen Jewish men. There was too much confused noise from the Temple Mount, and he was too far away to hear what was said. But postures and angry gestures told him harsh words were being exchanged.

The altercation ended abruptly when one of the soldiers seized the most demonstrative Jew by the neck and flung him to the ground. His companions advanced several paces with clenched fists but retreated when the soldiers drew their swords. The Jew's hands were bound behind his back, and he was marched away in the midst of the legionaries.

Marcus sighed and faced Quintus. "Do you blame them for hating us? It's likely one of those troopers was a Samaritan. The Jews probably object to his presence anywhere near their sacred ground."

Quintus gnawed his lower lip. Marcus read his guard sergeant's quandary. He would not argue with Marcus as his superior officer, but neither was he ready to sympathize with hardheaded Jews.

"Discipline and control," Marcus declared. "When the new governor arrives in a few weeks, we will hand him a controlled situation. What he makes of it thereafter is up to him. Did you hear anything useful in the souk today, Carta?"

Dressed in a plain tunic, with his shaggy mop of dark auburn hair, Carta could go anywhere without arousing suspicion. Marcus had no problem using the boy as his eyes and ears.

Carta frowned with thought. "They say there is a new prophet out in the wilderness, near the Jordan River. Some say he preaches about right and wrong. God judging us, too."

"So far he sounds like every rabbi in this country," Marcus said.

"But some rich men . . . the ones who wear the leather things on their foreheads?"

"Pharisees? Yes, boy, go on."

"They say the preacher better be careful." Carta shivered. "He says Herod has married his brother's wife, and God will smite him for that. They say Herod will call it treason."

"Caesar would," Quintus observed. He casually dragged his thumb across his neck.

Marcus countered, "The plot of every Greek tragedy. Who really cares about a crazy man out in the wild?"

Carta shuffled his feet. "His name is John. John the Baptizer. Very popular with common folk. But Herod hates him, and Herodias hates him even more."

Catching Marcus's eye, Quintus raised one brow in reminder of their conversation about Herod's queen. In the month since their arrival in Judea, Marcus had worked hard to stay out of reach of the Herodian spider's web . . . and her daughter's.

Carta concluded, "The cheesemaker told the fig seller that Herod's wife . . . she will have John killed one of these days."

Marcus stiffened. With that much talk in the marketplace about a crazy preacher, perhaps he had been too quick in dismissing the threat this John the Baptizer posed to law and order. If the preacher had popular support and ended up dead via the hand of the vixen Herodias, there could be riots.

"Possible Jewish rebellion," Quintus noted.

"Possible trouble anyway," Marcus agreed. "Good work, Carta. Keep your ears open and your mouth shut."

Carta nodded, his face beaming with joy at the praise.

"What do you say, Quintus?" Marcus asked. "Is a Jewish preacher worth riding into the wilderness to investigate? Whether he is prophet or traitor? Better to let the new governor know what he's facing, eh?"

Chapter 12

A four-foot swell broke against the cutwater of the ship. Though named after the winged god Mercury, the galley was anything but swift. The hull balanced on each crest and then plunged into the following trough. Clean, bracing spray raced aft along the deck.

Seated with Claudia on crates lashed just behind the ship's prow, Philo lifted his chin into the spindrift. The grinning boy relished the rise and fall of the ship's motion. Seemingly endless days, nights, and weeks of ceaseless, monotonous rowing by three banks of oarsmen had been required to carry the merchant vessel from Rome and then into and out of Alexandria, Egypt, thus far.

While Jono and Pilate groaned in seasick misery below deck, Philo and Claudia enjoyed the ride. Starling chirped with joy as her cage swung from a peg of the mast. Hope!

Does the bird sense that each mile carries her closer to her flock? Claudia wondered.

On the last leg of the journey to Judea, it seemed their luck had finally changed. The pair of sails, one forward and one amidships, bulged with the force of the breeze, and the *Mercury* raced northward.

The favorable wind dismantled Claudia's coil of hair, but she did not mind. Getting her son's attention, Claudia directed his gaze to the carved winged helmet capping the swan's-neck-shaped stern post. "It seems the patron god of this ship is finally showing us his ability."

An elderly Jewish passenger emerged from the companionway leading belowdecks. Claudia recognized him as one who came aboard at the Egyptian port. As if an unseen hand tugged him toward the land of the Jews, his flowing white hair and beard preceded him as he joined them beside the rail.

"It seems we are the only passengers able to stand," the old man noted to Philo. Then his eyes fell on the crooked bare foot of the boy.

"I cannot stand, sir. But today I am flying," Philo said happily. "Like my bird will fly when her wing is mended."

This reply pleased the elder. "And . . . what is your name, young sir, and where are you headed?"

Philo was polite but eager to share his joy. "Philo is my name."

The newcomer tilted his head to one side so that the gale cleared the long strands from his eyes. He addressed a question to Claudia. "Philo? The name of a noble Jewish scholar in Alexandria. Golden eyes, like your little bird. A rare color. Golden eyes are a feature I have seen only among my people. Are you perhaps also Jewish?"

"My mother. And her mother was a Jewess from Alexandria. I never met her. My son and I are from Rome."

"Ah? Well, then. In the words of the Almighty to Father Abraham, 'Count the stars if you can.' Because of your mother and grandmother, you and your son are children of Abraham."

Brushing spray from her face, Claudia continued, "My mother died when I was just a child. A great beauty, yet a woman of great sorrow." Claudia frowned, concerned she had been too open with this stranger. She shrugged. "But I know nothing more about her religion."

"Well, young Philo," the man said, smiling at the boy, "carry your name with pride. The philosopher with whom you share a name has written, 'Be kind to all, for everyone you meet is fighting a great battle.'"

Claudia was pleased. "He sounds like a kind man, as well as a wise one, this Philo. And since we are to live in the land of the Jews, I'm very glad to hear what you say."

The older man bowed deeply. "Pardon me for not introducing myself already. I am Josephus the Elder, scribe and teacher of Jewish law. Bound for Jerusalem, where"—he lifted a bony finger into the gale—"great change is in the wind."

"We're going to Jerusalem too," Philo piped. "My father is taking us there."

"Ah? This wind carries you far from Rome."

Claudia explained, "I hope it isn't an ill wind. My husband, Pontius Pilate, is appointed by Caesar to be the new governor of Judea."

Raising his bushy eyebrows, Josephus scanned the deck for the Roman official or his guards.

Correctly interpreting the unspoken question, Claudia replied, "My husband is below. State business—"

"He's sick," Philo interjected. "Ever since the ship started going up and down. But I love it!"

Josephus nodded gravely. "I will bring his health before the Almighty in my prayers," he promised. Then to Claudia he added, "And I will pray your husband governs your grandmother's people, our people, with justice and mercy. That he will be every bit as just as you are beautiful."

Claudia stiffened, and her face reddened with more than the wind's kiss. "My husband is . . ."

Philo looked up sharply, attentive to what his mother was about to say.

Claudia relaxed her shoulders and concluded, "Is just a man, like any other man."

Josephus put a hand on Philo's shoulder and patted it gently. "Our Philo also teaches that the choices made by ordinary men and women can profoundly alter the course of history. If true, then all words spoken and deeds, done or not done, may be important."

Claudia was grateful for the cooling mist. She nodded but said no more.

∽∾∾

Despite Marcus's vow to investigate the prophet named John the Baptizer, other matters had claimed his attention.

Bandits and rebels attacking caravans drew the *Primus Pilus* far from Jerusalem.

Day after dusty day, he brought order to the area, capturing the rabble-rousers. Cynical, hostile expressions of the common folk followed Marcus and his legionaries. Even at night, he didn't relax his guard.

But every once in a while, he would dream of a beautiful red-haired woman. He would remember the feel of her in his arms, her heart beating next to his, like a fragile bird, safe in his nest. He would turn to kiss her and . . .

It was always at that moment he would awake with a deep ache to the reality of the hard ground of Judea under him, wishing their story had a different ending.

Chapter 13

When order had been restored to Judea, Marcus, accompanied by Carta, Quintus, and a cohort of legionaries, marched out of Jerusalem and down into the valley of the Jordan. They tramped over stones worn smooth by generations of pilgrims. The air was still filled with dust compounded of goat droppings and camel dung from the many who had traversed the path recently, seeking the preacher.

Stopping a traveler coming away from the river, Marcus asked, "Do you know where the man called 'the Baptizer' is preaching?"

The response was a fearful stare, a vacant shrug, and a violent shake of the head.

"John the Baptizer? Have you seen him?" Quintus inquired of a group at a crossroads. A Jewish mother snatched up her toddler, and her husband put a protective arm around them both. No one replied.

Marcus glimpsed pure hatred in the man's eyes.

At a spot marked by the stump of an oak fully eight feet across, knots of people converged from both north and south. The buzz of eager conversation was squelched by the arrival of the Romans, but not before Marcus learned what he wanted. "This is the spot, right enough. The man called John is down at the river."

The armed soldiers wheeled onto the smaller road. Many in the crowd turned back. Other onlookers parted sullenly, standing amid the clumps of willows and glaring silently as the Roman troops passed.

"Quintus," Marcus said, "they think we're coming to arrest him. I won't learn anything if we scare him off. Leave the squad here. You, Carta, and I will go on alone."

Carta was all eagerness. Marcus trusted that two men and a servant boy, even if sent by Rome, did not pose any threat.

John was heard long before he was seen.

The trail skirted a knoll covered in red anemones and golden poppies. The rising and falling cadence of a stridently piercing voice cascaded above the buzz of the crowd.[1]

"The time has come for you to change your hearts!" a stern, masculine voice declared. "Look inside. You know the truth about yourselves. Rend your hearts, and not your garments. The Almighty is giving you one last chance!"

Leaning toward the centurion, Quintus muttered, "Your pardon if I'm out of line, sir, but if this is a sample of his preaching, he's no threat as a leader. People want to hear pleasant things, not harsh words."

"True most places," Marcus returned, "but these are Jews, remember? Perhaps only pointed speech like that penetrates their hard skulls."

At the next turning of the trail they saw him—broadly built, like a laborer in a stone quarry, with a wild mop of coal-black hair hanging below his shoulders. He wore a simple tunic of camel skin, with a wide leather belt around his middle. His sable beard was long, parted, and braided, and his skin bronzed from the harsh Judean sun. He stood on a boulder a few yards out in the water, gripping a smooth wooden staff in his left hand.

Tugging Marcus's elbow, Carta inquired fearfully, "Is he Cherusci? He looks like one of the wild men of the forest."

Planting himself a little above and to the side of the crowd stretched along the riverbank, Marcus studied the audience while the prophet with dark, brooding eyes raved on.

"You steal and betray and cheat the people you are supposed to be leading. You sons of vipers!" Lifting an arm that displayed muscles like corded rope, John reached his right hand toward a knot of well-dressed onlookers. "How do you think you will escape the wrath of the Son of David when he comes?"

The crowd was made up of many different parts of Jewish life—wealthy and poor, powerful and humble, meek and menacingly hostile. Despite being elbow to elbow and jostling for a better view, these groups did not mingle but remained distinct from one another.

A barrel-chested man wearing the headgear that identified a member of the Pharisee sect objected to John's words. "Watch how you speak. We are true sons of Abraham!"

John nodded gravely as if carefully considering the

reply. Then, even louder than before and more scathing yet, he said, "And you *comfort* yourself with such words . . . while you *conspire* with foreigners to *rob* the *true* sons of Abraham." Thrusting his staff aloft, he stamped it forcefully three times on the boulder with a sound of hammer blows. "Listen—the Almighty can make better sons of Abraham out of these stones. Because they are already washed clean while you remain wallowing in your filth!"

The members of the pious brotherhood of Pharisees scowled. The crowd laughed at their discomfort, and the Pharisees grimaced all the more.

Quintus remarked, "This fellow's more abusive than a nagging wife!"

Shaking his head, Marcus turned away from the spectacle. "And so he is no one Rome or Herod Antipas need worry about. The common folk may laugh at his antics, but soon enough the Pharisees and the other rich Jews will kill him. Carta, come, boy. We're leaving."

"Prepare yourself. Turn from sin. The kingdom of God is at hand. Repent of your sins and be baptized to show your change of heart," John urged. A surge of poorly dressed onlookers splashed into the current to stand knee deep in the river around his stony pulpit.

John's bellowing voice followed Marcus, Quintus, and Carta back up the draw almost as far as the main road. "Messiah is already at work among us and will soon be revealed. You will know the true master of God's vineyard by his fruit. Come. Repent and come to the water. Let the mercy of the Almighty wash you clean!"

The squad of soldiers lounging in the shade leapt to their feet. Marcus told Quintus, "Prophets are ten for a penny in this cursed land. This John will have his moment of fame and then vanish like a straw floating down the Jordan."

John the Baptizer was no threat to Rome, Marcus told himself again as he, Quintus, and Carta headed back to the Antonia. Still, he pondered the man known as a Jewish prophet. "Do you see anything mysterious about him?" he asked Quintus.

"Strange, yes; mysterious, no," Quintus returned. "They say he refuses wine and lives with the wild beasts by choice!" The guard sergeant tapped his forehead. "Diviners in Rome live in fine houses and keep servants. Clearly, this mad fellow is failing at his trade."

Marcus agreed there was nothing mysterious about the man, except perhaps how he managed to offend the powerful and still continue breathing.

Pavor, Marcus's fiery black stallion whose name meant "terror," snorted as a starling flew out of a clump of brambles.

John the Baptizer claimed no special access to the gods. He did not offer any miracles as proof of a divine appointment. He thundered against wrongdoing, but accusing the Temple authorities of greed only restated what all the common Jews already believed.

No, he was no threat. An annoyance, no doubt, but no threat. As soon as the weather turned rougher either with heat and scorching wind or with violent rain, John's popularity would end, Marcus decided. The crowds would desert him for someone in more attractive surroundings.

"I have heard of Abraham," Carta said suddenly. "The Jews talk about him. But who is the Son of David?"

Marcus knew little about the beliefs of the Jews, except what he had learned from a bit of reading and his own observations since arriving in Judea. Even so, this was a question he could answer. "The Jews have a story . . . a legend, really," he explained. "It's in their holy books. It tells of a liberator called a messiah. The stories tell how he will appear and restore their nation to greatness, like it was in the age of a great Hebrew king named David. So, Son of David. It's a myth. Nothing more."

"Messiah," Carta repeated.

Quintus growled, "Some men have claimed that title before."

Marcus nodded. "Yes, and been imprisoned or executed for their claims."

A band of high, lacework clouds raced past overhead, though no wind could be felt at ground level. Glancing up, Marcus had the sudden impression that the sky was holding steady and the earth moving very rapidly beneath it. Something evidently communicated this sense to Pavor too. The black warhorse stomped nervously. His hooves drummed on the hard earth.

"As soon as each was arrested, the mobs melted like gobs of fat on a blazing altar." Marcus laughed. "The rabble may think they want a liberator, but they will not tolerate a loser. It's been two hundred years since the last Jewish leader gathered an army that lasted more than a single summer."

"Master," Carta said, "I hear people talking in the market. They hate Herod."

Marcus shrugged. "He's fat and lazy and not a Jew."

"They also hate their high priest," Carta added. "Just like that man back there said."

Now the wind from aloft reached the valley floor. A dusty spiral dashed toward the soldiers as if challenging them for the road. The vortex leapt aside right before reaching them. A sharp smell was carried by the breeze. It reminded Marcus of those nose-piercing unguents preferred by athletes for massages. It was not unpleasant but seemed out of place somehow.

"The high priest of the Jews is supposed to come from only one of their twelve tribes," Marcus explained. "And it should be handed down, father to son. This man, Caiaphas, like his father-in-law before him, bought the office from Rome."

"So he's an impostor," Quintus observed.

Marcus agreed. "Both a merchant and a thug. The highest bidder, and the one who bowed the lowest to Rome. Even so, the people can't do anything to change it."

"So the Baptizer is right?" Carta asked.

Once more, Marcus agreed. "Yes, he speaks the truth. But to no purpose."

"But," Carta mused aloud, "if he's telling the truth about the Jewish rulers, maybe he's telling the truth about their messiah?"

Mockingly, Marcus returned a fair imitation of John the Baptizer's hoarse cry. "Get ready—Messiah is coming! The Jewish warrior-king approaches!"

The foremost pair of soldiers in the column snickered.

Quintus barked, "Quiet, there, unless you want flogging!"

Instantly they fell silent.

"Empty promises to draw crowds," Marcus argued. Yet unfortunately, he knew, such hollow nonsense could become the soil in which rebellion took root. Was the Jewish holy man really no threat?

A clump of thornbrush, torn free and swirling on the wind, smacked Quintus in the face. Savagely he yanked it away and flung it down. The double file of troops following stomped it underfoot. "By all the gods," he swore. "From seed to root to branch, this is a rotten, bloody land."

"True," Marcus responded. "But Judean wine pleases Rome's emperor. So Judean vineyards will be pruned by the sword as needed and watered with Jewish blood. Quintus, let's get out of this dust storm. Pick up the pace." Pavor already offered to perform a parade canter, as if facing an enemy.

"You heard the centurion," Quintus bellowed. "Lively, now. Quick march!"

The dust in the air did not dilute the piercing, unknown aroma. Despite his scoffing words, Marcus felt an unease that had not been present before. It was as if what he scented on the Judean wind was change . . . unexpected, dangerous change.

Chapter 14

Had there ever been so many stars? Claudia leaned back against the mast and turned her face heavenward.

The black curtain of the sky arched over the ship like a diamond-studded dome. The flat sea was without horizons. There were no hills or treetops to conceal the whole picture of glory.

Claudia's mother had once told her that there was only One God, the creator of the heavens and the earth. Before there had ever been an empire created by man, the Hebrew God of her ancestors had counted the stars and knew them by name.

Tonight, in the silence of the voyage, Claudia looked up, remembered, and could almost let herself believe in One Great God above all. There was a temple dedicated in Rome to the Unknown God. Why did the Hebrews not name their God? Could the two be the same?

The starry pantheon of Rome's gods marched through the constellations from east to west. Mars, the God of War, gleamed blood red in the west above Venus, the Goddess of Love. The two bright points of light hovered just above the edge of the western sea.

Is Marcus looking up at these same stars? Does he remember? she wondered.

On such a night as this, when Love and War shared the constellation of the Virgin, Claudia had first pledged herself to Marcus. Under an ancient tamarind tree, they had made a covenant of eternal love with each other.

But what were vows and eternal love compared to the will of Tiberius Caesar?

She had watched as the love Marcus had felt for her transformed to hate when Caesar decreed she would marry Pilate or die.

After that, Marcus had turned his eyes from her when she passed by. She wrote him about the child within her, but he did not reply. Only when Marcus sent the slave Jono as a gift to her and the boy did she know he had not forgotten her. Every day since then, Jono, the gentle giant, had been a reminder of the man who had once loved her.

Might he love her still? Her heart quickened at the possibility. His kiss on her fingertips at the seacoast and the flicker in his expression said he did. But his gruff stepping back and saying it would be better for them not to meet again had cut as keenly as a knife. Reality . . . Rome . . . had once again intruded.

Except for the cheerful company of her son since his birth, her life had been unbearably lonely. There was an emptiness in her heart that no one could fill.

Tonight Claudia whispered a new prayer. "Unknown God, God of my mother, I do not know your name, but she told me of your greatness. I do not know you, and yet, if you made the heavens and the earth, surely then you must know my name. And I long to know if you exist. I am asking . . ."

The rigging of the ship creaked. Ropes and sails groaned against the tugging of the wind.

Was that an answer? She strained to hear God's voice.

∽✿∾

Mars and Venus. Two stars hung in the west beyond Jerusalem. Restless at the thought of Claudia's impending arrival, Marcus paced along the parapet of the Antonia. He could just see the governor's palace where she would be living. It was a cruel irony—to have her so close, yet unreachable.

When she came to Jerusalem, would she walk on her balcony and gaze up through the lattice to see his fortress? Would she think of him and long for him? Would her love draw him like a torch draws moths to their deaths?

What would the penalty be, he wondered, *for loving the wife of a brute like Pontius Pilate?*

He shook his head. He was a soldier, a hardened man of war. Besides, who was so insane that they would die for love? Marcus had long ago decided that he would rather live and keep alive the possibility that somewhere there was a woman he might love as he had once loved Claudia.

Perhaps he had already found her—Miryam, the beautiful Jewish widow in Galilee who had become his mistress. At least she pleased him and made him forget for a time, even if she frequently tended to mention a young man she loved in her youth.

But as the time for the arrival of Pilate's ship drew near, his thoughts turned back to the conjunction of Mars and Venus, a fire in the western sky.

Marcus told himself he hated Claudia for marrying a man she detested. There was no comfort in the knowledge that she did not choose Pilate. No relief that she was locked in a loveless union with a second-rate politician.

Marcus was her first love, he knew, and she was his. Perhaps she was the only one he had ever truly loved. His heart twinged with the memory of the day they had been torn apart because of Pilate's betrayal. How had he not seen the true colors of his friend—that he was a man of no loyalty when it came to raising his own position—until that day? If Marcus could go back, do it all over again . . .

But no, there was no going back. There was only pain in the recalling.

Later, after she had been hastily married to Pilate, she had written him about the child. He had read her letter and steeled his emotions. He did not dare reply. He could not permit himself to come so near the edge of love's abyss. One step too close to her, and he would tumble to a bloody death.

Marcus knew Pilate well enough to be certain he did not love Claudia. But Pilate owned her, like he owned his horse or his vineyard or his slaves. And Pilate, being a man who cherished power over people and things, would never let her go.

So it was hopeless.

The stars may have twinkled in the sky the unforgettable night Marcus and Claudia swore they were one soul. But vows made before heaven had been broken by the reality of earth.

Marcus, more restless than ever, gazed out over the sleeping city. When she arrived, he would do what he could to protect her and Philo . . . and what he must for the man who had betrayed them. But Marcus knew he could never again give in to the weakness of touching her. Those days were gone forever.

As he stared up at Mars and Venus again, despair swept over him. His loneliness peaked.

Then he thought of the perfumed air and soft moonlight on the water of the Sea of Galilee. He could reach the home of his Jewish mistress by morning. She would be more than happy to help him forget . . . at least for a time.

"Carta." He called his servant from a sound sleep.

The boy appeared after a moment. "Yes, sir?"

"Saddle my horse. I have urgent business in the north."

Chapter 15

The *Mercury* docked in Cyprus to resupply. Jono carried Philo down the gangway onto the quay and Claudia followed close behind.

The solid ground beneath her feet seemed to move as though she were still standing on the deck of the ship. She swayed a moment, then reached out to steady herself on a bale of cotton. "I fare better on the ship, I think."

"You have your sea legs," the captain congratulated her. "A true sailor, Lady Claudia. Better than most passengers on this journey." With an amused smile he stepped back and saluted as Pilate, gaunt and pale, staggered onto shore.

Pilate cursed. "Can it be I am to endure weeks more of this misery? Then step on dry land and find I am just as miserable as I was on the galley?"

"It will soon be over, sir," the captain assured him.

"If I am to die, I hope it is over soon." Pilate squared his shoulders in an ineffectual attempt to regain authority. "It is in our orders from Caesar that we are to board a passenger in this port. A Praetorian. Vara is his name. Caesar's finest. He will be my personal assistant."

"I see him," Jono said dully.

Claudia followed Jono's unhappy gaze to a bald, coarse-featured Roman officer who waded through the bustling crowds toward the ship. Vara was notorious for his cruelty among the guards of Rome. Like his master, Tiberius Caesar, he was known for and feared for his brutality.

Claudia leaned close to Pilate. "I was not told of this."

"Your dear father thinks so highly of us, my love, that he has sent his worst to watch over us."

That Vara was the worst, Claudia knew. But she also knew the truth, through the chatter of women in Rome. Vara had raped a Roman merchant's daughter and thus was being banished to the province of Judea. Accompanying Pilate was merely an excuse to move him effortlessly into a land where his brutish behavior at least wasn't within sight of Rome. The only reason he was still alive was because he was a distant kin to Lucius Sejanus, the head of the Praetorian Guard. But that relationship also made Vara even more dangerous. He would be trying to buy himself back into Commander Sejanus's good graces. Claudia shivered.

Vara came near. He brushed past Jono with a sneer. Vara's dark-eyed gaze lingered too long on Claudia's throat. Thin lips curved in a half smile. He saluted. "Governor. Lady Claudia. Beautiful as ever. I trust you are well."

Pilate, dry mouthed, struggled to speak. "I'm not well. The sea is no friend of mine."

Vara nodded. "You are a man of terra firma. The sea is for the merchant class, Jews and wanderers and those unsteady in life. Like that one . . ."

At that moment a white-bearded old Jew led his porter up the plank and onto the ship.

Pilate seized the opportunity to insult Claudia. "That explains it. So Claudia, my wife, fares better than I on this journey. She is born to the swells and squalls of the ocean."

"Thank you." Claudia bowed slightly. "My merchant-class ancestors gave me the stomach to conquer even the most unpleasant experiences . . . and the vilest of company. On land or sea."

Vara brushed the remark off and addressed Pilate. "You shall soon have your legs under you, sir. Judea is a brutal land, filled with rebels and ruled by impostors who are not Jews, but one step beneath . . . Idumeans. I have crucified many Jews and many Idumeans. The Jews die with less shouting, but they die all the same. Judea is a land that must be governed by a man like you. Caesar has chosen well."

Claudia could not resist asking, "And you, Praetorian Vara, how well do you manage on the sea?"

He bowed slightly. "I am a Roman, Lady Claudia. I pray to the gods I will sleep from here to port. And when I awaken, I will wake with the strength of a dragon."

❧

It was stifling in the dark cabin. Starling peeped as the ship rocked gently.

Philo stuck his finger through the bars of the cage and stroked her head. "I know. It has been a very long journey. Only a few days more, and then we make port."

Pilate moaned in his sleep. He was too ill to get out of his bunk.

Philo noticed that his mother was not in the cabin. As the *Mercury* had sped farther south and the nights grew warmer, Claudia had spent almost every night on deck beneath the stars. By now, it had become a habit.

Philo called Jono, who slept in the corridor across the threshold.

The big man rumbled his sleepy reply. "What is it, young master?"

"I want to go up and see the stars."

The hinges squeaked as Jono cracked open the door and scooped cushions, boy, and birdcage in a single motion.

As they climbed the gangway, the big man said, "I was hoping to sleep beneath the stars tonight. Somehow that makes the nausea less."

"I think Mother shall miss the sea when we are on land again."

"And so shall you, eh, boy?" Jono emerged into the warm wind and breathed in deeply.

"Yes. Our journey will soon end, the captain said today. We are very close. What will it be like, Jono? You were there long ago. You know the land of the Jews."

Jono stood quietly a minute, as if scanning for Claudia. Philo spotted her silhouette near the bow and almost instantaneously Jono moved toward it, as if servant and boy were symbiotic.

"The people are a strange lot. As the old man has told you, they have only one god and they will not eat the meat of a pig, though they be starving." Jono jerked his thumb toward the heavens. "And they believe that stars tell a tale of paradise yet to come and a great righteous King who will rule the world. They call it the Promised Land, where we are going. Yes, I know it all sounds foolish, but they seem to be a happy people with many festivals and feasts." He picked his way over rope coils and cargo. "And when they are not happy, they also have many riots and rebellions. They do not like to pay Roman taxes. For this reason your father must govern them. And they hate the gods of Rome."

"Mother," Philo called, "you are sleeping beneath the stars?"

"Come," she instructed Jono. "Put him down here beside me."

Jono deposited Philo on her lap. "If you do not mind, my lady, I will rest in the bow and keep watch over you and the young master until day breaks."

She nodded her permission.

"Philo," she murmured, "if only we could stay in this moment and never sleep again. There is some mysterious wonder that stirs my heart tonight. As though I am about to live an adventure much greater than anything I ever dreamed."

Philo rested his head against her. "I feel it too. Excitement. Like everything is going to change for us. What can it be, Mother?"

They sat in wordless awe at the vision of so many stars. By and by Jono slept in the bow. His snoring rumbled like quiet thunder.

Philo grew suddenly very sleepy. He did not remember when he drifted off . . .

๛

It seemed like only minutes had passed before the dawn penetrated Philo's dreams. His eyes opened to see gulls circling and crying overhead.

His mother was awake. She looked like she hadn't slept. Now she searched the horizon. "Good morning, Philo," she said with some hint of sadness.

He looked up at her and smiled. "Good morning, Mother."

"I think we have spent our last night upon the sea." She raised her hand and pointed. "Look there."

He lifted his head. In the distance, the outline of the land of the Hebrews loomed. "The Promised Land."

"Yes. At first light. I think it may be."

Starling chirped as white-winged gulls cried and floated above them in the breeze.

"Do you smell that?" Claudia asked.

Philo inhaled the scent of the new land. "It smells like . . . what is it? Not like Rome."

She caressed his hair. "Adventure, Philo. Vineyards, orchards, oak trees, and a whiff of cedar and blue sage. Yes." She laughed, raising her face to the rising sun. "It smells like home, I think."

๛

Jono held Philo up to face the wind in the bow of the ship. The ebony giant smiled and held a quiet conversation with the child. Claudia could not hear their words, but it did not matter. Philo was smiling.

Josephus sat beside Claudia.

"I can smell the land." The elderly Jew raised his nose to the wind.

"I don't welcome arriving." Claudia shrugged.

"You have had peace, these weeks, at least. Pilate and Vara sick together. Perhaps there is justice in that." He smiled at her. "And mercy for you of sturdy merchant stock on board our little island paradise." He patted her hand.

"I do love the solitude on board ship." She hesitated. "There is no love lost between me and Vara, the interrogator of Caesar's court." She didn't mention why Vara was really being sent to Judea.

"That is unmistakable, Lady Claudia." Josephus lifted a brow. "And perhaps an understatement."

Claudia managed a grin. "Vara is the sort of creature that, if the gods entered into the bodies of men, he would be inhabited by the very blackest, most evil god of all."

"I believe he has slept most of the way with the help of the juice of crushed poppies. And he is generous in one area—he offered your husband a vial for himself." Josephus's eyes twinkled.

"At least they have been quiet," she added. "But I dread the moment when they will wake up and cast their dark eyes around the world."

Josephus inclined his head in understanding. "You will

find that the affairs of state will keep them very occupied. You will have little contact with Vara."

"And my husband?"

"Ah. Governor Pilate. I tell you truly, he will hardly have an instant to rest. Your palace is in the old home of Herod the Great. It is a dark and dank place full of the memories of murderous deeds. But your time there will be limited. You will have a home in the port of Caesarea and perhaps another in the new city named after your father, the city of Tiberias in Galilee. A beautiful place. And there, perhaps, you will be away from the plotting and vanity of the Herodian Court."

"I loved our country home outside of Rome."

"Well, then, there you have it. Galilee shall be your refuge."

Claudia was silent awhile. It was not a bad prospect. Perhaps she would seldom see Pilate and never see Praetorian Vara.

"You will survive, Lady Claudia." Josephus's empathy, understanding, and wisdom had been a gift to her since their first meeting. Now his eyes spoke courage and hope into her soul.

"I have heard the stars in the heavens are the same in Galilee as they are in Rome. I will look up at night," she said wistfully, "and imagine I am somewhere else."

If only it could be with Marcus, under that ancient tamarind tree, and their destinies could change . . .

Chapter 16

*D*oes *Marcus see me?* Claudia wondered. He seemed to steadfastly look away as though their ship was still far out to sea. Lined up at attention in precise rows on the docks of Caesarea Maritima, the Roman soldiers sweated in their full dress uniforms. However, Marcus, mounted on Pavor, betrayed no sign of discomfort, despite the intensity of the Judean sun. Behind the Roman legionaries, a pair of Jewish officials from Herod's court stood beneath the shelter of an awning.

The oak-planked deck of the *Mercury* glowed white in the blazing light. It almost matched the marble dome of the Temple of Augustus that dominated the harbor. Beneath the meager shade cast by a furled sail was Pontius Pilate, dressed in the purple-bordered toga befitting his station. He accepted a goblet of wine from a kneeling servant and handed it to Claudia. He then took one for himself.

Standing several paces behind his parents, Philo darted nervous glances at his mother and fidgeted in Jono's arms. The towering black man was planted like a tree beside Josephus the Elder. Josephus patted Philo's shoulder reassuringly.

Pilate raised the cup toward the Temple, then toward the Judean landscape. "To new beginnings," he said, taking a swallow of the wine.

Claudia also lifted a cup. Her smile was almost imperceptible as she nodded toward her son and the aged Jew. "To justice and mercy and right choices," she said gently.

Pilate stared at her with skeptical curiosity.

Avoiding his gaze, Claudia sipped her wine.

"Six weeks at sea," Pilate said. "Learning the customs of those I will govern has been good for you."

Claudia nodded. "There has been a shift in the wind."

"Tiberius would be pleased at your change of heart toward our posting," Pilate observed, speaking over the top of her comment.

Lightly Claudia offered a touch of sarcasm. "You are surprised, my love? Should I not toast the coming ruler of my father's kingdom?"

Pilate studied Josephus. The scholar returned the governor's stare. "Then we must hire the old Jew as a tutor, since he lifts the dark clouds of despair."

"It is a new day," Claudia affirmed, taking another sip of wine.

A ringing blast of Roman trumpets interrupted the banter.

Claudia watched as Marcus barely touched the warhorse with his heel. Pavor moved six paces forward, stopping again as Marcus dismounted.

Pilate's gaze darted from Marcus to Claudia and back, as if attempting to catch them in some betrayal. Failing at this still left bitterness imprinted on Pilate's brow.

A peremptory gesture from Pilate ordered Claudia to descend the gangplank with him. Jono with Philo and Josephus followed. Motioning for the others to stop when they reached the dock, Pilate continued forward toward Marcus.

Marcus's hand thumped his breastplate. "Hail, Caesar. And welcome to Pontius Pilate, the arm of Rome in Judea." With a bow, Marcus added, "And welcome to his gracious lady."

There was an instant when Marcus looked past Pilate at Claudia, then immediately away. Even so, Claudia witnessed a flash of renewed hatred on her husband's face. "Once again, Marcus Longinus," Pilate said with a sneer, "it seems you have explored the land I govern before me. From the ship I found my view of the shore barren and unpleasant."

Claudia held her breath, but Marcus merely returned, "Then you do not truly know it, Governor."

Lowering his voice so that only Claudia and Marcus could hear, Pilate continued, "Tiberius appointed me to rule a land that delights in rebellion. Have no doubt. I will govern that which is in my hand."

Seizing Claudia's fingers, he squeezed them hard enough to hurt. She winced with the pressure and struggled discreetly to free herself. The space of three heartbeats passed, and then Pilate relaxed his grip.

Trying to cover her discomfort, Claudia summoned Jono to bring Philo forward. Pacing alongside her, Jono inclined his head gravely toward Marcus, though he did not speak.

"Look, Philo," Claudia said. "Look who has come to greet us. Marcus Longinus, the Hero of Idistaviso."

"Hail, Centurion," Philo piped. "Where's your battle crown?"

Marcus bowed to Philo and smiled. "Hail, Philo. I will let you wear it when you visit the legion in Jerusalem."

The Herodian officials, hearing Jerusalem mentioned, stepped forward to pay their respects to the new governor. "Which will be soon," one obsequious-sounding court steward intoned.

A second man in brocade robe and turban added, "Hail, Caesar! Hail, Governor Pilate!"

The first official continued, "We who serve the great tetrarch, Herod Antipas, greet the power and might and protection of Rome, come to us in the flesh."

Pilate said sourly, "Protection. Yes. Your master is in need of Rome's protection, I hear."

The Herodian courtiers exchanged an uneasy look. "We . . . that is, this is a land of rebels and . . . yes. Tetrarch Herod is grateful for . . . welcomes Rome's protection."

Pilate replied, "The only thing between Herod and rebellion . . ."

Claudia was grateful when he stopped himself from saying something undiplomatic.

Pilate continued, "I look forward to renewing my . . . friendship . . . with your master. I was a boy, but I remember Herod and his brothers as young men in the household of Caesar in Rome."

Both of the tetrarch's representatives took a relieved breath. One resumed in his most fawning tone, "Jerusalem eagerly awaits the arrival of the glory of Rome in our midst."

ᘏᘖ

Drawing back the curtain of the sedan chair, Claudia stared in amazement at Jerusalem's Temple of the Almighty. Framed in the vehicle's entry, and seen from the northwest of the city, the sanctuary of Zion loomed over the city like a snowcapped peak. Along the caravan route leading from the seacoast to the citadel of holiness bustled thousands of Jerusalem residents and thousands more pilgrims.

On one side of the conveyance strode Jono, fiercely scanning for any threat. On the other placidly rode Josephus the Elder on a red donkey.

The scholar leaned over toward Claudia to describe the scenery. "See how the gold lining the edge of the sanctuary roof catches the light? Gold leaf, each page separated by the breath of the artist and applied with a peacock feather brush. There is no more beautiful sight in all the earth."

Philo was seated on his mother's lap. Claudia felt the boy shivering with excitement.

Pilate rode a white horse at the head of the marching legionaries, while Marcus and Cassius rode farther back on the sides of the column.

Claudia heard Marcus order the procession to halt. "Standards down. Cover the images and into the cart with them. Lively, now!"

Lowering the pole-mounted medallions, the soldiers were quick to obey.

Wheeling his mount and trotting back, Pilate commanded, "Stop this at once!"

One image was already shrouded with canvas and another halfway into its protective wrapping, Claudia saw. She also spotted confusion on the faces of the men.

Marcus addressed Pilate. "It is Jewish law. We must not carry images of Tiberius openly into the city."

"What are you saying?" Pilate demanded. "What?"

"We risk a riot," Marcus explained in a lower tone.

Pilate glared at Josephus, as if the old man was personally responsible for this affront. "What is this madness?"

Calmly the scholar replied, "The centurion is correct. Jews are a people who believe in one invisible God."

Pilate retorted, "Caesar is the only god that matters."

"To display the image of your emperor," Josephus continued, "is a grave violation of our religion. I will not enter the holy city with you if you choose to continue with this offense."

His face reddening and his jaw working, Pilate snapped, "Ignorance! The Emperor Tiberius is the son of god, the divine Augustus. These standards were made new for this day. I begin my governance by honoring Tiberius. There is no territory, no matter how insignificant," Pilate added with a sneer, "that does not acknowledge his authority. It will be so here as well. I will have full display of Caesar's images!"

At a curt nod from Marcus, the soldiers obeyed, removing the standards once more from the cart and lifting them high once again. With no word of farewell, Josephus turned and rode away on the donkey.

Arrogance and pride stamped on his features, Pilate galloped back to the head of the procession and ordered it to resume its progress. Too softly for Pilate to catch, but near enough to the sedan chair for Claudia to overhear, Marcus muttered, "Pilate, you do your office, yourself, and the government in Rome no favors here today."

❧

The procession advanced another four hundred yards nearer the gate of the city. In that space Claudia witnessed the visage of the onlookers change from a wary crowd to a hostile, angry mob. The pounding of possessive Roman drums and the blare of assertive, domineering Roman trumpets echoed from the walls as if Jerusalem were throwing back the challenge in Pilate's face.

Herod's entourage, walking immediately behind Claudia's sedan chair, looked apprehensive.

Pilate struggled to control his prancing horse.

At a command from Cassius, the files of legionaries spread apart. The outermost columns of men shifted their javelins from their shoulders to their sides, iron points prepared to ward off any attack.

Despite the obvious danger, Pilate carried himself with no emotion visible to Claudia except overarching pride. His jaw was set and his shoulders braced. Claudia had seen that look before. No retreat was possible from the position he had taken.

"Blasphemy!" someone shouted.

"Blasphemy," other voices shrilled. "Take them down. Blasphemy!"

A piece of rotten fruit arched overhead to smack wetly against Pilate's armor.

"No images of foreign gods in Jerusalem," the mob demanded. "Pagan kings. Pagan gods. Take them down! Images of Caesar. Take them down!"

Philo clutched his mother's arm. Claudia cried out as rocks struck the canopy and curtains of the chair.

Wrenching a walking stick from someone in the crowd, Jono brandished it like a war club. Loudly, he bellowed, "Get back. Keep back!"

From both sides of the procession mobs surged toward the soldiers carrying the standards. Many Jewish hands sought to wrench the offending images free from the Roman soldiers.

A long, slim dagger stabbed downward toward a standard-bearer. Before the blow landed, another legionary smashed the attacker's arm with the butt of his lance, then pinned the man to the ground with its point.

"Cassius!" Marcus ordered. "Ride ahead! Turn out the garrison! Go!"

Hugging Philo tightly to her, Claudia covered the boy's head with her hands. She bent over to shield him further as the sedan chair rocked with the press of the crowd.

Jono lay about him with his improvised club, bludgeoning with one blow any who got too close.

More knives flashed in the sun, countered by thrusting Roman spears. A rioter screamed and clutched his stomach. A soldier, knocked to the ground by a stone, was trampled in the melee surging around the images.

Rushing forward, a quartet of rioters toppled Pilate from his horse.

Marcus spurred Pavor into the middle of the group. Slashing with his sword first on one side and then the other, he felled one man and scattered the rest. Leaping down, Marcus seized the bridle of the terrified white horse just before it bolted and assisted Pilate in remounting the animal.

Spurring back toward Claudia, Marcus ordered the soldiers to close ranks and make for the gate. "Quick march. At the double. Move!"

Legionaries and sedan chair bearers alike jogged forward while the outer files of soldiers continued to slash and thrust and clear the path.

Blood spattered up and into the curtained alcove, where Claudia covered Philo's eyes.

Charging legionaries, led by Cassius, surged out of Jerusalem's gate. Indiscriminately hacking with their swords, the soldiers struck down many who had only been trying to flee from the carnage.

The two groups of troopers met. At Marcus's direction they charged the remaining knots of rioters, putting them to flight. The procession made it inside the high-walled entry of the governor's compound and the thick oak and iron gates were shut against any further danger.

Jono carried Philo and half-carried Claudia, whose shaking legs would scarcely bear her weight. They reached the foyer of the governor's palace.

Pontius Pilate had arrived to take up his duty governing the Jewish nation.

Chapter 17

Marcus stood one step up from the bottom of the prison. The illumination shed by flickering torches did little to brighten the depths of the Antonia's dungeon. The spiral stone staircase that was the only access to the pit was referred to as the Gates of Hell. Everyone who descended the steps, including Marcus, risked his neck.

In the large, central chamber at the bottom of the shaft huddled a hundred disheveled, beaten, and bloody prisoners. Their hands tied behind their backs, they were so dispirited at their likely fate that a half score of Roman soldiers was enough to guard them.

Marcus observed them. Waving Cassius to his side, he noted quietly, "Shopkeepers. Shopkeepers and farmers swept up in the net."

Cassius nodded. "These are not assassins. Most of them didn't even have weapons. This was planned by someone else."

Marcus agreed. "Someone who got away. We'll find out who's behind it."

Marcus turned to exit the pit. The gleams of light were

not enough for him to distinguish the features of the prisoners, yet the shadows were not deep enough to hide the fear on every face.

Carta held Pavor's reins in the courtyard of the Antonia Fortress. Marcus remounted the animal to ride across the city to Pilate's palace to make his report.

The streets surrounding the luxurious grounds built for Herod the Great were crammed with hundreds of anxious Jews. Many were women and children and others elderly men. Younger men, of the age being held in the dungeon, were understandably absent.

The protestors stood or sat, stoically awaiting word of their loved ones.

On the black horse in his blood-spattered uniform, even in the growing twilight, Marcus was conspicuous. Trying to make his way through the crowd, Marcus walked the mount carefully in order not to crush people.

"There's one of them," an old man's voice quavered.

A women cried out, "Where have you taken my son? Where is he?"

Beside her, another woman, her face streaked with tears, called, "My husband! Reuben the Leather Worker. Where is he?"

The elderly Jew shouted, "Let them go! They did nothing wrong."

Reuben's wife begged, "Let him go. Why did you arrest him? He's no rebel!"

The aged man added, "They only defend our faith," not aware that his words indicted the arrested ones.

The crowd began to chant, "Let them go! Let them go!"

Marcus urged Pavor forward, forcing the protestors to move aside. The closer to the walls of the palace he came, the thicker the throng. There was barely enough space for Marcus to pass, and the mob quickly closed in again behind him.

Watchmen called out from the walls. The gates ponderously swung open. A squad of ten soldiers brandishing lances emerged and formed a lane for Marcus to enter.

"Welcome back, sir," the Decurion in charge of the gate guard offered, holding the horse for Marcus to dismount.

The close of the portal reduced the volume of the chant but could not block it out. The cry of "Let them go! Let them go!" continued ringing in Marcus's ears as he entered the palace.

The new governor was under siege.

࿔

Pontius Pilate strode up and down the length of his stone-floored office, crisscrossing the inlaid-mosaic pattern of glass cubes and precious stones. He stepped on the image of ripe clusters of purple grapes hanging from thick golden vines adorned with emerald-hued leaves as if attempting to crush the fruit underfoot.

Pilate was dressed in fresh clothes and toga.

Marcus remained unwashed from the battle.

"They just keep coming!" Pilate fretted aloud. "Hundreds more every hour. Thousands! Will they storm the palace?"

Marcus did not answer the governor's anxious query. Instead he said, "They want their men. That's all they want."

"They are rebels!" Pilate's attempt to inject firmness of tone was spoiled in Marcus's ear by the fact that it was a half octave higher than Pilate's normal voice.

"They are simple folk," Marcus corrected. "Simple folk who happened to be in the street when the Zealots struck."

Thumping one fist into the palm of the other hand, Pilate pronounced, "We'll crucify them in the morning as rebels. All of them. An example."

Patiently, striving to keep the weariness he felt from overflowing into expressing frustration at Pilate's stupidity, Marcus clarified, "Then the mob *will* come over these walls. You will be dead or deposed by tomorrow evening."

"They are worse than the Cherusci," Pilate lamented. "Because these Jews look civilized!"

Remaining as matter-of-fact as he was able, Marcus suggested, "You were warned. About the standards. You played into their hands."

Spinning on his heel so that his sandal squeaked on an amethyst grape, Pilate shouted, "What was I to do? Insult Caesar? Hide his images as if we were frightened to enter Jerusalem? This city belongs to Rome, and Tiberius *is* Rome. This is his property, isn't it?"

Marcus opted not to reply to the string of rhetorical questions.

Pilate continued expressing his exasperation. "How can such a people be governed? Every other province accepts the gods of Rome and the emperor along with their own customs. Why not these Jews?"

Marcus saw in this question an opportunity to prevent further bloodshed. "Turn the prisoners over to High Priest

Caiaphas. It is a religious matter. Demand a ransom, a bond of peace, from the high priest. A religious tax. Caiaphas will pay it, the prisoners will be released, the mob will go home, and the matter will be settled. Let Herod and the high priest offend their own people, while you collect revenue for Rome . . . and maintain the peace, as Caesar requires."

"Tiberius set me up to fail," Pilate lamented. "He knew this would happen."

Marcus frowned as he disagreed. "He hopes you'll show yourself wise."

"Tiberius laughs openly and calls me a fool!"

Marcus could stand no more of this miserable self-pity. The words slipped out before he could restrain them. "Today you proved him right."

Whirling again, Pilate snatched a sword from off his desk and advanced on Marcus. "Maybe you arranged our welcome. Maybe you caused this!"

Glaring into each other's eyes from two paces apart, neither man turned at the sound of a side door to the chamber being opened.

Claudia's voice was thick with disgust. "Don't be a fool!" she said to her husband. "If Marcus wanted you dead, he wouldn't need a mob to throw stones. Or my father to send an assassin."

Not taking his gaze from Pilate's, Marcus watched indecision replace anger. Pilate's will crumbled. Turning away from both Marcus and his wife, he tossed the short sword toward the desk. It landed on the edge, then clattered to the floor. The point struck a spark from a vine leaf and made the chamber echo with a hollow metallic ring.

"We were friends once," Pilate stated.

Marcus ignored that comment. Instead he said, "For the sake of Claudia . . . and the child, prove Tiberius wrong."

"You think I'm a fool. Both of you!"

"You are wise enough to know that if Claudia is harmed because of your arrogance, Tiberius will have your head sent back to Rome in a jar of olive oil. And I will be the one to cut it off and send it to him!" Marcus's words had the quality of cold iron.

Pilate bent toward the sword as if he would seize it and threaten Marcus again. His fingers touched the hilt just as Philo limped into the office from behind his mother. Eyes wide at the confrontation, he asked, "Mama?"

"Yes, my darling?" Claudia embraced her son, who buried his face in her neck.

"Josephus rode away on his donkey. Will he come back?"

"I hope so, Philo." Claudia glowered at her husband. "I do hope so. We have very few friends in this land." Her words were spoken to her son but directed at Pilate. "Very few indeed. We must not alienate that handful only because they speak unpleasant truths."

∽∾∽

At the far northwestern corner of the Temple Mount was a platform from which the plaza in front of the Antonia could be seen. Several stories below where High Priest Caiaphas stood was a throng of manacled prisoners. Coming out from within the fortress, they halted, blinking in the daylight.

Facing them was a score of Temple guards in their green tunics and conical helmets. Caiaphas watched as a Roman officer waved an order and legionary jailers started unchaining the captives.

Turning to his guard captain, Joachim, Caiaphas said sourly, "This new Roman governor has shifted blame for the riot onto my shoulders."

Joachim shook his head and murmured something about the corrupt and unscrupulous Romans. "Thirty pieces of silver . . . the price of a slave! . . . paid personally to Governor Pilate for each life spared. As if any of that rabble were worth a single denarius. Extortion!"

The captain of the Temple guard directed a file of his men to deposit obviously heavy sacks at the feet of the Roman officer. Then the Jewish guards took charge of the Jewish prisoners and marched them away from the Antonia.

The sounds of cheering and thanks being offered to the Almighty rose up from the streets of Jerusalem.

Ponderously shaking his head, Caiaphas likewise deplored the ransom demand. "A bond of peace, the Romans say. I say, even if they have to sell their own children to repay the Temple treasury, every man . . . every one of those prisoners . . . will pay back the price of bond plus fifty percent for my trouble."

～～

Claudia watched as her husband stalked back and forth across the stage in the palace's audience chamber like a prowling lion. The room in which Pilate received diplomatic visits contained an elevated dais. On it sat his chair of state. When Pilate delivered a pronouncement or made an official proclamation, it was given while seated in that chair. Any ruling from that position was backed up by the might of Rome. From there Pilate spoke in the name of Tiberius Caesar.

Every second or third time he passed the chair, he patted its arms as if to reassure himself of its potency. On the wall behind the X-shaped furniture hung the offensive standards bearing the likeness of Tiberius himself. Claudia reasoned Pilate was pleased with himself, since he regarded the images with satisfaction. It was as if he had exactly planned the events all along.

The steward announced the arrival of Tetrarch Herod and High Priest Caiaphas at the same moment. Lifting his chin, the governor seated himself in the chair of state and Claudia took a chair right behind his right shoulder.

Herod and Caiaphas may have come at the same time, but it was clear to Claudia from the way they stood apart from each other that they were not together.

Herod cleared his throat to speak, but Caiaphas was quicker. "You kept us waiting. We"—the inclusive word was offered unwillingly—"longed to welcome you."

With a snap of his fingers, Caiaphas summoned a line of servants carrying gifts for the governor. On a table in the center of the room they placed bowls of the finest dates, figs, and pomegranates. Beside these were bolts of woven linen in colors of blue, white, and scarlet. In the midst was a seven-branched golden candelabra Claudia recognized as a menorah.

Pilate waved it all away. "My wife and son might have been killed, and now you offer trinkets. Is that how you welcome Caesar's governor? High priest? Tetrarch?"

Clearing his throat again, Herod spoke. "Those people . . . ignorant cattle, my lord Pilate. A religious riot . . . not my domain."

Herod's disclaim of any responsibility confirmed what Claudia already suspected. Each man would try to shift the blame to the other.

Pilate addressed Caiaphas. "Religion. So it is your domain as high priest, eh, Caiaphas? Your herd stampedes and tramples their own calves in the street? Yet it has come to my attention that you dare to blame Rome?"

Caiaphas spread his broad palms in a gesture of denial. "What can be done with such ignorance and superstition? They flock to mystics in the wilderness. John the Baptizer . . ."

Herod visibly stiffened at the mention of the prophet's name.

"John the Baptizer speaks," Caiaphas continued, "and the common Jews believe he proclaims the words of the invisible God." The high priest waved a bejeweled finger toward the chair in which Pilate sat.

Scowling, the governor challenged, "You are their high

priest. Does your Jewish god demand his worshippers spill their own blood to dishonor Caesar?"

Caiaphas made a sweeping gesture that seemed to encompass all of Jerusalem. "We who rule the Temple built by Herod the Great honor Caesar and Rome. My priests offer our Jewish divinity a sacrifice for Tiberius Caesar every day. This," Caiaphas added with a certain smugness, "we have done since long before Emperor Tiberius requested it."

Herod rumbled unhappily, "Good religion is one-third superstition and one-third business. The rest is politics."

"And which third do you practice?" Pilate demanded.

Caiaphas clearly did not want Herod speaking for him, so he hastily offered, "We who rule the Jewish Temple are men of reason. We practice good business. That requires that we use superstition and politics to best advantage in order to control the people."

"Which makes you politicians," Herod observed with a curl of his lip.

Caiaphas refused to be baited. "A delicate balance," he agreed.

"Console them, control them . . . and pick their pockets, eh?" Pilate said to Caiaphas.

The high priest did not reply. Claudia frowned.

Pilate next addressed Herod. "Caesar appointed you tetrarch out of respect for your father. He was called 'the Great,' but he earned that title."

Herod lamented, "John the Baptizer stirs up the people against me."

"A lone voice, crying in the wilderness? One man?

What would your father have done? What would Herod the Great have done?"

Claudia shivered. She felt she had just overheard a conspiracy of murder.

Chapter 18

Herod the Great had built twelve courtyards within the compound of his Jerusalem palace. Most were filled with fountains and designed for strolling amid shrubbery and fruit trees. The private apartments used by Pilate and his family overlooked several of these, but now Claudia was seated on a balcony above a square marked off with white stones. At one end were targets for archery and javelin practice. The nearer quarter was a flat pavement designed for fencing.

Pilate wore a quilted, padded suit, padded gloves, and a gladiator's helmet with curved cheek pieces protecting nose and mouth. He was practicing swordsmanship with his trainer. Heracles was a member of the Praetorian company assigned as Pilate's bodyguard. Like his namesake, Heracles was immensely strong, but not quick of either foot or wit. Still, Claudia knew, the man was smart enough to let Pilate win most of the time.

Claudia watched as Pilate feinted to his right. Heracles countered the move with a lunge toward that side. With his opponent off balance and out of position, Pilate swung his blunt practice sword in a backhanded arc. The blow struck Heracles in his sword hand, making the trainer drop his weapon.

Pilate's face showed smug satisfaction.

The strike, though causing no real damage, stung. Heracles stood holding one wrist in the other, but still he asked, "Will you have another bout, sir?"

Shaking off the protective gloves, Pilate wiped sweat from his face and peered up at the position of the sun. "No, not today. You are dismissed."

Heracles saluted Claudia on the balcony and departed down a long tunnel leading to the bodyguard barracks. Pilate helped himself to a chalice of wine from a pitcher that stood on a nearby table. He lifted the cup toward Claudia before drinking.

"When we were boys," he called to her, "my father took Marcus and me to watch the gladiators. Then we would play at being swordsmen."

"Philo begs to see the legionaries drill at the Antonia. I think it would comfort him to know he is well protected while you are away in Caesarea."

Pilate lifted his eyebrows. "If it pleases you."

"There is little enough for entertainment here," she observed. "I wonder what my friends in Rome are doing."

A movement in the access tunnel must have caught Pilate's attention. He turned to peer that direction, though Claudia could not see who or what it was.

"Speaking of him, the *Primus Pilus* is coming," he explained.

"The centurion will be advising us on military matters . . . and spying on us for your father too, no doubt."

Marcus emerged from the tunnel. He must have seen Claudia on the veranda, but he did not even look at her, much less greet her. After acknowledging Pilate, he said, "You asked to see me?"

"You almost missed the fun. I was dueling with Heracles, and Claudia is . . . homesick."

Stepping swiftly to a cabinet that held a selection of weapons, Pilate chose two swords and tossed one to Marcus.

It was a challenge. "Shall we have a bout?" Pilate asked. "I was just telling Claudia about our childhood. She might find a demonstration enjoyable."

Marcus examined the short sword's point and edge and looked at Pilate's to see that they matched.

Claudia's breath caught in her throat when she realized they were not practice weapons, but real unguarded blades.

Whipping off his cloak, Marcus was revealed as clad in a tunic without armor. Since he had accepted the challenge, Marcus no longer ignored Claudia. "How is the boy?" he asked her.

"Frightened," she returned. "Since the incident when we arrived, he has nightmares. He weeps because he must sleep alone."

Pilate asserted, "We can't give in to such foolishness. We must toughen him up."

Advancing to two sword-lengths from Pilate, Marcus took a position ready to begin the contest. "Life will make the boy hard soon enough," he clarified.

Pilate scowled. "He is a weakling physically. He must be made strong in other ways. What use is a lame son? He cannot even walk."

Without further comment or word of warning, Pilate lashed out with his sword and the contest was on. Marcus gave back a pace under Pilate's furious onslaught, but he did not appear concerned.

"If I were his father," Marcus said, countering a blow with a parry, then aiming a thrust at Pilate's face that made him jerk his head aside, "I would buy him a pony and teach him to ride."

"If you were his father," Pilate grunted, "you could do as you please with him." He swung a two-handed, chopping blow and the swords clanged together, driving Marcus's guard down.

Flipping the tip of his weapon back up, Pilate's point scored a hit on Marcus's left arm. The scratch filled with blood.

Stepping back a pace, Pilate admired his accomplishment. "Are you out of practice?" He lunged forward again, aiming a thrust at Marcus's midsection that the centurion batted aside.

Claudia saw the moment Marcus realized this was not a game. The centurion's face hardened as he knew he was fighting for his life. How could this end? Claudia was consumed with fear for Marcus. He could not kill Pilate, or even wound the governor, or he would face crucifixion.

Stamping his foot like Pavor charging an enemy, Marcus

drove forward, sword flashing in the sunlight. Pilate gave ground—one pace, another, and then a third. In a moment the two sword grips clanged together. Pilate and Marcus were face-to-face.

Disengaging, Marcus backed up a step so the combat could resume.

Immediately, Pilate went on the attack, attempting the same move he had used to defeat Heracles. Driving hard to Marcus's right, Pilate expected the centurion to be off balance for the conclusive, backhanded swipe.

Instead Marcus countered the move with a faster sweep of his own weapon. Pilate, overextended, lost his grip on the sword, which went flying out of his hand.

Both men stared into each other's eyes. Both were panting heavily. There was a long beat, during which Claudia held her breath. Then Marcus raised his sword in salute and allowed the point to drop toward the ground.

Claudia gave a sigh of relief.

With yet one more salute Marcus turned his back on Pilate and strode away down the tunnel.

Pilate joined Claudia on the terrace above the dueling yard. When she saw him slowly ascending the stairs, her heart was gripped by a cold fury.

Claudia tried not to let this emotion show on her face, but Pilate had no such restraint. Raw hatred suffused Pilate's cheeks.

Stripping off his protective gear, Pilate carelessly tossed it aside. He snatched up another pitcher of wine and poured a mug so full that dark crimson drops splashed onto the floor. Draining it, Pilate poured himself another before either of them spoke.

"He could have killed you," Claudia said flatly.

Pilate sneered. "But he didn't. Marcus Longinus is no fool. And now I am certain. All that is mine . . ."

Claudia jerked away from his touch, but Pilate grasped her shoulder and squeezed. Forcing her to submit to the bruising pressure, he left the imprint of all his fingers on her flesh. "All that is mine is safe in the hands of the centurion. He will not dare anything different."

An hour later, Claudia watched her husband ride out of Jerusalem at the head of a column of bodyguards, leaving Marcus in charge of the garrison and the security of Jerusalem.

Chapter 19

*P*hilo's face gleamed with excitement as Marcus carried the boy from exercise to exercise within the Antonia's parade ground. Sensing this was not a time for a mother to hover, Claudia and two of her attendants retired to an interior room from which they could observe.

The fortress provided a training ground similar to the area in Pilate's palace. The plaza within the Jerusalem barracks was much larger, much plainer, and much dirtier. In one corner of the yard, legionaries armed with wooden swords dueled under the critical eye of their decurion. Elsewhere soldiers threw javelins at a rank of five human figures stuffed with straw and hung upright on wooden crosses.

❧❧❧❧❧

Quintus followed Marcus and Philo. When the trio approached the lances, Marcus asked, "Would you like to see me throw one?"

At the child's eager nod, Marcus handed him to Quintus.

149

Selecting a lance that was straight from wooden shaft to blade tip, Marcus hefted it in his hand. Without any further hesitation, Marcus launched the spear toward the center target. Though the distance was fifty paces, the javelin flew straight, piercing the heart of the target so that the point protruded from its back.

"Bravo!" Philo applauded.

While part of the garrison drilled, the rest cleaned armor, sharpened weapons, and oiled leather harnesses. A few, having completed their duties, knelt around a game of dice. Again carrying Philo, Marcus passed the gambling. A series of boxes and circles had been scored into the flagstones, together with a center circle into which the image of a tower had been etched.

Noting the boy's interest, Marcus explained, "Basilicus. The 'king' game. You throw the dice and move your token toward the center tower."

At that moment one of the troopers tossed the dice, then exulted, "Ha! Six, seven, eight! See? I win! Flavius, run up to the mess hall and bring me a flagon of wine. Quickly, or I'll have you flogged."

Marcus commented, "He is the 'king,' you see. The others must do as he says until they play again." The soldier named Flavius got to his feet and gave a sweeping bow to his "king" before turning and presenting his backside to the temporary monarch.

"There is a lot of jesting and mockery too," Marcus concluded.

Later, still carrying Philo, Marcus escorted Claudia and

her ladies to his quarters. At a gesture from Marcus, Carta handed Philo the *corona obsidionalis*.

"Not even Tiberius Caesar has such a crown," Claudia noted for Philo.

The boy held the bronzed circlet of spiked leaves as if it were a great treasure, turning it over and over in his small, pale hands. "I heard the soldiers say there is no general as brave as Marcus Longinus. My friend Josephus says in Hebrew, *Aluf Ha'Alufim.*"

"Champion of champions," Claudia translated.

Marcus reached toward Philo, and the boy reluctantly relinquished the corona. But Marcus was not taking it away. Instead he placed the crown on Philo's head. "Your father and I fought back to back that night. Pilate slaughtered a hundred Cherusci warriors."

"At Idistaviso Centurion Marcus Longinus captured two thousand," Carta added. "And liberated me."

The crippled child listened eagerly as the servant boy recounted what he had witnessed in Germania, and his dramatic rescue by Marcus. Leaving them to replay the memorable battle, Marcus accompanied Claudia to the window overlooking the courts of the Temple. The flagstones bustled with white-robed priests and the many-hued garb of worshippers.

Claudia said, "There is so much to learn about these people. What to eat, what not to eat. Festivals and holy days. More than six hundred commandments, I hear. How does one ever learn them all, let alone keep them all? But I must try. Tomorrow evening I will need an escort. It is arranged. I have begun lessons at the home of Josephus the Elder."

"Why doesn't he come to the palace?"

"Josephus is a devout Jew and won't come to the home of a Gentile, lest he violate his religion. And after what happened with the riot . . ." Claudia shrugged. "He says he will instruct me in the ways of the Jews so I can be of help to Pilate."

Marcus could think of nothing to say in response, there in the presence of the ladies of Pilate's court, except, "I'm sure he will be grateful for your counsel. And as to your safety tomorrow night, I will see to it myself."

Chapter 20

*E*ven though the home of Josephus the Elder was in one of the more fashionable districts of the city, its location gave it no better access to light on this moonless night. Claudia and Marcus, cloaked and hooded, traversed streets steeped in gloom. Traveling through the valleys that comprised the Holy City, the sky was as barred over them as the shutters securing the windows of the houses. Tiny glimpses of starlight filtered through from above. Fragments of yellow gleams escaped the locked shades.

The only illumination for Marcus and Claudia was shed by torches in the hands of two ragamuffin linkboys— Jerusalem Sparrows, Claudia heard them called. Occasionally they passed men warming themselves over flickering braziers or speaking in muted tones beside even darker alleyways. No one spoke loudly enough to be overheard.

Once at the door of Josephus's house, Claudia knocked. An elderly female servant admitted her. Posting himself beside the entry and dismissing the Sparrows with thanks and copper coins, Marcus told her, "Take as long as you want. I'll be here when you're done."

Inside the house, Claudia was conducted to the study. In marked contrast to the night, a wave of light poured out of the room. Oil lamps in sconces drove back the shadows. The chamber was ringed on three sides by tables dripping with partially open scrolls. Beside a center table gaped a wooden chest brimming with additional parchments. On the remaining side of the chamber a charcoal fire glowed fitfully. After greeting Claudia, Josephus invited her to sit while he rummaged through the chest in search of a particular roll.

"I visited the prophetess of Apollo in Rome," Claudia said cautiously, unsure if referring to a pagan god would mortally offend her mentor.

"Oh?" Josephus returned.

"She says there lives a true King of the Jews. Not Herod. A man in disguise among the people."

Josephus stopped rooting among the parchments for a minute. "King of the Jews? The stuff of legends among the pagans, but reality to us. Thirty years ago court astrologers came from Persia and Greece and Ethiopia in search of a newborn Jewish king."

"And did they find this Jewish king?"

"They made the mistake of inquiring first at the palace of Herod the Great. I beg pardon, your palace, as it is now. And Herod, fearing competition for his throne—he had already killed his own wives and children he suspected of disloyalty—sent soldiers to Bethlehem." Josephus waited to see if Claudia would comment. When she remained silent, he continued, "Sent them to search out and slaughter every male child under the age of two years, just as happened in the time of our Lawgiver, Moses."

Squinting into the chest, Josephus finally located the roll he sought. He pulled it out and gestured with it. "And now Herod's dissipated son sits on a throne as tetrarch of the Galil. As brutal and as terrified of the prophecies of our coming king as his father was."

Claudia stared at a tiny orange flame leaping from coal to coal. "The old prophetess says if Rome openly crowns the true King of the Jews, then here in Jerusalem there will be peace."

Josephus nodded while rolling and unrolling the scroll, searching for a particular passage. "Our scripture also has a prophecy. A moment, please. Isaiah. Aha! Here—'Therefore the Lord himself will give you a sign: The virgin will conceive and give birth to a son, and will call him Immanuel,'[2] which means, 'God with us.'"

Claudia laughed softly. "A virgin will give birth? That's not the way it works."

Josephus seemed unoffended by her gentle mocking. "True. But what kind of sign would it be if the prophet merely said, 'A child will be born'? Do not Romans hold that their founders, Romulus and Remus, were born to a virgin and the god Mars? The babies were set adrift on the river but rescued and suckled by a she-wolf. Now I ask you . . ."

Claudia laughed again, more freely this time. "I see your point."

Setting down the first parchment, Josephus produced

another and flourished it aloft. "And here is the prophecy of the prophet Micah that predicts Messiah would be born in the city of David. It was this message that turned Herod's jackals loose to butcher the babes of Bethlehem. Listen—'But you, Bethlehem . . . out of you will come for me one who will be ruler over Israel, whose origins are from of old, from ancient times.'"[3]

Musing aloud Claudia noted, "Caesar does not care who occupies old Herod's throne in Jerusalem. Not as long as the tithes and taxes are shared with Rome."

Josephus nodded. "And the high priest fears the people. He cares only for his share of the tithes."

"And Herod Antipas?" Claudia asked.

Combing his long, white beard with both hands, Josephus replied, "Like his father, this Herod truly fears the coming of the Jewish Messiah—this unknown king who will rise up and destroy the Herodian dynasty." Returning to the earlier scroll, the scholar found the place and read, "'For unto us a child is born, unto us a son is given . . . and his name shall be called Wonderful, Counsellor, The mighty God, The everlasting Father, The Prince of Peace.'"[4]

There was a pause in which both teacher and student pondered the words. Some bit of moisture in the fire escaped as hissing steam.

At length Josephus resumed, "I heard the infant king escaped Herod's slaughter and was taken to Egypt, to Alexandria, for safety. I also went to Alexandria and stayed. And now they say the king has returned. By his suffering, Isaiah says, he will redeem his people Israel."

"Prince of Peace," Claudia repeated aloud. "Can there be such a one? Can there ever be a time of peace?"

∼✑✑✓∼

Marcus heard the footsteps before he saw three dark-robed figures that appeared from out of the blackness. Their attempt to be secretive put Marcus on his guard. A dagger hung around his neck in a leather sheath, and his favorite short sword was out of sight, hanging by his side beneath his cloak. But the centurion drew neither of these weapons as yet.

The men were Galileans, judging by their accents as they spoke to one another. All were brawny, with hefty shoulders. Fishermen, perhaps. They appeared squatter in body and less agile than Marcus. Then again, they outnumbered him three to one.

"Unless you have business here, I suggest you keep moving," Marcus said calmly. Now the sword flashed out. Marcus also drew the dagger with his left hand but let it remain by his side.

Long, skinny-bladed knives emerged from their clothing. One brigand was close enough to remark, "I've seen this fellow."

A second added, "Sounds like a Roman."

Their companion noted, "Look there—the sword of a Roman soldier."

Marcus lifted his sword to assassin's eye level and swung it slowly from face-to-face. "Unless you want to make its closer acquaintance, you should leave now."

The first to speak, apparently the leader, ignored Marcus's words. "I do know this man. He rode with Pilate. Slew my cousin and arrested my brother! And the woman inside this house . . ." His eyes glinted with interest. "Pilate's wife."

"A fine haul in this net," the second exulted. "We'll take the woman and this one . . . or his body . . . to bar Abba. A pretty ransom!"

The trio of brigands moved in. The leader had only a moment to be shocked that, instead of backing away, Marcus ran toward him. Marcus's hobnailed boot kicked him hard in the gut, doubling him over. The weapon clanged on the cobbles.

Another stabbed downward with his dagger. Marcus's sword flashed out, chopping an arm between wrist and elbow. The fellow screamed loudly, dropped his knife, and scurried into the shadows.

At the same moment, Marcus used his other blade to parry a thrust from the third attacker. The man slipped under the blow and thrust upward.

With no time for a fancy fencing move, Marcus dropped his shoulder and rammed into his assailant, knocking him back against the wall of the house. The attacker's dagger flew from his grasp.

Marcus drove the hilt of his sword into his opponent's jaw. The blow caused the man's head to snap back and crack loudly on the stones.

Turning, Marcus saw the leader crawling toward his weapon. Stepping toward him, Marcus planted his foot on the man's hand, then placed the point of his sword to the assailant's throat. "I wouldn't try that if I were you," he warned.

A quartet of legionaries rushed up out of the night. Two more followed, dragging the last of the three cutthroats between them.

"What took you so long?" Marcus demanded.

"Your pardon, Centurion," one said. "But you told us not to come too soon and scare them away."

"True," Marcus agreed. "Take them to the Antonia. I'll be along soon."

The legionaries departed with the prisoners, one unconscious and two moaning with pain.

Minutes later, the door to Josephus's house opened. Marcus, again wrapped in his cloak, greeted Claudia and the Jewish scholar.

"Shalom, my dear, and good night," Josephus said.

"Shalom and thanks," Claudia returned.

Marcus was glad she appeared completely unaware of the skirmish outside the old scholar's door.

∽≈∽

Marcus gave a sharp whistle, then a second. Jerusalem Sparrows ran into view, their firebrands fanned by the breeze of their motion.

Claudia was impressed. "Torch boys. You had them wait?"

"There's a place where they can stay warm and still hear my call," Marcus said. "So, Josephus the Elder. Are you enlightened?"

Was Marcus breathing a bit hard? Had he been exercising while he waited for her? Claudia flicked a glance his way. Torches and enlightenment. That sounded like the teasing Marcus of old.

Claudia joined in. "I leave my lesson with a burning question. Could a new Jewish king spark rebellion among the common people?" It was such a relief to speak straightforwardly, without sidestepping the intrigues and dangers of political life in Rome or Jerusalem. She knew she could trust Marcus.

"The fields of hatred," Marcus said, "are dry tinder. If they were able, first the Zealots would stone Herod. Then murder the corrupt Temple officials in their beds . . . and plant them deep."

Despite the puns, the conversation was serious. "Pilate should find this secret King of the Jews and recruit him," Claudia murmured. "Rome will share power for peace. Whatever keeps the taxes flowing Rome will support."

"Secret king," Marcus scoffed. "Superstition."

"And if it is not superstition?" Claudia challenged.

"The Legion is ready to crush the rebellion and bring the peace of Rome to this place. Your idea is not bad, but it is in the wrong order. First Rome imposes peace, and then it anoints the strongest candidate to keep the peace. Hope for anything else is a wisp"—Marcus motioned toward the sputtering torches—"of smoke."

Marcus's breathing had returned to normal by the time he, Claudia, and their youthful torchbearers arrived back at the governor's mansion. Marcus never explained the cause, nor did Claudia ask. She found her own breath came quicker in his presence, but Marcus was at most times so proper and formal that his emotions seemed to be on ice.

"I am pleased that the evening was so peaceful," Claudia ventured at the entry to the family apartments. "Josephus says next time he will come to the palace. He is content, he says, so long as our meeting is outside, in the garden."

Marcus gestured that the meeting location was of no consequence to him. "I had a half dozen legionaries posted along our route tonight, in case of trouble."

"Thank you," Claudia returned. Now, how to conclude? "Thank you . . . my friend."

Taking the Sparrows with him, Marcus saluted, turned on his heel, and departed.

Thoughts of a Jewish messiah, the riots provoked by her husband's egotistical arrogance and foolishness, and her keen and continuing desire for Marcus produced a storm of conflicting thoughts and emotions. Claudia opted to concentrate on the one peaceful island in a troubled sea—Philo.

Claudia stood beside her son's bed and gazed at him tenderly as he slept. Carefully, so as not to wake him, she stroked his hair and felt her heart overflow with love. In this moment she could set aside all the other turmoil.

When he reached out in his sleep, she wondered if the boy somehow knew that she needed him as much as he needed her.

⌒⌒⌒

A short while later, no more than three quarters of a mile from the governor's mansion, Marcus evaluated the scene in the dungeon of the Antonia. One of the captured Zealots was chained to the wall with his arms raised above his head. His head lolled on his chest.

Grasping the brigand's hair, Cassius yanked his head up and examined the battered face. "This one's still alive."

The two others captured after the attack on Marcus lay on the damp floor. Their bare backs were striped in blood, and they lay curled and limp. One was dead. The other nearly so.

Cassius kicked the live one. "Took some persuasion," he told Marcus, "but they talked. Sicarii, all right. Dagger men. Zealots."

Marcus frowned. "That name they mentioned—bar Abba. Their leader?"

"Camps on the east bank of the Jordan. No exact location. Probably moves often. How did you know they'd attack tonight?"

"No great prophetic gift. Since the riot, we knew they would watch for easy targets to strike. I suspect they watch the governor's palace all the time." Marcus indicated the one hanging in the manacles. "Attacking a Roman officer. Punishable by death. Flog this one publicly in the morning, then crucify him." Indicating the one still alive but prone on the flagstones, he added, "Keep this one alive. Find his family. Bring them in. He'll do whatever we need."

Chapter 21

A final turn in the steep climb brought the cavalry troop to the top of the hill overlooking the Sea of Galilee. There, a mile or so away, lay the harp-shaped lake. It looked tranquil, deceptively tranquil, to harbor the rebels Marcus was seeking.

The Roman troopers shared the road with a throng of pilgrims. Scanning them with a suspicious eye, Marcus noted a cart carrying a sick man whose complexion was the color of sand and a blind man with bandaged face being led by another.

The rest of the throng was common folk—women, children, elderly. No threat seemed possible from any of these.

A quartet of cavalry riding ahead of the rest cleared a path for the contingent that followed. "Make way, there. Move aside," they repeated over and over. Slowly, the travelers moved apart for the soldiers.

The faces that turned toward this command showed weariness and some resentment, but very little anger. To Marcus's surprise, many of them—like the cripple being carried on a pallet, his legs twisted like corkscrews—reflected determination that bordered on hope.

"Let them fall out and rest the mounts, Quintus," Marcus ordered.

Spurring Pavor forward, Marcus confronted a man leading a donkey. On the animal rode a woman holding a boy about Philo's age. The child's head was tucked unnaturally against one shoulder. His hands were clawlike and his face a grimace.

"Where are you going?" Marcus demanded.

The woman was clearly frightened. Without speaking, she clutched the boy's head and hugged him closer than before.

Cassius, riding beside Marcus, repeated the demand. "You heard the centurion! Where are you headed?"

The man leading the donkey replied, "Taking our son to the healer."

"Healer? Where is he?"

"By the Sea of Galilee, we have heard," the man replied.

Cassius corrected, "Lake Tiberias it is now called."

"Your pardon, Officer," the father said. "I meant no offense. No matter what you call it, we hear a rabbi named Jesus of Nazareth is there. Teaching our people the ways of peace."

The mother lifted tired, scared eyes to study Marcus's expression. "They say he heals many diseases by the power of God. Our boy, he is . . . we are taking our son there."

Marcus waved the family to move on. Was that what this entire procession was about? A parade of cripples, diseased, blind, and broken, going to see a healer?

A swirl of wind brought an acrid, rancid scent with it. Even the warhorse lifted his head and flared his nostrils. Passing by two score of yards apart from the rest of the pilgrims hobbled a band of lepers. Clothed in rags, every bit of flesh or limb that showed was hideous to see.

"An army of cripples," Marcus concluded.

"Seeking a teacher who claims to heal," Cassius added. "Pitiful."

"A man of peace as well? Then not our man. Let's get away from the stench. We've seen enough. Ride on. Back to Jerusalem."

❧

Marcus, arriving on Pavor from the Antonia, snorted and shook his head, an expression duplicated by the black horse. Both man and beast felt frustrated disbelief at the confusion in the streets of Jerusalem. The scene playing out in front of them was the perfect expression of everything that was wrong with the Holy City of the Jews.

Two processions that had no intention of arriving together were entangled and blocking everyone's passage. Neither High Priest Caiaphas nor Tetrarch Herod Antipas would yield precedence to the other. The result was that when their files of porters and ceremonial guards simultaneously reached the battlements constructed by Herod the Great, there was much pushing and shoving. Moreover, the disturbance took place on Pilate's doorstep, just outside the entry to his palace.

Herodian guards blew their trumpets as if noise alone

gave them special rights. The Levite attendants of Caiaphas fought back with trumpets of their own. The din was deafening.

Religion, civil authority, ambition, greed, and foreign rule all competed beneath the arches constructed by Herod. What a mess this province was! Marcus couldn't really feel sympathy for Pilate, who had brought this posting on himself, but it was a nightmare and no mistake.

Driven out of their own streets, crushed into doorways and alleyways, the occupants of Jerusalem shot undisguised glares of disgust at their high priest and the would-be monarch. There were also those, Marcus noted, whose expressions went beyond dislike and disapproval to hatred and malice. Those were the ones who would bear watching.

The cacophony put Pilate's attendants on notice. The gates to the palace courtyard swung hurriedly open, as if begging the arriving guests to stop the racket. The retinues of both Jewish leaders were crammed into the plaza. Marcus remained outside, watching, while Herod and Caiaphas entered the official suite for a conference with the governor. A captain of Pilate's Praetorian guards bellowed for quiet. The angry exchanges between priests and guards did not stop, but the volume decreased.

Traffic in the street outside resumed a more normal aspect. Marcus noted two things. The common folk hurried past, as if anticipating further trouble, and some hard-looking characters continued lurking nearby, seemingly oblivious to any worry.

Minutes passed, then Pilate, accompanying Herod and the high priest, reemerged. Marcus nudged Pavor forward enough to overhear their final exchange.

In his high, arrogant tone, Caiaphas said to the governor, "If Rome is to govern, you must not be ignorant of the superstition that drives the Jews."

Pilate was not impressed. "Because of the teaching of a mystic, I am threatened by the population you govern. And the life of Caesar's daughter is put in danger. Tiberius Caesar may well question if you are capable of controlling your own rebellious people. Or perhaps Rome should appoint a beloved prophet . . . instead of either of you . . . as both a Jewish king and as high priest. I understand there is historical precedent. Perhaps someone completely new who will manage the people and the profits in your places?"

Marcus noticed the threat strike home. Herod's flabby jowls quivered, and Caiaphas's neck stiffened. The two men exchanged an unhappy, anxious glance.

"Take better care of your responsibilities," Pilate concluded, "or I will find those who can." With that the governor reentered his palace with head held high, leaving priest and king both awkwardly stunned, and each ready to blame the other.

"John the Baptizer!" Caiaphas spat accusingly. "What is he? Why bring him up to Pilate? One religious fanatic in a line of a thousand fanatics. And that other one in Galilee? Galilee's your province, isn't it?"

Herod returned, "Appointed by John. Both claim to be religious men. Religion's your area, not mine."

"His reputation grows," Caiaphas conceded. "I've sent agents to discredit him."

"The wrath of Rome is called down on our heads," Herod lamented. "What have I to do with Jerusalem?"

Caiaphas retorted, "You and Herodias are as much targets as I."

The caravans, untangled at last, proceeded to resume their travel. Ensconced in their respective sedan chairs, Caiaphas and Herod continued their loud banter. "The riot was entirely a religious matter! Yet I am equally blamed," Herod spouted.

"John the Baptizer," Caiaphas clarified, "speaks more against you than me. He's as much your problem as mine. If I fall, so will you."

Even while listening to the mutual recriminations, Marcus studied the road about a block ahead. He had not failed to notice how the men he glimpsed earlier, who had remained in the alleyways, now moved closer to the street. They shoved other bystanders out of the way and thrust their hands into the lapels of their robes as if grasping something concealed there.

It was time to act. Calling up to the guard patrolling on the walkway above the gate, Marcus commanded, "Ho, sentry!"

"Yes, Centurion?"

"Turn out the guard. Armor, swords, and lances. Two dozen men should do. Quickly!"

"At once, yes, sir!" Within the palace grounds an alarm bell clanged violently.

Immediately, the expressions of Caiaphas and Herod turned to terror. Demanding a return to the safety of Pilate's courtyard, the two groups once more fought each other, striving to reenter the gate.

The blades of Zealot daggers flung back the sunlight at the same moment it was reflected from twenty-four burnished Roman helmets. Roman soldiers trotted out, lances at the ready.

The sicarii must have caught sight of this rapid reaction, because they broke off their attack. Now escaping crucifixion was all that mattered. The rebels broke for the crowd, with the legionaries in pursuit.

Pleased with the response by the troops, Marcus could not help mocking the servants of the Jewish officials. "So," he said to the captain of Herod's guard, "trumpets to fight Zealots?"

"To warn the people to move aside," the man stammered.

"Ah. Well, a dozen rusty blades were waiting to be drawn to find the heart of your master in the street. How is it you did not post sentries on watch outside the gates?"

The street, so jammed with bustling shoppers and pilgrims earlier, was now completely deserted. "I stand corrected," Marcus said. "Your trumpets worked."

Five of the would-be attackers were caught, dragged back to the palace, and held at spearpoint at Marcus's feet. "Take them to the Antonia," he ordered. "Also, detail squads to accompany Lord Caiaphas and Lord Herod and their . . . musicians . . . to their respective destinations." Lowering his tone, he addressed the guard captain alone. "And double the watch around the palace tonight. Patrol the streets. You understand?"

"It shall be done," the officer returned.

Marcus didn't hear any more banter between Herod and Caiaphas as their interrupted journey continued at last.

∽∾∾

Pilate and Claudia were in their apartments when the alarm sounded. Emerging onto a balcony, they saw the pursuit in the streets. "A near disaster well handled, I think," Pilate commented in self-congratulation.

"A near disaster, yes," Claudia agreed.

Pilate's continued praise of himself allowed Claudia's sarcasm to pass unnoticed. "I may wash my hands of those two idiots."

Claudia saw Marcus giving directions regarding the prisoners and the sentries. When she spoke again, it was to say, "You must learn the ways of the Jews."

Shaking his head, Pilate countered, "This is what I need to know—how to keep the Zealots under control and how to keep the high priest and Herod squabbling among themselves until we can depose them both and install a new high priest and Jewish king."

A servant announced, "Centurion Marcus Longinus is here to report."

"Let him enter."

Marcus spoke to Pilate, but his words were for Claudia. "You are safe and well?"

"Perfectly," Pilate said. "There was never any real danger."

"And the boy?" Marcus asked.

Claudia looked away. It was unlike Marcus to address himself to her in front of Pilate. "Well enough," she returned.

"Caiaphas and Herod will both survive another day, it seems," Marcus concluded.

Standing straighter in his pride, Pilate announced, "They have been warned to keep their houses in order."

"I heard them refer to another prophet in Galilee," Marcus added. "From the Baptizer fellow out east, to this man in the north." Claudia caught a look from Marcus and gave a quick nod in return. "The whole country is stirring. Everyone is following after this new fellow named Jesus. The blind . . . the lame. Lepers. We saw them all flocking the roads to hear him preach."

Pilate scoffed, "Escaped inmates from a leper colony and blind beggars are not an army. No threat to Rome."

"There are Zealots among them," Marcus countered. "My legionaries were . . . noticed."

"The Baptizer seems to be the root of all rebellion," Pilate observed. "You must go out to see him again. But this time, go as a common man, seeking answers from a prophet in these troubled times."

Pilate was very pleased with himself, Claudia saw with a rush of anxiety. It was at times like this that Pilate created more difficulties for himself and everyone around him.

Chapter 22

The music and drums from the Tiberias palace of Tetrarch Herod Antipas invaded the quiet landscape of Galilee. Claudia, seated beside Pilate in the carriage, looked over her shoulder at the tranquil Sea of Galilee as they passed through the gates of the walled estate.

"They are already drunk, I suppose," Pilate muttered. "We will put in our appearance, stay long enough for decorum, and then flee from the tetrarch's female viper back to our refuge."

Claudia nodded. In the matter of Herod and Herodias, Claudia agreed with Pilate. In the year since they had arrived in Judea, anything unpleasant in Claudia's world was called *Herodias*.

Pilate remarked, "How I miss the feasts of Rome. I am bored already. Truly, if there was any way to avoid this gathering of pompous Jewish elite, you know I would do so."

"She detests me," Claudia noted.

Pilate lifted her chin. "Perhaps it is because you carry more Jewish blood in your veins than she does?"

"She does not carry any blood in her veins whatsoever.

172

Jewish or otherwise." Claudia smiled. "I hear if she is cut, she bleeds vinegar."

"Well, Herod finds something interesting in her."

"Herod is a fool."

"We know that. We have always known that." Pilate paused and considered Claudia. "But your father is not a fool. He knows well your mother was a Jewess. And so perhaps he thought your heritage would be a tonic to soothe these rebellious, stiff-necked Jews."

"I prefer the company of men and women who are truly of the lineage of Abraham. These people who fawn and preen in the court of Herod are impostors, just as Herodias is an impostor."

The carriage drew to the courtyard. Raucous laughter emanated from within. Claudia grinned. "Speaking of braying mules, Herodias speaks."

He grinned back. "Always the first voice we hear in Herod's court. Herodias."

Claudia stepped onto the paving stones of the outer foyer. Her smile froze. There, before her in the torchlight, was Marcus, and beside him was a woman of extraordinary beauty.

Pilate seemed pleased at her reaction. "She looks like you in many ways—beautiful, slender, catching the eye of every man—except her hair is dark, her eyes a deep, rich brown, and her breasts are a bit larger than yours," he mocked.

"You planned this. After all these months, Pilate . . ."

"Ah, you didn't know, my love?"

Claudia resisted the urge to flee. "Know what?" she

snapped. She was angry with herself because her voice trembled.

"Speaking of impostors, you pretend not to care? You pretend you never cared?"

"He's nothing to me."

"Well, then, here's news. Your centurion—he who wears the *corona obsidionalis*—has a Jewish queen. She is his idol, his paramour. Look hard at them. Doesn't the color of that gown perfectly set off her tawny skin? This is reality. He beds this rich widow of Magdala. Miryam, they call her. Her wine and produce supply our garrison in Galilee. The wine we drink tonight will be from her vineyards."

"Why should I care?" Claudia felt the blood rush from her head as they walked toward the mingling guests.

Marcus turned his eyes toward Claudia. Cold and uncaring, he raised his cup in mock salute, then turned his attention back to Miryam.

The sensuous woman smiled and drank him in with wide brown eyes. He was clearly intoxicated by her.

"Here's news." Claudia raised her chin and swept toward the torch-lit courtyard. "Not only do I not care, I consider Marcus Longinus among the scum of the earth."

"So at last we agree on something. Come, you must meet her," Pilate insisted.

"I would not bother myself. She is nothing but a lowborn courtesan."

"So was your mother." Pilate laughed.

She resisted the urge to slap him. "I hate him." Tears stung her eyes.

"Tears, my love? Jealous, my lady?"

"You insulted my mother, and I-I hate him, and I will not—"

"Careful, Claudia." Pilate lowered his voice. "Someone may notice. Your hatred reveals your love."

∾◦∾

A pair of noble, aged, gnarled olive trees had been transplanted onto Pilate's new estate in Tiberias. Josephus the Elder fit well into the setting, like a third venerable tree.

Claudia and Josephus sat in the shade. A gravel path wound in and out among knolls tufted with reeds bordering artificial ponds and flowering clumps of red anemones and golden poppies.

Josephus gestured toward Philo, who was being led on pony back along the garden track. The boy's grin was as wide as his ears and his face as luminous with joy as the sheen on the chestnut horse. "Your son loves his new companion. Four sound legs under him."

Claudia's gaze darted to a balcony of the two-story villa. On it Pilate stood, glowering at the scene. Claudia nodded slowly and lowered her voice, even though no one was nearby to overhear. "A gift . . . from Centurion Marcus Longinus."

"First time I've seen the boy smile," Josephus continued, "since we left the ship."

"Philo loves it here," Claudia agreed. "The air, I think. And the water. Pure and sweet. Not like Rome, or Jerusalem. Oh, I'm sorry."

175

The old man laughed. "No need. Jerusalem may be the Holy City, but it requires a week of constant rain for it to be called clean."

Philo looked to see if his mother was watching. When he caught her eye, he waved ecstatically.

Claudia returned the gesture and smiled back at him.

"The common folk suffer in this land, the same as in Rome," Josephus said.

"Many innocent people are dying in chains."

Josephus caressed the open scroll lying on the oak table in front of them. Tapping it lightly, he said, "God's Word cannot be chained." Lifting his hand, he swept it over Galilee. "The water of our land may be sweet, but there is no water pure enough to wash away the blood on Herod's hands."

"I thank God there is no blood on the hands of Pilate . . . yet," Claudia said fervently. Unsaid was her thought, *Pilate already has enough for which to answer.*

Josephus turned his bushy-browed eyes to regard her seriously. "The soldiers of Herod are notorious for their brutality. From the time of Herod the Great, even until now. Pagans and mercenaries. Not Jews. They are jackals, not men, chosen for their love of slaughter. Samaritans and Idumeans, selected for their hatred of Jews."

Claudia fastened her focus on her son. Was there a god who could answer the prayers of her heart for his safety and happiness? "While the leaders of this land feast, mothers weep for their children."

∽✣∽

Pontius Pilate was in his office when Marcus arrived at the palace. The single word "Enter," uttered in Pilate's abrupt, snappish manner, responded to the centurion's knock. There was no greeting. Pilate was bent over a sheaf of maps, leaving Marcus standing beside the door.

"I know that step," Pilate said. "As familiar to me as the sounds of the birds outside my window at home."

With a pair of calipers Pilate traced the distance from Caesarea to Mount Carmel and then from a place south of the tiny hamlet of Bethlehem to Jerusalem.

"You asked for me?" Marcus inquired.

"I summoned you," Pilate emphasized.

Acknowledging their roles, Marcus offered a formal salute, which Pilate returned halfheartedly. He stabbed the calipers into the desktop, pinning Mount Moriah to the oak plank. "Philo rides his pony every day," Pilate said.

Is that the reason for the summons? Marcus wondered. He nodded. "When a boy cannot walk, it is good to let him gallop."

Placing his palms flat on either side of Jerusalem on the map of Judea, Pilate stated accusingly, "You meddle in the affairs of my house. Your business is solely to assist me in ruling this place for Caesar. Nothing more."

Marcus locked eyes with the governor. Neither would be first to look away. It was hard for Marcus to recall how he had ever thought of this man as a friend. "As is the way of fools," Marcus countered. The pause was long enough for the message to be clear, but he continued before Pilate leapt on it. "Soon Caiaphas and Herod will pull down their house with their own hands."

Pilate chose to ignore the jibe. "We do well to keep Rome at arm's length from the petty squabbles of priests and prophets."

"The Baptizer would have made a better high priest than Caiaphas."

"More honest, perhaps. Not better," Pilate corrected. "Caiaphas accepts bribes. John would not." The governor extended his hand, palm upward. "Rome requires a man of commerce to be the Jewish high priest—a man with a more practical outlook on religion."

When no answer was forthcoming from Marcus, Pilate shifted his view northward on the map and jabbed a thumb downward at Lake Tiberias. It was the same gesture Caesar used in the arena to order death for a fallen combatant. "What about the one in Galilee? Jesus?"

Trying not to give his comment any particular emphasis, Marcus merely replied, "A carpenter's son. A man of peace."

Pilate laughed. "Not the stuff kings or high priests are made of, then? So who shall we appoint as the new king of the Jews?"

Part Three

He will bring to light what is hidden in darkness and will expose the motives of the heart.

1 CORINTHIANS 4:5

Chapter 23

Marcus had been buried in all the aspects of running the military district of Galilee. First Cohort was never idle. Because bandits still looted, he increased the number of patrols. His activities kept him so busy that he barely had time to think about his last turbulent meeting with his mistress, Miryam, at her villa.

Yet the moment he'd learned her startling news still haunted him . . .

"Marcus? I am pregnant," she had said quietly.

He drew back from her. "And who is the father?"

She gasped. "You, Marcus! There has been no one but you!"

Disbelieving, he studied her with contempt. "You said the name of your precious Barak bar Halfi in your sleep last night, Miryam."

Furious, Marcus had ridden away from her home. He might have believed that the child was his, except for her calling out the name of her former lover in her sleep. His anger boiled so hotly that it was only his mission from Pilate that kept him from strangling her for her infidelity.

Pilate had been worried that during Herod Antipas's "arrest" of John the Baptizer, the prophet would "accidentally" be killed while resisting arrest. Pilate didn't want Herod to create any martyrs. So Marcus's job was to meet Herod's men at Selim on the Jordan and accompany them—not participate—in their capture of the Baptizer. He was to be an observer only, with no authority. But Marcus also knew he'd likely become the Baptizer's protector. If not, the Baptizer would die and Marcus would have to answer to Pilate for that. Interfering with Herod's men, though, would cause Herod to complain to Pilate and land Marcus in trouble. It was a double bind, with Praetorian Vara waiting to take advantage of such a time.

With Marcus on horseback and Carta on a donkey, the two traveled swiftly over the next two days. They didn't overtake Herod's soldiers at Selim, though, so they headed farther south. It wasn't until the morning of the third day, at the Jordan River crossing between Jericho and the Perean city of Julias, that Marcus spotted them.

He wasn't surprised that the tetrarch's four soldiers resembled the worst cutthroats from the bazaars of Damascus. "I am here as the personal representative of Governor Pilate and by his order," Marcus announced.

"Am I supposed to be impressed?" sneered the Herodian trooper who appeared to be in charge.

Marcus's anger at Miryam that had lingered throughout his journey now boiled over at the imbecility of the man. In one swift move, Marcus drew his blade and poised the tip of the dagger under the man's chin. "Yes, you are,"

Marcus said bluntly. "Now, let's begin again. What are you doing here?"

"We are here to seize the troublemaker known as John the Baptizer," the leader stated, his face pale with fear.

"Understood," Marcus agreed. "Provided the Baptizer is on this side of the river. Otherwise you are not to disturb him in any way. And if you do manage to arrest him, I will accompany you for a time . . . just to see that he doesn't break free and injure you, or call down fire upon your heads."

The other three soldiers exchanged secretive looks. In an instant, from seeing the leather strings about their necks that concealed their daggers, Marcus knew the truth. Pilate had been right. Herod had sent hired killers to take care of John the Baptizer. And from their murderous expressions, Marcus recognized that his own life was in danger as well.

"I'll have those weapons," Marcus ordered. "And I'll go with you. Move out."

Half a mile upstream from the river crossing they found John the Baptizer, still on the Perean side of the border.

The prophet's voice rang out. "Don't use your authority to force money from people. Don't arrest men on trumped-up charges and tell lies about them to get a reward."

The Herodian soldiers spat in disgust. "How much of this do we have to hear?" Grabbing their spears from Carta's donkey, the mercenaries pushed through the crowd of spectators. Marcus could not legally interfere, as much as he wanted to.

People in the crowd yelled to the Baptizer to flee. The

guard in the water retrieved his weapon and stood ready to defend the Baptizer. Bloodshed was only a second or two away.

"Master," Carta begged, "do something!"

But it was the Baptizer himself who intervened. He waded ashore and walked toward the soldiers. When the crowd surrounded him, protecting him against the mercenaries, he spoke to them like a father would to beloved children. "I knew this time would come. Go where I told you and find the one I told you to find. Then do what he says to do. Don't worry about me. Nothing can happen to me that is not written long ago."

Herod's men grasped the Baptizer and hustled him up the slope and out of sight of the crowd.

On the way to Herod's citadel in Machaerus, seven miles east of the Dead Sea, Marcus encountered a company of Fourth Cohort troopers returning from Arabia. Conscripting them to accompany him, both Marcus and the Baptizer arrived alive at their destination.

Machaerus was an inescapable prison, positioned on a rocky hill and enclosed on all sides by ravines.

Before Marcus took his leave of the fort, he told the Baptizer, "You did a brave thing, surrendering as you did. If you had fought, you might have escaped, but many in the crowd would have been killed." Marcus had seen the man's character in that moment—his unshakable courage, his caring for the people over himself.

The Baptizer shrugged. "It is for the Almighty to decide if my work on this earth is done."

Marcus blinked in confusion. "Who is this mysterious other you are talking about? The one you ordered your followers to find?"

The Baptizer stared directly at Marcus. "Jesus of Nazareth."

∾∾∾

It had been on the return trip from Machaerus to Galilee that Marcus saw Jesus. Marcus and Carta had slept overnight near one of the forks of the Jordan. They awoke to large crowds of people gathering nearby.

"This may be the man John the Baptizer spoke of," he told Carta. "We will go listen."

As they walked into the crowd, Marcus asked an old woman, "Where is the teacher?"

She eyed his Roman uniform briefly, then rested a gnarled hand on her cane and smiled. "Just find the biggest group of children. He'll be there."

He was indeed, sitting on the sloping sand with a couple of young children on his lap and three others close by. They were playing a game.

Just then Marcus saw a father carrying a child who was seized with convulsions toward Jesus. The father's expression was set with a single-minded purpose—to get his son to Jesus. In Rome, such children would have been left to die on the banks of the Tiber. Even here, the crowd parted as if the family had leprosy.

But Jesus moved the two children off his lap, then leapt

up, moving toward the father and catching him midstride. His arms embraced both the child and the man. The trio sank to their knees. Looking up at Jesus with a pleading expression, the father at last relinquished his grip on his child out of fatigue.

By now the mother had joined the group. For a while, all was silent, as if the wind itself and the chirping birds nearby had stilled. Then something extraordinary occurred. Marcus knew exactly when it had, for the mother's eyes brimmed with unbelievable joy!

When Jesus stood, holding the child, the boy's legs hung straight.

"Thirsty, Mama, thirsty," the child called.

She raced toward him and gathered the boy from Jesus' arms.

But the father remained prone on the sand. He reached for Jesus' ankles and grasped them. Jesus lifted the man up and blessed him. For what? A love that wouldn't give up?

Bewildered and uncomfortable, Marcus sought out one of the burly fishermen beside the river. "Tell your master that John the Baptizer has been arrested and taken to Machaerus." Then he couldn't resist adding, "And he may be in danger himself. . . ."

ॐ

After Marcus and Carta left Jesus by the river, both were silent. At last Carta asked, "Master, what exactly happened?"

What indeed? Marcus had pondered that question

ever since the child had been healed. In front of hundreds, something supernatural had happened. A child had been healed. The grief of the parents had been real. So had the contortions of the child. Clearly, they were not charlatans.

What bothered Marcus even more than the miracle, though, was the love in the mother's and father's eyes. The father's expression stated that he gladly would have given his own life in exchange for his son's healing.

Might Miryam's baby be mine after all? he wondered. *Did I speak too hastily? Did I wrong her? Is it time for me to become a father?*

That internal debate unnerved him.

Chapter 24

Marcus and Carta halted at the crossroads near Neapolis. There, near the edge of the reeking garbage dump, were two crosses, with bodies hanging from them. It sometimes took the men days to die. If anyone was caught trying to aid a crucified man, he would incur the same penalty. With that deterrent, only a single guard was left on duty.

"What are these guilty of?" Marcus demanded.

"Hail, Centurion." The legionary saluted. "They are guilty of *maeistas*."

Maeistas was a charge of defaming the state or the emperor. All it took was a testimony of two "witnesses" for anyone to get rid of a potential enemy, whether he was guilty or not.

Marcus peered up at the men's faces and was startled when he recognized them—brothers from near Pella. When the younger brother had been forced into Roman service and had attempted to flee, the older brother had swung a sickle to defend him . . . and been flogged as a result. Now the younger brother was already dead. The older brother nearly so. Neither were rebels.

"Who ordered this?" Marcus demanded.

"Praetorian Vara," the legionary replied. "For offending

the dignity of Rome. They are to be made examples. He himself witnessed the carrying out of the sentence."

Behind Marcus he heard a whimper. Turning, he spotted Carta, his face a frozen mask. But his body was trembling with pity and terror.

Marcus's anger flared further. He had grown increasingly wary and disgusted with Praetorian Vara's horrific treatment of the Jews, especially arresting them for trumped-up charges. Now he was crucifying the innocent?

"Take the boy down," Marcus ordered. "He is already dead."

"But the other is not," the guard argued. "The order says both must die before either is removed."

Marcus looked again into the eyes of the protective older brother, who had passed beyond being able to speak. But his expression of mute appeal was clear.

"Break his legs," Marcus demanded.

The older brother closed his eyes, as if satisfied.

It was the only act of mercy Marcus could provide, since it would hasten death. Flinging his coin purse at the soldier's feet, he said, "See that they are properly buried . . . not thrown in the quarry." He drew himself up to his full centurion stature. "When I return here, I will ask. And my order better have been obeyed, or I shall find you."

⁓⁓⁓

It was in Caesarea where Marcus caught up with Vara, at the construction site of a granite building. Marcus grabbed him from the edge of a crowd and yanked him out of sight behind a scaffolding. "Are you mad? For the past year, every effort has been aimed at keeping the peace, and now you jeopardize it? Why?"

"Take your hands off me," Vara demanded coldly. "So, you came across the rebels I executed at Neapolis."

Marcus tightened his fist. "What rebels? Those Galilean farmers—one of them barely a man?"

"Really?" Vara fired back. "They were seen in the governor's courtyard with the ringleader bar Abba and were also part of the disturbance in Jerusalem. We caught them fleeing after bar Abba escaped."

"They weren't fleeing," Marcus clarified, "they were simply going home! They live near Pella. Did they offer any defense?"

Vara lifted his chin. "Against *maiestas*?"

Marcus crossed his arms. "Let me guess. You were one of the two witnesses. Who was the other?"

"Tribune Felix," Vara stated, watching Marcus's reaction.

Marcus was stunned. The one honorable young Roman officer Marcus knew had been turned? Had he been bribed or threatened?

Marcus pushed away from Vara in disgust. After he'd made his report about John the Baptizer to Pilate's secretary, Marcus and Carta immediately left Caesarea.

～⊙～

Marcus and Carta stopped by his mistress Miryam's estate. With dreams of ending their previous quarrel and stepping into the role of father, he quietly mounted the stairs to her room. But she was not there.

He was exploring the items on her dresser when he spotted something protruding from the shelf beneath the desktop. When Marcus tugged at it, it came free. It was a scroll of parchment, with Miryam's handwriting.

Dearest Barak, it said. In that instant the horror of her betrayal pierced him more keenly than any arrow ever had.

Marcus waited three hours before Miryam returned home.

"Where have you been?" he barked at her.

"With Joanna," she explained, smiling.

"Liar!" he yelled, charging at her and grabbing her arms in a vise grip.

"Marcus, let go of me! You're hurting me!" she pleaded. "All right, I wasn't at Joanna's. I went . . . to get rid of . . . the baby!"

Her confession hit him like a body blow. His anger dissipated, replaced with . . . something else. Flickers of Jesus with the children swam across his vision. He felt a keen sense of loss.

"It's not . . . what I wanted," he murmured.

At those words, she transformed into a wild creature, kicking, hitting, and scratching him. He held her off easily until at last she crumpled, exhausted, on the floor.

Then he looked up at the heavens. "Is this all there is?"

He stumbled from her room and out of the villa.

"Master," Carta said, as soon as he saw Marcus, "your face?"

Marcus put his fingertips to his cheek and they came

191

away bloody from where her nails had scratched him. "It's nothing. To Tiberias, swiftly." He knew he had to be there when the news came out that Miryam had betrayed him and he had rejected her. He would paint the picture that he was tired of her, nothing more.

No one needed to know of the wounds other than those on his cheek . . . the deep wounds in his soul.

Chapter 25

Marcus had never liked having to attend Herod's feasts. Now he liked them even less. Miryam no longer accompanied him. Rumors swirled about her and her onset of madness. Marcus sidestepped them all. But it was growing more difficult to sidestep Herodias's lascivious daughter, Salome. Pilate appeared to delight in summoning Marcus to report on the progress in the Galil at such feasts, perhaps to ensure that Claudia noticed Salome's advances on her former lover.

For Marcus, dining had become a dangerous affair.

❦

Claudia detested Herod's banquets in the Galil even more than she did those of Rome. The only part to be enjoyed was the food. Even that, though, gave her indigestion on nights like this, when Pilate seemed to be fixed on vexing her. She was always seated in direct view of Marcus.

This night, as soon as she saw Marcus, she very deliberately turned from him. From her vantage point she noted Salome staring at Marcus, devouring him with her eyes.

Pilate also must have noticed the display of attention. "All the elite of the region are here." Then, to needle Claudia, he added, "Politics creates strange bedfellows, they say."

Claudia smiled through gritted teeth. "Spoken from personal experience, my love?"

"The centurion owes me a report," Pilate noted. "Shall I call him over?"

Above Claudia's protests, Pilate did so. Marcus and Claudia barely made eye contact when he reached their table, and both looked away immediately.

"So, Centurion," Pilate commented, "what news from the frontier? Is Rome safe from a Jewish savior?"

"I will answer your question with three of my own," Marcus responded. "What if there were a general who could feed an army of thousands on a single basket of bread? What if he could heal his wounded soldiers? Even raise up those killed in battle to fight again?"

Claudia grappled with this story. What was Marcus doing?

"Anyone we know?" Pilate inquired blandly. "Is this part of a Jewish myth . . . or merely lavish sampling of Herod's refreshment?"

"It is a man of no significance to the rulers of this world. The son of a carpenter."

Claudia still could not understand what this was about.

Pilate laughed and helped himself to an ample portion of the refreshment. His cup was immediately refilled by a slave posted behind him. "I thought you were serious! Then he will not call down fire from heaven?"

"If he wished to, I believe he could."

Pilate narrowed his eyes. "Then I see no reason you shouldn't continue to serve Rome in the Outlands. Samaria. Galilee. The wilderness. You may serve me more effectively there, keeping a close eye on the matter." His eyes flicked to Claudia and then back to Marcus. "That way—"

His next words ended abruptly since Herod chose that moment to raise his glass and begin his usual long round of toasts. When the crowd responded loudly and got to their feet to cheer, Marcus took the opportunity to bow himself away from Pilate and Claudia and exit the stuffy hall out into the garden, where he could breathe again.

All that was on his mind now was making his way as quietly and quickly as possible toward the stables. Going through the garden ensured that none would take notice of his leave. After the round of toasts, the already intoxicated guests would be too filled with wine to notice his absence.

When a footstep sounded on the pathway, though, he paused.

ᏜᏜᏜ

As Marcus took his leave, Claudia felt the room grow too warm and stifling. With a nod toward Pilate, she wove her way to the side of the room and then out the door to the garden.

Once outside, she walked rapidly toward a bench that appeared rarely used, since it was hidden in the shadows by day and nearly impossible to find at night. There she could rest awhile, away from the clamor.

Then a shadow loomed, one the size of a man, on the pathway.

Her heart beat rapidly. "Who's there?" she demanded.

"Marcus," came the answer.

Marcus. She knew she was safe. But then anger flashed. "Go away. You are the last person I want to see again . . . ever."

His shadow moved closer. "Yes. Well, I am leaving again shortly."

"I'm glad." She wiped tears from her cheeks. "Then you will be safe."

She *was* strangely relieved. The politics of Herod and Pilate grew more dangerous every day.

Marcus lowered his voice. "No one is safe. I know that. I have known it my whole life." His tone was gentle, tender . . . the way it used to be with her.

She switched the subject. "There's a rumor that you have grown too fond of the Jews." Her eyes met his.

"Miryam, you mean." He shook his head. "She is a madwoman. In love with someone else from her youth. I can't live with that."

"An old story."

"A woman without discretion. I have no more time for romantic games."

Why, Claudia wondered, *am I pleased to hear that the love affair between Marcus and the woman is over?* "Philo . . . will miss you."

"The boy is no part of Pilate, Claudia."

"No. Not at all like Pilate." She avoided his gaze. "So where will you go?"

"Religious leaders draw rebels like moths to flame. Your *husband* favors the military tactics of Praetorian Vara to keep order here in Jerusalem."

She flinched at Marcus's emphasis on *husband*. "Terror and intolerance, you mean," she fired back.

"That sums it up," he stated simply. "But temperance in ruling the Jews is the only hope Rome has to keep a Jewish rebellion from exploding."

"Pilate is hardly a man of temperance," Claudia remarked.

"You, on the other hand . . . I believe Tiberius had a purpose for requiring you and the boy to come here. You offer another perspective on what is happening in Israel." He paused. "Perhaps it would be wise for you, personally, to keep him informed."

She nodded. "That I will."

"I am glad you are here," Marcus murmured.

Claudia saw a flicker of admiration in his eyes, and it was too much—too much pain to think of what might have been. She took a step away from him. "How are things going in the far outpost you are now banished to?" she flung toward him.

"We hunt rebels . . . and spy on prophets," he stated. "John the Baptizer is imprisoned now, but new prophets arise. One is Jesus of Nazareth, the Baptizer's cousin."

"I would like to see these prophets in action."

He tilted his head toward her. "For the sake of Rome?"

"For the sake of truth," she replied.

"Truth." He sighed. "I'll let you know if ever I find it."

"Good luck to you, Marcus. And to us all."

He turned to go, then swiveled back toward her. "If you are able, Claudia, get the boy out of Jerusalem. Trouble is coming. This is a city of riots and assassins and violence. You can find a peaceful life away from the plotting here. Go to the governor's residence in the city of Tiberias. If Pilate needs an explanation, tell him the air is sweeter in Galilee."

"My very thoughts tonight," she agreed.

"Then farewell, Claudia. " He strode away into the darkness as a cloud covered the moon.

Chapter 26

As soon as Marcus received the urgent message, he and Carta left for Kuza and Joanna's home. Kuza, Herod's one sensible steward, and his wife had become friends of Marcus and Miryam during his post in Galilee. Their little boy, Boaz, was dying. His grieving mother sat on the floor beside him, holding his limp hand. The sadness in the room was palpable and crushing.

Marcus was standing by a window in the boy's bedchamber when Miryam rushed in and knelt by Joanna's side.

"Oh, Miryam," Joanna sobbed. "The light is going from my life . . ." She collapsed in her friend's arms.

At that moment, Kuza fell to his knees. "We are being punished by the Eternal!"

Marcus stiffened. "What kind of god would murder children?"

"It is his will," Kuza whispered.

"You're all crazy." Marcus crossed the room and lowered himself to take Boaz's hand. In a tender voice, he said, "Maybe there is something . . . someone who could help.

In Judea I saw a rabbi heal a child—a cripple—with my own eyes."

Kuza lifted his eyes. "Where is he? I will crawl on my knees, if only . . ."

Marcus got to his feet. "By last report, he's staying in Cana. Come on, Kuza. We'll ride all night. Fetch him back here. He'll work his miracle on Boaz."

∽✺∽

Marcus and Kuza traveled from Capernaum to Magdala. But when they entered the boulder-strewn road to Cana that wound upward into the hills, their horses became winded. Since it was dark, they set their course by a star . . . and soon were lost.

Is this a fool's errand? Will the boy die before we can even reach Jesus? Marcus wondered, but he had to do something to help his friend. Kuza was clearly exhausted, only his desperation driving him on when his own strength had failed.

It wasn't until noon the next day that Marcus and Kuza reached Cana. Jesus was speaking in a rocky field. Kuza stumbled forward. When faces turned hostile because of Marcus's Roman dress, he halted at the back of the gathering and let Kuza go on alone.

"Sir," the steward called out, "will you help me? My only son is dying!"

Mutters of resentment swept the crowd at this request. Then a man shouted, "Your master arrested John the Baptizer. You have no right to ask for anything!"

Kuza cried out to Jesus, "I have no one else who can help me!"

The crowd quieted when Jesus got to his feet.

"Please, I have traveled all night to find you. If you can help him," Kuza pleaded.

Jesus scooped up a boy about the same size and age of Boaz and hefted him high onto his shoulder for the crowd to see.

The crowd evidently got the unspoken message. *The life of a child is all this father is asking for.* The muttering ceased.

Kuza fell at Jesus' feet. Jesus handed the boy on his shoulders to one of his talmidim. Then he grasped Kuza's arms and lifted him.

As tears flowed down Kuza's face, Jesus said, "Go on home. Your son is alive."

Marcus was stunned and dismayed. That was all? The healer would not come with them to touch Boaz? He thought about the journey home and the great weight of sadness to follow. Had Kuza lost his wits? Accepting merely the promise of this country rabbi? How devastated would he be when he returned home . . . and found Boaz food for worms?

But, strangely, Kuza was smiling. "Thank you. When you come to Capernaum," he told Jesus, "you must stay with me."

～⌒～

The entire journey back to Capernaum, Marcus wrestled with his emotions. He had sensed something unusual happening at the Jordan when the young crippled boy had been healed. But he had not known that sick child personally.

This time the beloved son of his friends was ill. Marcus understood the hole that would be left in his parents' hearts if the boy died.

He and Kuza were by the outskirts of Magdala when he spotted Carta, riding out with all speed to meet them. Marcus's heart sank. So it was over.

"Master!" Carta called. "Lord Kuza! Boaz is alive!"

The reunion of parents and child a short while later was indescribable. Marcus looked with longing at the scene, then gazed at Miryam, who stood in a corner of the room. But when he touched her arm, she ignored him and left the house.

He followed her into the grapevine arbor. A light rain fell.

"Miryam," he said softly, "come with me to see the power of this man. To hear him. Maybe he can help."

"Go see this healer yourself!" she spat back. "I'm not sick. You're the one, not me."

Marcus slumped. Rain now sluiced down. "Yes, you're right. I wasn't saying it's only you. Maybe it's everyone. Me too. The truth is, I'm a Roman . . . not even worthy to ask him."

She crossed her arms. "I'm content with my life the way it is."

His heart ached for her, for him, for what might have been—first, with Claudia, and next, with Miryam. Was every possibility for love and family for Marcus destined to be a failure?

"I have been a fool," he stated dully.

Then he hurried up the steps into the torchlight of the house and took his leave.

A couple of days later Marcus visited Kuza's Capernaum home again. Joanna and Boaz were off to Nazareth to see the healer, Jesus, and to bring him gifts. The two men had the opportunity to talk in a straightforward manner.

"Herod Antipas is furious I went to Jesus to beg a favor," Kuza explained. "I am being accused of using bad judgment."

Marcus frowned. "Are you in danger?"

"No," Kuza said, but he still looked worried. "I need to stay out of sight for a while, though. Perhaps Herod will forget about my indiscretion if nothing new reminds him of it. But, my friend, I understand if you want to keep away from me."

Marcus lifted a brow. "Rome has no particular interest in Jesus. Being your friend won't harm me."

"Don't be hasty with that decision," Kuza corrected. "Herod is looking for any reason to execute John the Baptizer, and he will find one. Anyone connected to the Baptizer will be suspect . . . especially Jesus, his cousin."

Marcus thought about Vara's use of the charge of *maiestas* as a method of eliminating people. What if Herod applied the same accusation to Jesus? Marcus's mind leaped to the natural conclusion. *And I, a Roman officer, was the one who took Kuza, Herod's steward, to meet with Jesus.* Rumors of suspicion would then seal Marcus's fate. Kuza's forewarning was founded. Now Marcus more fully understood the situation. But it wouldn't stop him from acting when he needed to.

So when Kuza suggested that he pay for a new roof for the synagogue in Capernaum—in gratefulness for Boaz's healing—and asked Marcus if he would oversee the repairs, the centurion agreed heartily.

It was the least he could do to express his own thanks for the life of the boy who had become like a nephew to him . . . even if it would raise rumors that his sympathies lay with the beleaguered Jews over Rome's interests.

Chapter 27

Supervising the restoration of the synagogue in Capernaum took every spare minute Marcus had. He'd discovered that in order to hold the refurbished roof, the structure's walls needed bracing, and he had secretly contributed from his own funds. The legionaries in Marcus's command—Syrians and Samaritans—couldn't understand why a Roman would show so much interest in the project. When Marcus made them haul and stack building material, the Samaritans were incensed. When goods were damaged, Marcus had to keep an even more careful eye on his own troopers.

Marcus was across the street at a tavern, reviewing plans and drawings, when he heard a skirmish. Rushing outside, he eyed the situation and came to his own conclusions. Several Samaritan legionaries had been throwing rocks at the Jewish laborers. Then one had kicked the scaffolding when a laborer was carrying bricks. The Jew had fallen fifteen feet. He hadn't been killed, but his arm was clearly broken.

Furious, Marcus burst into the laughing group of soldiers. He grabbed the first one and threw him headfirst into a wall. He punched the second one in the face.

The remaining soldier pleaded, "We meant no harm. A bit of fun, is all."

Marcus narrowed his eyes. "Fun, is it? I'll have your hide off—"

At that instant, from behind him, he heard, "Centurion Longinus!"

He turned. Praetorian Vara had arrived, with Tribune Felix at his side.

"Brawling with your own men?" Vara said scathingly.

"Disciplining," Marcus shot back. "No concern of yours."

"Oh, but it is," Vara clarified. "A word with you." He dismounted and entered the tavern.

Marcus glared at the legionaries, wanting to finish business with them. But he had to follow.

Once Marcus was inside, Vara lost no time in berating him for not catching the rebel leader bar Abba yet, then added, "And you're wasting time working on a Jewish synagogue? You took one of Herod's royal stewards to consult with a Jewish preacher? Very questionable." He frowned. "Finally, I've learned that you had a previous encounter with the two rebels I executed at Neapolis, yet you let them go unpunished. You didn't report the matter to headquarters."

That's when Marcus knew that the tribune, Felix, had betrayed him. No one else knew.

"If it were up to me," Vara threatened, "I'd break you

completely, or worse. But Pilate has instead decided to merely reduce your rank. You will still be a centurion of First Cohort, but no longer *Primus Pilus.* Your new assignment will be overseeing the collection of taxes for Capernaum." He stared at Marcus. "While keeping an eye out for rebels, of course."

A menial job. But Marcus couldn't argue. It would bring the same punishment as disobeying an order. He remained silent.

"By the way, I enjoyed your Jewish mistress," Vara threw in. "She fought back just enough to be diverting."

Marcus was sickened. No woman deserved to be taken against her will, and Vara was known for his brutality. Was Miryam all right? Marcus clenched and unclenched his fists. One move toward the bully, and he would be executed. He could not, did not, rise to the bait.

So Vara tried again. "I'm sure you can't afford a servant in your reduced circumstances. I fancy the boy. Why not sell him to me for, say, thirty denarii?"

"Get out," Marcus said. His words were steel, even if his body didn't move.

Vara laughed as he left.

﹏

After his demotion, Marcus continued his efforts to refurbish the synagogue. By now the Jews of Capernaum were used to seeing him around their city. Some actually smiled at him.

Capernaum also welcomed Jesus of Nazareth, the Baptizer's cousin, with open arms. At first he spoke only in the synagogue, sitting in the midst of the scaffolding and work in progress. Marcus avoided hearing the rabbi's teaching. No need to further gain the attention of Rome and Praetorian Vara.

As stories of the miraculous healings spread, the synagogue could no longer house all who wanted to hear Jesus, so he started to preach out of doors.

One day Marcus and Carta were journeying back from Tiberias when they came to a cove of the Sea of Galilee. Jesus arrived from the opposite direction.

"Can we stop and hear him, Master?" Carta asked.

Marcus agreed, if they could stay at the back of the throng. Two fishermen brothers were repairing some rigging on their sail when Jesus approached. Marcus laughed as he watched. Anything Jesus wanted, he surely wouldn't get from Shim'on, the big burly fisherman who always scowled at Marcus in the marketplace. It was rumored he was already angry that his brother was spending too much time listening to Jesus and less time with their business.

The teacher motioned toward Shim'on's boat and appeared to ask a question.

The big fisherman shook his shaggy head and jammed his pointer finger toward the net.

Jesus seemed to ask again.

Finally, Shim'on's brother, Andrew, called out, "What will it hurt? Let the master use the boat while we work on the nets."

Shim'on scowled but gave in. Together the two brothers pushed the vessel out from shore. Then, immediately, Jesus began speaking to the crowd that continued to gather.

"The time has come! God's kingdom is near!"

At the word *kingdom* Marcus paled. Had he misjudged Jesus as harmless? Using such a word could be dangerous.

Jesus then added, "Turn to God from your sins and believe the good news!"

Marcus relaxed. What the teacher went on to say sounded similar to the message of John the Baptizer. But there was one puzzling difference. The Baptizer had talked about getting ready for what was coming. Jesus spoke as if that something was already here.

When Jesus finished speaking, the crowd dissipated. He thanked Shim'on for the use of the boat. Then he said, "Row out, and let down your nets."

Marcus chuckled at the look Shim'on shot his brother. *Clearly, this guy is crazy.* But outwardly, Shim'on blustered, "We already fished all night. Worked hard too."

Then something happened. As Shim'on looked up into Yeshua's face, his ranting faltered.

Marcus moved closer to overhear the fisherman's next words. "But if you say so, I'll let down the nets again."

Jesus got into the boat with Shim'on and Andrew. When he raised his hand, they lowered the net over the side. Then the two brothers rowed in a circle to close the loop of net back on itself.

Suddenly, Shim'on's face turned red with the strain of trying to pull the bundle of net. "Hey," he bellowed out in joy across the water. "Ya'acov, get John! Bring the other boat. We need help out here!"

When the two boats were alongside each other, all four men struggled to draw in the net. The area between the boats seemed to be boiling with leaping fish! The fishermen drew basket upon basket of fish into Shim'on's boat until it was settling low in the water. Then they heaped more fish into the other boat. There were still more.

Marcus watched in wonder as Shim'on sank to his knees in front of Jesus. Jesus put his hands on the fisherman's shoulders.

What words passed between them? Marcus couldn't hear. But he too knew this was more than just a lucky catch. He had watched such fishermen with their catches. This one was far more bountiful—by seven times—than the best one he had ever seen.

When he and Carta turned to go, Marcus was still pondering.

◇◇◇

Though Marcus had been demoted, no one had been assigned to replace him. But he'd lost the accommodations that had gone with his title of *Primus Pilus*. His new home in Capernaum was four tiny rooms. In one of them was a stand for Marcus's armor, with the *corona obsidionalis*—the bronzed wreath that marked a hero—hanging on top of it. It was the only thing that remained of his pride in his years of service to Rome. In his darkest hours, he wondered if his loyalty had been misplaced.

One day Carta announced, "Two Jews are here to see you, Master."

Marcus sighed. Likely it was something to do with the synagogue. "Ask them to come in."

"I already did," Carta replied. "They respectfully declined because it would defile them."

He sighed again, then got up and stepped outside his dwelling. One of the men he recognized—Avram, a disciple of John the Baptizer. The other announced himself as Philip of Bethsaida.

"We have heard that you are a fair man who deals justly with the Jews," Philip said. "We were talmidim of the Baptizer. Now we follow Jesus."

Now they had Marcus's attention. "Go on," he urged.

When Philip explained they had not heard from John since he was arrested and that they were concerned he might be ill, Marcus nodded. He well remembered the conditions of the Machaerus prison.

"Be ready to travel fast," Marcus said. "We leave tomorrow at dawn. It will take a week for the round-trip journey."

This time he directed Carta to stay. He knew the boy was intrigued to hear Yeshua speak and wanted to allow him the opportunity.

~∞~

Several days later, Marcus gained entrance easily to the Machaerus prison by implying this was an official visit. Marcus had seen imprisoned men in terrible condition before, but the changes he saw in the prophet were shocking.

The Baptizer's voice was barely recognizable, and his once-sturdy arms were reed thin.

Furious, Marcus swiveled toward the jailer. "You were to see that no harm came to this man. Why has he been starved?"

The jailer cowered. "I leave his bowl full, but when I return it hasn't been touched."

Marcus understood now. The Baptizer had been used to living under the stars, roaming freely, and bathing in the streams. Now he was confined and in nearly continual darkness in the dungeon.

"Master," Philip said gently. "It is me, Philip."

The Baptizer at last looked up. "No one will give me any news," he pleaded. "Was I wrong, Philip? Should we be looking for someone else? Or is he the one?"

"Are you talking about Jesus?" Marcus interjected. "What do you mean, is he the one? The one what?"

The Baptizer turned his eyes on Marcus. "You were here before . . . the Roman." He lifted a bony arm. "The Deliverer sent by the Almighty to reconcile mankind to himself. Go to him. Ask him," he begged. "And send me word of what you see and hear. But I want the truth, not what you think I want to hear."

His request went against all laws of Herod Antipas. Captives were not allowed to have information.

"I will," Marcus agreed, much to his own surprise. Perhaps the Baptizer wasn't the only one who wanted the truth.

And then, for some unexplained reason, Marcus felt he should return to Galilee with haste. "I'll ride ahead," he told his traveling companions.

If he rode hard, he could be back in Capernaum in two days.

Chapter 28

It was everything Claudia had feared. Pilate's jealousy of Jono's kind affection for Philo had finally taken root and grown into hatred.

Pilate paced the length of the bedchamber and back. Claudia fought panic as she brushed her hair and tried to soften his dark mood.

"This slave, Jono. The boy is too dependent on him. For everything."

Claudia defended the pair. "Don't let your imagination sweep away reason. Jono is nothing more than a slave to Philo. Jono carries him. He is our son's legs."

"The boy speaks to his black creature as he might speak to a companion."

"It is only natural, Pilate. Philo has no friends. He has no companions. And Jono was presented as a gift to Philo."

"A gift from the centurion to a cripple—to mock me. Philo, the cripple, son of Pontius Pilate!"

"Jono belongs to Philo. And in the document I am the administrator."

Pilate grasped her wrist and pulled her close to his scowling face. "But you would not dare oppose me."

"I am still the daughter of Tiberius Caesar. Release me."

He flung her away. "And your illustrious father banished you as surely as he banished me."

"We are not exiled so far that he does not hear of your every mood and every move, Pilate. He will not tolerate your abuse of his flesh any longer."

For a moment the thought of Caesar's retribution appeared to sting the governor of Judea. He considered her unveiled threat in silence.

"The buying and selling of a slave is of no concern to Rome. I can find a hundred slaves like this Ethiopian. Philo will become used to another. The boy thinks too well of the slave. A servant is a servant. Seen and not heard."

"And I would say to my father that Jono is a trusted bodyguard. He would die for the boy. And for me."

"And so he will die, if he is not sold in the slave market. Some mysterious illness, perhaps. Or a viper in his bed. Tiberius Caesar understands how accidents can happen."

"You are a jackal at heart, Pilate." She glared at him, certain his threat was a reality. "You will have what you want, I see, and there is no one who can turn you back."

"At least we can agree on that. I will not permit a common slave to usurp the child's affection for me. The slave must be sold."

Pilate stalked from the room, slamming the door behind him.

Claudia covered her face with her hands and wept.

"I do not know what to do." Claudia's eyes misted with tears as she sat across from Josephus.

The old man studied her by the firelight. "But you know what must be done."

"Pilate will sell Jono if I insist he must remain with my son. Who would dispute the bill of sale signed by the Roman governor?"

Josephus raised his finger. "By your own Roman law you are accorded some legal rights. If you do not permit the sale . . . ?"

"Then, truly, my husband will have him killed. By stealth, so no one can accuse. I considered bringing him to your service. But Jono may not remain in Jerusalem. Wherever he is, Jono is a dead man in the eyes of Pilate."

"You know of the Roman document of manumission. The freeing of a slave by his master?"

"Yes. I technically retain right of ownership until Philo comes of age. I brought the documents of ownership." She fumbled in her leather pouch and laid the parchment scroll on the table before the old man.

Josephus unrolled the scroll and studied the wording for a long time. "It is clear the right is yours and yours alone to grant the slave his freedom. A simple document of manumission and he will be released to go. And further he will be granted the rights of Roman citizenship." He indicated her gold ring with Claudia's seal engraved upon it. "You carry the seal of your rank."

"Yes. My signet, as you see."

"Then it is in your authority to use your seal for good."

Claudia considered briefly the punishment she would likely receive at Pilate's hands if she granted Jono his freedom. Then she smiled mischievously. "All right, then. Freedom," she answered quietly. "I do not know where Jono will go, but he will be free."

Josephus smoothed his white beard. "Home, I would suppose. The instincts of a wild bird will carry him back to the nest where he was hatched."

"Ethiopia. He was a champion and a royal prince of Ethiopia. Defeated in battle by Centurion Marcus Longinus and presented as a gift to my son. Philo has been in his arms since he was a baby. This will be difficult." She sighed. "And I do not even know where Ethiopia is. Or how long it takes to travel to such a land."

Josephus replied, "It is said that once the queen of Ethiopia came personally to pay homage to our great King Solomon. And from that meeting she carried back a son of Solomon in her womb. Their offspring still rule there to this very day. Ah, yes. Ethiopia. A fine destination. And if he is a prince descended from the Queen of Sheba and Solomon, then surely such a man as this must be given his freedom."

"So be it."

Josephus sharpened his quill pen and smoothed a fresh square of lambskin out before him. "The skin of a lamb will withstand the adventures such a fellow is likely to face on his way home to Ethiopia. You must write this in your own hand in Latin. And then I will write in Aramaic and

Greek and Hebrew to follow. And with your signet ring pressed onto red wax, you will set the prince upon his journey home."

⌒⌒⌒

Starling's feathers glowed iridescent purple in the early morning sunlight the next morning.

The lambskin scroll on the table was signed by Claudia and countersigned in the childlike handwriting of Philo. It was sealed with the red wax and signet ring of Claudia.

Claudia raised her chin and dared to speak. "Jono is a free man. Philo, your father has gone on business in Caesarea. Before he returns, we must let Jono fly from us."

Philo's chin quivered as he and his mother shared their last breakfast with the big man.

Tears traced the ravines of his ebony face. "You have been in my arms since you were a frail infant." Jono struggled to speak. He looked at Claudia. "As if he were my child . . . . Oh, forgive me if I am too bold in speech, but my broken heart overflows like waters." He wiped his tears with the back of his hand.

Philo laid his cheek against Jono's hand and kissed it. The two embraced. "Oh, who will carry me here and there, Mother? With Jono I was not a cripple. I walked and ran faster than any other boy."

Claudia said, "Look. Starling's wing is healed. She can fly, but we keep her locked in this cage. How will she ever find her children? Her family?"

The boy was silent as he studied the little bird. "Then Jono should take Starling with him on his journey. And when he finds her flock, he must let her go."

The big man nodded. He sniffed and choked back sobs. "Oh, my dear, dear boy! I will do this. She will keep me company and sing to me on my way home."

The parting was hard. Philo, seated by the parapet, watched as Jono, carrying Starling's cage, strode from the palace gates and out into the crowds of Jerusalem. His shoulders were above the heads of the tallest Jews. Philo called out, "Jono!"

The Ethiopian prince stopped and looked back. The citizens of Jerusalem flowed around him as though he were a boulder in the center of a vast river. Lifting Starling high, he waved at the little boy on the parapet and placed the birdcage on his shoulder.

"Always remember I love you," Jono boomed. Then he turned and walked away, vanishing around the corner.

Satisfaction flowed over Claudia. No matter what she suffered as a result, she had done what she could now to ensure the safety of their beloved Jono. But not a day would pass that she and Philo would not miss his gentle, comforting, and strong presence.

Chapter 29

*J*ono, prince and mighty warrior of Ethiopia, strode across the face of Israel with Starling's cage dangling from his index finger.

How long had it been since he was permitted to speak in his own language? To speak Amharic in the presence of his captors was forbidden, lest he speak treason against Rome. It had been ten years since he had heard his own voice utter even one familiar word in his mother tongue. But now he was a free man. The scroll of his freedom was safely tucked into his belt.

What Amharic word would he speak first? What phrase could contain the fullness of his joy?

He pondered this as he studied the little bird in her cage. What did Starling long for more than anything else?

The word broke forth from Jono's throat unbidden.

"Amarachi!" he cried in his own language for the first time since his exile. "God's grace!" Then he laughed and shouted, *"Abidemi!* I have seen the world!"

Yes, he had seen the world and survived, and now he

would come home again, where every spoken word was like an old friend.

He had one promise to keep before he set his face toward Ethiopia.

Jono stopped at a well in Galilee. He drew water and drank deeply, then offered drops to Starling until she was satisfied.

Climbing the highest knoll, he shaded his eyes against the sun to find his bearings. There was the Sea of Galilee, shining like a silver plate beneath the blue, blue sky.

"Ah. *Wazzala*—beautiful and elegant!"

And then he spotted something above the western bank. In the far distance rose a dark spiral cloud, like living smoke. It was the starling flock, spinning synchronized patterns in the sky.

The little bird at the end of Jono's great arm sang and ruffled her inky feathers. She shook herself and hopped onto her perch in excitement. Hope!

Jono held her up to see and put his lips to the cage. He smiled broadly. "You hear them too? So these are truly your own family, Starling? They speak your language. I see. I see. They have flown from Rome to the skies above Galilee, and now, at last, we come upon them perhaps only twenty miles from where we stand. Since you are alone, if I turn you loose now, perhaps some hawk will spy you as you sit upon a rock and you will be eaten. No. I will carry you to the flock as I carried your little master. And I will open the cage door only when you are safe and you may fly to your family."

Twenty miles was a small distance for the legs of Jono. A day's journey at most. He took off his head covering and tied it around the metal bars to give Starling shade against the heat.

Singing a song of freedom and hope, he set out.

∽∾∾

Hours later Claudia sat before her mirror, brushing her hair and aching from the beating Pilate had given her after discovering she had set Jono free. Even her status as Tiberius Caesar's daughter had not saved her this time. Her clothing would have to be chosen carefully for Herod's birthday feast that evening to hide the marks of the deep bruises that were immediately apparent. Knowing Jono was safe and free, though, dulled the pain.

Pilate had railed at her. "Imbecile. Worthless woman! What made you think you could thwart my desires? You are powerless. Under my control."

Yes, he had made her pay. And then, when he hadn't crushed her spirit along with injuring her body, he'd threatened to send his soldiers after Jono.

Claudia's heart had quickened in dread, but she had steeled her expression. An idea flickered. "Herod's feast. We must not be late," she had reminded him from where she lay prone on the floor.

He had paused over her, foot poised to deliver another kick. "There's that." Then he'd stepped back, scowling in disgust. "He was just a slave. Not worth fretting over. Other things have precedence. Get up. Get dressed. We have Herod's birthday to attend."

Claudia had never been so thankful for an event she hated.

Chapter 30

*T*he rainy season had watered the dust in the streets of Jerusalem and reduced the smell of sheep and camel dung. But the change of weather had done little to improve the aroma of Herod's palace, Claudia thought. Damp and drafty, the odors of mold competed with overused incense to create a sickly, stinking atmosphere.

The celebrants of Herod's birthday feast were mostly already too drunk to notice. Claudia and Pilate, along with visiting dignitaries from Nabatea and Parthia, were seated in places of honor near Herod, his wife, Herodias, and her daughter, Salome. Wealthy merchants and prominent Temple officials received special treatment as well.

Pilate, his usual morose self, stared into the ruby-hued wine as if using it to divine his future in the region he hated.

His reverie was interrupted by Herod, who raised a glass and loudly called, "To our friend. My friend. The governor. A true friend of Caesar. To Pontius Pilate." The entire company echoed the sentiment, drinking deeply.

Pilate, his words already slightly slurred, responded

to Herod's toast. "And to our friend and Caesar's, Herod Antipas! A man of action who has no fear as he rids us of troublesome prophets! The tetrarch Herod Antipas!"

Pilate's sarcasm seemed not to register with Herod at all, Claudia noticed. But with Herodias, it was otherwise. If possible, Herodias's features sharpened and her eyes took on a dangerous gleam. Claudia watched her whisper something to Salome, receive a quick nod in return, then quietly address Herod.

Herod clapped his hands. "Now, for our pleasure and the pleasure of our distinguished guests, my daughter, Salome, will dance for us . . . as Queen Esther danced before her king to save her people."

Salome stood, swayed slightly until every eye was on her, then addressed Herod. "As Queen Esther was granted her wish, I expect a reward from my father."

Herod replied, "Anything for you, sweet Salome! Your heart's desire. Up to half my kingdom."

Claudia had read the story of Esther. She recognized these exact words from that account, but she doubted that a motive like Esther's existed in Salome's wicked little heart. And, clearly, Herod had already drunk too much wine.

Herodias and Salome exchanged evil, devious smiles. Something bad was happening, but what?

"For my reward," Salome said, "all I want is . . . the head of John the Baptizer, on a platter!"

Herod guffawed loudly. Some in the crowd laughed nervously.

Claudia's heart pattered. This could not be real.

Still chuckling, Herod turned to see his wife's eyes boring holes into him.

"Well?" Salome demanded. "Is this not a small gift to restore the honor of my mother?"

The audience held its collective breath.

Fear, guilt, and pride chased each other across Herod's yellow skin. Herod's gaze darted about the room, but he found no assistance for his dilemma. In an almost inaudible voice he said, "Let it be done."

Herodias summoned one of her husband's soldiers while Herod drained a cup of wine, refilled it, and drained it again.

Claudia felt sick. Couldn't Pilate do something to stop this?

Raising her slender arm in a triumphal wave, Herodias directed the musicians to play. A drum began to pound and Claudia's head throbbed in time with it. Layers of mind-numbing sound were added—flutes, lyres, horns . . . and tambourines that hissed like snakes.

Salome danced her way around the room, lingering near the most attractive unmarried men to run her hands over their shoulders. When the cadence of the music slowed, Salome slithered back to her place beside her mother. A servant, bearing a large silver platter, entered the chamber, accompanied by the Herodian soldier.

Claudia looked everywhere at once, not wanting to experience what was about to happen. No emotion she witnessed mirrored her own. Herod looked fearful, Herodias victorious, Pilate between bored and amused.

Her thoughts flickered to Marcus. How would he respond if he were here? He'd be angry—angry enough to draw his sword and kill the whole Herodian clan. Perhaps it was best he'd been banished to a far outpost.

The platter was placed before Herod, who turned away. Herodias waved for the cover to be removed. It was.

Claudia was nauseated. Overwhelmed with shock and revulsion, she gasped. Tears streaming, she did not wait for Pilate but stumbled blindly from the palace.

∽∾∽

As Herod's party continued as though nothing unusual had taken place, Claudia wept in the garden beneath the stars. She knew that the beheading of a prophet for the pleasure of a spoiled girl and her plotting mother would be forgotten tomorrow. Such executions happened in the court of Tiberius with some regularity. Herod was, after all, modeling his rule after the customs of his Roman patron. Still, the savagery of life was something Claudia could not get used to.

Marcus was right. Nowhere was safe. The Baptizer had died for speaking his mind about Herodias. Even while he'd been standing in the middle of a river in the wilderness, it seemed she heard every whisper. Finally she had taken her revenge. As more prophets arose, such as the Baptizer's cousin, where would the bloodshed end? Was Jesus of Nazareth next?

She would do as Marcus had suggested—keep Tiberius

informed. She'd tell him about what had happened at the feast tonight. The senselessness of Herod's behavior. That Herod as tetrarch was a disaster to the Jews . . . to anyone who wished to live in peace. That it was no surprise rebellion brewed among the common folk as a result of such treatment.

∽∾

Claudia walked beside Josephus the Elder in the palace garden in Jerusalem the next day. The courtyard in which they strolled had a massive central fountain made of white marble with gold veins, set off by a diamond pattern of inlaid onyx. Jets of water spurted from the mouths of gracefully carved dolphins.

The plaza was ringed by pomegranate, olive, and fig trees. Birds sang in the branches.

Stopping where a fine mist from the fountain cooled the heat of the day, Claudia asked, "On the ship you spoke of another prophecy. A Jewish king, suffering for his people, the glory of the Lord revealed . . . the Messiah."

Josephus laid his hand on the surface of cool stone encircling the fountain and gestured toward the pool. "I went to see John at the Jordan before his arrest. I saw him baptize a young rabbi . . . a *tzadik*."

"*Tzadik*?" Claudia repeated. "What is the meaning?"

"A righteous man," the scholar explained.

"Is there such a thing?" Claudia challenged. "A righteous man? Truly righteous?"

"Perhaps one," he returned.

"And do your prophecies name him?" Claudia asked. "How will he be known? When will he come?"

"He will be called *Immanuel*, which means 'God with us.' But that is not his name. He will be called Son of David, but that is not his name, either," Josephus explained.

"If you know, please tell me," Claudia urged. "I must learn it."

"I believe . . ." The elderly man pursed his lips in thought. "His name is Jesus. A Nazarene. *Yeshua* in Hebrew. And his name means 'salvation.' He is a descendant of Israel's greatest king, David. They are saying by the many miracles he performs that this Jesus may be the savior the prophets foretold. It is written of the Messiah by the prophet Isaiah, 'Then the eyes of the blind will be opened and the ears of the deaf will be unstopped. Then the lame will leap like a deer.'"[5]

"Yes!" Claudia said eagerly. "What else?"

"Say to those with fearful hearts, 'Be strong, do not fear.'[6] Messiah will bring salvation from heaven to all people. He will freely offer mercy, forgiveness, and eternal life to all who believe in him."

Claudia stared straight into the old man's eyes. "Do you believe this? Truly?"

Josephus took a deep breath before replying. "It is written in the Holy Books. When the Son of David reigns as king in Jerusalem . . ."

Philo, released from his lessons in Latin and Greek, limped painfully into the sunshine of the garden.

BODIE & BROCK THOENE

"When that day comes," Josephus continued, "he will heal every sickness and the lame will leap and dance for joy."[7]

Another servant, leading Philo's pony, brought boy and horse together. Philo's face lit up with purest joy as he stroked the animal's nose.

"To dance," Claudia said with longing in her voice. "A beautiful dream."

Lifting his lined face toward a bird singing in the nearest olive tree, Josephus observed, "Do not lightly dismiss dreams. Sometimes dreams are the bright shadows of reality."

Claudia straightened her back and shoulders. "Where is this man whose name means Salvation?" she asked firmly.

"Galilee, they say."

"I want to meet him." She gazed wistfully at her son. "If only it were true . . . and the lame could dance."

230

Part Four

"I will restore you to health and heal your wounds," declares the LORD.

JEREMIAH 30:17

Chapter 31

Marcus thundered on Pavor toward his Capernaum home, driven by an uncanny sense that something was amiss. As soon as he reached it, a little after sunrise, he unbridled the horse, let him drink from the watering trough, then led him into the pen. A minute later, he plunged his head and shoulders into the same trough to remove the sweat and dust of Galilee.

When he called for Carta, though, the boy didn't come. Instead his friend Kuza emerged from the house.

"The boy is . . . ," Kuza began haltingly.

Marcus strode toward Kuza. "Carta is what?"

"The boy has been hurt . . . badly. Joanna is with him."

The sense of dread that had grown on the journey from Machaerus weighed Marcus's next words. "Hurt? How?"

Kuza beckoned Marcus. "Look inside."

Marcus was stunned. The small front room was a mess—cooking pots overturned, burst wineskins. He moved to his bedroom. The door hung from one hinge, and his clothing was flung around the room. The stand that held his *corona obsidionalis* was broken. Red splotches were scattered over the floor and walls. Marcus knew blood when he saw it.

"You don't want to see this," Joanna warned when he moved toward the doorway of Carta's cubicle.

What Marcus saw next shocked him to the core. The figure that lay on the cot was barely recognizable as Carta, he was so beaten.

Carta started to sob. "I tried, Master, to fight him. But he was too strong . . . hurt me, bad."

Marcus whirled on Kuza. "Did anyone see who did it?"

"Some say a Roman wearing black rode away after they heard screams."

Vara!

Joanna's anger glimmered in her eyes. "Yes, it was Vara. A beast did these things, not a man. An animal that could do unspeakable things to the boy."

At those words, Marcus's gut wrenched. He understood what she meant. Carta had been not only battered but horribly violated. He was likely crippled . . . if he lived.

"And now his neck is broken," Joanna continued. "He cannot move arms or legs."

Marcus could not stand to hear any more. He had only one mission now—revenge. He would find Vara and make him pay.

He pushed out of the house, despite Kuza's pleading, and ran straight to the pen to saddle Pavor.

∽◦∽

The twenty miles had passed pleasantly for Jono and Starling the first day of his freedom. When dusk had settled in, they had made their bed in the fields, and both had slept soundly. It was the first time since Philo's babyhood that Jono had not awakened during the night to be the boy's legs.

This morning, above the hills of Galilee, the great cloud of starlings swarmed through the sky again in synchronized spirals. Jono spoke to the little bird as he walked the dusty road. "We will continue to follow your family, my friend."

Soon the path became packed with other travelers, all moving in the same direction. "Where is everyone going?" Jono asked a family nearby.

The young peasant pointed toward the flock of birds. "We are bringing our little girl to the great healer. Yeshua is his name . . . Gentiles call him Jesus. Look there! Even the birds of the air follow him."

Jono's gaze swung to the peasant's wife, who carried a small, paralyzed girl. "Great healer? A sorcerer is here in the Galil?"

"No sorcerer. A man of God. Where have you been that you don't know about Jesus?"

Jono answered, "Home. Ethiopia. Then Rome and in Jerusalem these past few months. I am a freeman now and traveling home."

The farmer replied, "Come and see his miracles! He heals all who come to him and ask. He speaks and the lame, the blind, the demon-possessed become well and whole."

"And you hope that this Jesus will raise your child to be whole?"

The mother nodded eagerly. "If we can get close enough, then I am sure he will."

Jono joined them. "I will come with you and see if this is true for myself."

"You will, after today, carry back a great story to your people," the peasant assured him.

Jono pressed forward with the throng as the ever-changing geometric patterns of birds moved out over the crystalline surface of the lake.

~~~

As Marcus galloped toward the barracks in Tiberias, his heart and conscience wrenched. He should have known Vara would try something. He should have taken Carta with him to Machaerus. On that ride he had realized that Carta was not merely his servant, or the boy he had rescued from the Cherusci during the Battle of Idistaviso. The boy was the closest thing Marcus had, and perhaps would ever have, to a son. He had trained the boy, seen him grow up, spent most of his days with him.

When he reached the officers' barracks, he tossed the reins into the air and leaped off Pavor even before the horse had halted.

Quintus attempted to block his entry. "Marcus," he reasoned, "I know what happened. But you can't go in—"

Marcus rammed the guard sergeant to the side and hissed, "Stay out of my way."

He stormed into the room. As soon as he started to close on Vara, though, the Praetorian stabbed Marcus's forearm with a knife. Ignoring the pain, Marcus punched Vara in the jaw, then started to strangle him.

A second later, Marcus felt a blow to the back of his head, and two legionaries pinned him to the ground.

Vara got up, rubbing his throat, and said with a raspy voice, "I'll see you crucified for this."

Then a voice spoke from the hallway. "Not so fast. What is this?"

Marcus looked up. Tribune Felix, the one who had betrayed him. What was he doing in Tiberias? Marcus now had nothing to lose. He'd be nailed to a cross by morning. "Ask him what he did to my servant . . . if you don't already know," he said with bitterness.

Felix frowned. "To Carta? No, I don't know."

Vara blustered, "When the centurion was not at his post, his slave refused to answer my questions about his whereabouts. So I punished him."

"He raped the boy and broke his neck," Marcus shouted.

"What of it? It's only a slave. Worth thirty silver denarii. Here, take it," Vara said callously. He flung a leather pouch on the floor.

Marcus struggled to rise, but the two legionaries continued to hold him down.

"Take the centurion to my office," Felix ordered. "Tie him to a chair for now." Turning to Vara, he said in a steely tone, "It is time for you to return to Caesarea. You have two hours' head start, to gather some guards to protect you. Now, get out!"

Once in his office, Felix ordered the legionaries to leave and shut the door. "Contrary to what you think, I did not betray you. Since my family has influence in Rome, Pilate decided to hedge his bets in case Sejanus falls out of favor with the emperor. So I am the new commander of First Cohort."

"Then what happens to me?" Marcus said through gritted teeth.

Felix untied Marcus's bonds. Removing his scarf, he used it to bind Marcus's injured arm. "Nothing. But that is on the condition that you go back to Capernaum. Leave the feud alone."

Marcus had no choice but to agree in order to go free. Then he took his leave without another word.

Pavor waited outside, grazing on the sparse tufts of grass near the barrack entrance. Marcus mounted, blood from the knife wound trickling down his arm despite the scarf binding it, and galloped away toward his home in Capernaum . . . and Carta.

Chapter 32

The man named Yeshua, or Jesus, sat on a hillside above the Sea of Galilee and addressed the crowds.

Jono guessed there were perhaps twenty thousand people between him and the prophet, even though at his great height, he towered above them all. Men, women, and children pressed in—as many Jews as an entire army.

Most of the people were well and whole. But others, like the child of the peasants walking next to him, were clearly unwell. All those around Jono seemed to be poor farmers, people of the land.

At that moment Jesus gestured toward the starling flock. His voice rang out clearly over the heads of the people. "No one can serve two masters. Either you will hate the one and love the other, or you will be devoted to the one and despise the other. You cannot serve both God and money.

"Therefore I tell you, do not worry about your life, what you will eat or drink; or about your body, what you will wear. Is not life more than food, and the body more than clothes? Look at the birds of the air; they do not sow or reap or store away in barns, and yet your heavenly Father feeds them. Are you not much more valuable than they? Can any one of you by worrying add a single hour to your life?

"And why do you worry about clothes? See how the flowers of the field grow. They do not labor or spin. Yet I tell you that not even Solomon in all his splendor was dressed like one of these. If that is how God clothes the grass of the field, which is here today and tomorrow is thrown into the fire, will he not much more clothe you—you of little faith?

"So do not worry, saying, 'What shall we eat?' or 'What shall we drink?' or 'What shall we wear?' For the pagans run after all these things, and your heavenly Father knows that you need them."[8]

When Jesus finished teaching and came down from the hillside, Jono joined the great multitudes that followed him.

Suddenly the crowds parted as the stench of a leper filled the air.

The leper made his way toward Jesus and knelt before him. "Lord, if you are willing, you can make me clean."

Jesus touched the leper. "I am willing. Be cleansed."

Immediately the man was cleansed of his leprosy.

And Jesus said to him, "Tell no one, but go your way. Show yourself to the priest and offer the gift that Moses commanded as a testimony to them."[9]

Astounded at what he witnessed, Jono followed closer, still carrying the starling in her cage on his shoulder.

∽∾∽

When Marcus returned to Capernaum, a large grouping of men and women were gathered around his door.

His heart leaped. *Did Carta die?* A deep ache set in. *Or is this the death watch?* If so, there was still hope.

But as he dismounted from Pavor, he saw what he never could have imagined—tears of compassion for him, a Roman. He bowed his head as his emotion threatened to overflow. Ranks parted in respect and friendship as he neared his front door.

Entering his home, he caught his breath. The nearness of losing Carta overwhelmed him.

Joanna held Carta's hand. He wheezed weakly. Marcus fell to his knees, took the boy's hand, and kissed his fingertips. He couldn't bear to look at Carta's face. The wounds of knowing what the boy had to suffer were too painful.

Marcus felt helpless. There was nothing he could do to stop death.

"Marcus, this is Mary of Nazareth," Joanna said. "She is watching and praying with me."

He glanced up. The woman gazed at him with compassion. She had dared to enter the home not only of a Gentile but of a Roman. His gratefulness knew no bounds. "Thank you."

Mary caressed Carta's auburn hair. "I have a son also."

"Carta is . . ." At last Marcus voiced the truth. ". . . like my son."

"Mary is the mother of Jesus. Staying at Shim'on's house," Joanna explained.

The burly fisherman welcomed Jesus' kin into his house now? Indeed things had changed.

Then the memory of Jesus healing the crippled child swept over Marcus. "Your son, dear lady, is the only hope

I have." He wept. "Which means I have no hope, for I am not a Jew. Why would Jesus help me?"

"You must ask," Mary said gently, "or you will never know. What you have been cannot change. Just be what you will be now. So get up, and go seek my son."

When she ushered Marcus to the door, Philip and Avram were waiting outside. Marcus's voice broke as he asked them, "Will you go to Jesus, on my behalf?"

That very minute Philip, Avram, and the elders of Capernaum left to seek Jesus.

❧

Jono made his way with the crowd toward nearby Capernaum. They stopped in an open field, and Jesus again began to speak.

"Love your enemies. Do good to those who hate you. Bless those who curse you. Pray for those who mistreat you . . . Do to others as you would have them do to you . . . The good person brings good things out of what is stored in his heart. The evil person brings evil things out of what is stored in his heart. For out of the overflow of the heart he speaks."[10]

Jono grappled to understand how one could love his enemy. That an evil person did evil was easy to grasp. But how to bring out the good in a good person in such a dangerous time? He saw himself as a good person, yet in his heart he knew he harbored hate.

For so many years, after he had fallen to the Roman

champion Marcus Longinus, he had been enslaved . . . until the goodness in Claudia had set him free. He had also grown to deeply respect Marcus, who had chosen life instead of death for Jono. Now that enemy was the closest thing he had to a friend.

Chapter 33

Marcus sat numbly by Carta's side while Joanna and Mary put his house in order—scrubbing the crimson stains from the walls and floor, sweeping the ashes into the fireplace. He knew they were preparing for the inevitable funeral.

What if what Marcus asked was impossible? Or improbable, because he and Carta were not Jews? He shuddered.

When Jesus had healed the crippled child, he had said that faith was what was most important. *Where do you find faith?* Marcus asked himself. *When a situation is completely out of your control?*

He thought of the crippled child's father and his actions. The man had staggered forward with the child, certain that if he could only reach Jesus, his son would be healed. Marcus thought of Kuza, falling at the feet of Jesus, begging for the rabbi's help.

So perhaps faith is believing that Jesus is able to do something and asking him to do so? Marcus pondered. *Even if what you ask seems impossible?* He buried his head in his hands.

Then he heard a loud shout from outside. "Jesus of Nazareth is coming!"

Marcus leaped up and ran out of the house even without gathering his sandals first. He squinted up the road. A crowd approached—so many that it appeared as if the road itself was moving. Jesus was at the forefront.

Hope surged, drowning out the hopelessness that had nearly crushed him.

ञ्चन्द्र

When Jono entered the village of Capernaum along with the crowd following Jesus, he was startled to see his former enemy and now friend, Centurion Marcus Longinus, running barefoot toward the healer.

And then, when he was merely feet away from Jesus, Marcus bowed his head, in the same manner of respect as he would give to a commanding officer. Jono had seen it before, many times.

"Sir?" Marcus hesitated. He looked up. Jesus' expression must have encouraged him to continue speaking. "My servant is paralyzed." He appeared to fight for control. "He has been terribly tormented." His voice was broken—not like the strong, battle-hardened Roman centurion Jono knew him to be.

His servant? Carta? Jono wondered. *What has happened to the bright boy who is always with Marcus?*

Jesus asked Marcus, "Shall I come and heal him?"

Marcus fell to one knee. "Lord, I am not worthy that

you should come under my roof. But only speak a word, and my servant will be healed. For I also am a man under authority, having soldiers under me. And I say to this one, 'Go,' and he goes; and to another, 'Come,' and he comes; and to my servant, 'Do this,' and he does it."

When Jesus heard Marcus, he marveled, and said to those who followed, "I have not found such great faith, not even in Israel. And I say to you that many will come from east and west, and sit down with Abraham, Isaac, and Jacob in the kingdom of heaven. But the sons of the kingdom will be cast out into outer darkness." Then Jesus said to Marcus, "Go your way; and as you have believed, so let it be done for you."

Jono, towering over the crowd, witnessed this and saw Quintus running to meet Marcus. "Centurion! Centurion! Carta is healed, sir!"[11]

The uproar in response to the healing swept through the crowds like a wave. Now everyone wanted to follow Jesus.

❧

Marcus looked back to where the crowd of mourners had gathered around the front of his home. Doubt edged into his mind. Marcus shoved it back. He walked back toward his home.

He fought with himself. *Be like Kuza and the father of the crippled boy. Jesus said it. I only need to believe it is so, and it will be so.*

Such faith went beyond all human reasoning, but Marcus chose to believe it.

As he neared the doorway, there was movement. Then a slender figure emerged. It was Carta! Alive and . . .

Marcus stared. Not even a bruise marred the boy's face.

"Master!" Carta called as he ran to meet Marcus. "Are you all right? Has something happened? Why is there such a crowd of people here?"

Marcus marveled. Even the boy's memory of the horrific event had been erased.

Tears coursed down Marcus's cheeks. He opened his arms to Carta and embraced him. He stroked his hair, then kissed the top of his head. "My boy, my boy! Yes . . . I am all right."

And now, finally, for the first time in his life, he was.

Chapter 34

Jono fought against the current of humanity to move closer to Marcus's home. At last, Starling in hand, he was only feet from the door when two burly men—fishermen by the smell of them—barred his way. They looked at the bird in the hand of the giant. By their expressions and swiftly exchanged glances, Jono thought that perhaps they considered mocking him. However, they'd likely thought better of it after eyeing Jono's size.

"Halt!" commanded the one who appeared to be in charge.

Jono lowered his chin and peered down his nose at the bulky fellow who seemed almost child-sized in his presence. "I have come to see Centurion Marcus Longinus," Jono growled.

"We know the centurion, but we do not know you."

"I am a freeman," Jono explained. "A citizen of Rome. I have a name he will remember from former days."

"Well?" The first fisherman stared at the starling. "There is much that has happened here today. I can't say he will care that there is a large black man here with a starling in his hand."

Jono drew himself up even taller. "Then tell Centurion Marcus Longinus this. His old enemy and dear friend, the freeman Jonathan Selasi, Prince and Champion of the King of Ethiopia, and citizen of Rome, stands in the heat at his door."

"With a little starling in a cage," laughed the second fisherman. "A princely companion indeed."

Jono replied, "The bird is a good omen among my people . . ." He paused, then decided to embellish the story a little, translating it in terms that might move these simple guards to action. "The sign of a messenger. And if a messenger with the importance of myself is turned back from the gate, a plague shall descend upon the one who rejects him."

This was not true, but the story indeed stirred the first man into action. He peered nervously around and then toward the skies, as if judgment might descend that instant. Then he stammered, "In that case . . . yes. I will tell him you have come." Within seconds, the fellow disappeared.

Jono glared at the remaining man, who backed away from him.

Minutes passed before the first man returned. "Centurion bids you come. He says . . ." The fisherman reddened. "I must welcome the bird heartily." He turned to the bird. "So, hail and welcome, little bird!"

Jono glowered. "That's more like it." With a few short steps, he rapped on the lintel.

With a joyful laugh, Marcus threw back his door and grasped the big man by his shoulders. "Welcome, Prince Jonathan, my dear enemy and friend! I hear you are a freeman now and a citizen." He quirked a brow. "I am indeed curious to know how such transpired." He gestured toward the starling. "And you have brought a good omen. Today my servant Carta is saved from death."

"I saw it all," Jono said. "You and this Jesus, the Jewish rabbi."

Jono placed the cage on Marcus's table and noted the *corona obsidionalis* that had been placed there.

"Jesus is more than a rabbi," Marcus said. "More than a teacher."

Jono smiled. "Something has happened to you since we last saw one another."

"More than I can say, my friend."

"I knew one day you would save the world and win the crown. But to see you also filled with the joy of life . . . that I did not think I would see."

"The foolishness of other men becomes the glory of another," Marcus noted. "But tell me, now that we may speak as equals, why have you come?"

"I am free but not by my own doing. You knew from the first when you sent me to guard your lady and the child that I would never leave the boy of my will. Having lost my own children in the wars, I have guarded the boy as if he were my own."

"Then what's this about?"

"The master of the house thought to sell me in the slave

250

market, so when he rode to the north on state business, Lady Claudia drew the document and set me free."

"Tell me what you know."

Marcus listened attentively, his brow furrowed, as Jono told him tales of Pilate's bullying and abuse. Jono added stoically, "He still beats her from time to time. She takes it very well, considering . . ."

"Considering what?" Marcus retorted.

Jono paused. "Perhaps you don't know. When you sent me to her when Philo was born, I saw and heard things . . ."

Marcus scowled. "Like what? Say it plainly."

Jono lifted his chin. "When Claudia was with child soon into their marriage, Pilate was not happy. He beat her daily, the servants told me. One day she fell down the stairs. He followed her down and kicked her in the belly. She nearly lost the baby. Once, when she was weeping, she told me she believed that was when Philo was injured, in her womb."

A wave of anger washed over Marcus. In that moment, he wanted to throttle Pilate until he was dead. But he could only stand clenching and unclenching his fists.

Claudia's words when she bade him good-bye at the docks filtered back. *"I can forgive him everything . . . even the worst that he has done to me, to Philo . . . but . . ."*

He sighed. So she too had suffered, much more than he'd imagined.

Jono touched his shoulder. "The boy. I love him as my own. Pilate has no love for Philo. Worse, he is ashamed of him. Philo will need some man to look in on him. To show an interest in him. Though he cannot walk, he is a brilliant little fellow with a heart that soars above the clouds."

Marcus nodded. "Then, yes. I will if I am able."

"And one more thing . . ." Jono shuffled his feet. He drew a breath, then looked directly at Marcus. "She often remarks that the boy has a beautiful heart . . . like his father. I am sure she cannot mean the governor. Nor can she mean Caesar, his grandfather. I do not know of whom she must be speaking. But I will attest to the truth that the boy's heart is kind and beautiful."

༄༅

The giant's words pierced Marcus like a lance. So Jono knew the truth.

After Marcus had received Claudia's letter that she was pregnant, he had steeled his heart and destroyed the parchment. She was, after all, married . . . even if Tiberius did force her hand. It was too dangerous for him, for Claudia, for the infant if the letter existed. He had never spoken of it to Claudia. The closest they had come was Marcus's statement in the garden. *"The boy is no part of Pilate."*

"No," she had replied. *"Not at all like Pilate."* Then she had avoided his gaze and switched the subject.

Jono continued to study Marcus with compassion. The secret was safe with the ebony giant, Marcus knew.

"For your sake then, old friend, and for Claudia's and the boy's, I will do all I can for him," Marcus promised. "You have seen the miracles of Jesus. I think we must find a way to bring Philo to him."

Chapter 35

Marcus and Jono clasped hands in farewell as the morning light gleamed golden on the Sea of Galilee. "Where will you go now?" Marcus asked.

"Home, I thought. But where is home?" Jono spread his arms wide. "My forefathers were once of this people many generations ago. There is a legend that the blood of King Solomon runs through the veins of the kings and princes of Ethiopia."

"Your blood."

"Perhaps it is true. Perhaps I will stay awhile and see how this story plays out." Jono held up the birdcage. Starling fluttered. "And this morning I will follow Starling's flock across the water to the country of the Gadarenes, where Jesus is."

Marcus replied, "From what I have witnessed of Jesus' authority and power, it will all end well for the Son of David. Who could stand against him?"

"Until all things are established, you must be careful of your words," Jono warned. "I have seen the danger. In the house of the Roman governor there is suspicion of Jesus.

Will he raise a rebellion? And in the house of Herod there is great fear and hatred."

Marcus nodded and placed a leather pouch of silver coins in Jono's hand. "Go to the shore. You will find a boat to carry you across the water."

～∽∽

The small fishing boat from Capernaum scudded across the water. The master of the boat was a slightly built, sun-dried man with the hide of an old sandal. He knew plenty about Jesus and also knew several of his disciples well.

Jono did not need to question him. As they sailed, the fellow talked, hardly pausing to take a breath.

"Peter and James left their father to manage all the business on his own. Poor fellow. But he does not seem to mind. He figures when the revolution comes and Jesus is king in Jerusalem, his boys will be part of the court. Judges at the very least and very wealthy. They can buy up every fishing boat on the lake and own a fishing empire. That's what he says, anyway. As for me, I won't sell my boat cheap."

Jono commented, "No one will have to work if the stories are true. Jesus makes bread out of thin air."

"It's true! It's true, right enough. No one goes hungry when he's around. Five loaves and two fish multiplied to feed thousands in his camp. Thousands!" The fisherman shook his head in awe. "There are miracles all around. The night he set sail with his followers to cross the water, his twelve talmidim were in the boat with him. A few dozen of us fishermen were chartered to carry others across after him. A whole fleet of fishing boats. I didn't go because I read the signs that there was a storm coming. I stayed put while every other fool set sail. And sure enough, a storm whipped up, as comes up here some days. Oh, how it blew! Everything I heard, even those most experienced thought they would sink."

"What happened?" Jono fed bread crumbs to the starling.

"I'll tell you, but you won't believe it. Wind, such wind, and waves as high as a house. Jesus stood and roared against the wind and the storm. Commanded the weather to be still, and it obeyed him!" The fisherman wore an expression of wonder. "Imagine that—the wind and the waves obeyed his voice. Suddenly, all grew calm. As calm as a pond on a summer day. The raging ceased and not one person perished." He adjusted the sail. "And so, everyone believes that Jesus can only be the Son of David. There is no other explanation."

"It must be so," Jono agreed. "But what will come of it? What does it mean? Will you be an army? Fight for him in Jerusalem? Take up your swords and battle the Romans and Herod's soldiers?"

"Mercy me! I don't have a sword. But I will follow him. He can heal the wounded. Raise the dead. Feed the army. Why wouldn't we follow such a general?"

The east shore loomed up, and the boat slid onto the sand among dozens of other boats that sailed with Jesus and his followers.

In the distance the cloud of starlings rose and spiraled like a whirlwind.

"Look there—even the birds of the air follow him," said the fisherman.

Jono paid the master and hurried up the slope of a hill to the peak. Jesus sat with his twelve disciples on a boulder on the opposite side of a valley. His voice resounded in the natural amphitheater. Below him was a throng of people as far as the eye could see.

Like an army, the thousands filled the valley.

Jono arrived just in time to hear Jesus resume addressing the crowd. "Therefore the kingdom of heaven is like a certain king who wanted to settle accounts with his servants. And when he had begun to settle accounts, one was brought to him who owed him ten thousand talents. But as he was not able to pay, his master commanded that he be sold, with his wife and children and all that he had, and that payment be made. The servant therefore fell down before him, saying, 'Master, have patience with me, and I will pay you all.' Then the master of that servant was moved with compassion, released him, and forgave him the debt."

The crowd buzzed with appreciation. What a kind master! What a lucky fellow!

"But wait," Jesus instructed. "Listen to what happened next. That servant went out and found one of his fellow servants who owed him a hundred denarii; and he laid hands on him and took him by the throat, saying, 'Pay me what you owe!' So his fellow servant fell down at his feet and begged him, saying, 'Have patience with me, and I will pay you all.' And he would not, but went and threw him into prison till he should pay the debt. So when his fellow servants saw what had been done, they were very grieved, and came and told their master all that had been done. Then his master, after he had called him, said to him, 'You wicked servant! I forgave you all that debt because you begged me. Should you not also have had compassion on your fellow servant, just as I had pity on you?' And his master was angry, and delivered him to the torturers until he should pay all that was due to him.

"So My heavenly Father also will do to you if each of you, from his heart, does not forgive his brother his trespasses."[12]

Once again the audience hummed as they discussed Jesus' words. God would only forgive in the same measure that we forgive others? Husbands and wives regarded each other with troubled expressions. Friends and business partners leaned their heads together, as if suddenly struck with unresolved issues to be discussed.

A hundred birds passed overhead and circled above the big man. Starling fluttered in her cage.

"All right then." Jono lifted her up. "Are these your family?"

He loosed the latch and threw open the door. "You are free! Look! Free!"

Starling hopped from her perch and paused only a moment at the open portal. Then, with a happy chirp and a flurry of wings, she leapt into the sky and joined the other birds.

Jono shielded his eyes against the sun and traced her flight until she merged with the flock. He placed the empty cage on a boulder and hiked down the path to take his place among the human flock.

Chapter 36

It was always a joy for Claudia when Pilate and his Praetorian henchman Vara rode off on government business to Caesarea. She had heeded Marcus's warning and had wheedled permission from Pilate to stay at the governor's mansion in Tiberias for a while. Though she was happy for the fresh air, she missed the bustle of Jerusalem and her lessons with Josephus.

Claudia had awakened early to the sound of myriad feet traveling the road outside the gates of the governor's estate. Philo was not yet awake.

"What is it?" Claudia asked her maid.

"Lady Claudia, the people are coming from all over Galilee to hear the teaching of Rabbi Yeshua, Jesus of Nazareth."

Claudia climbed to the roof garden for a better view. The mass of humanity traveling along the lakeshore seemed endless. She had not witnessed such crowds since the great events of the Roman Circus. The citizens of Rome had often come in tens of thousands to watch gladiators fight to the death, but in Galilee, the multitudes flocked to hear the teaching of a new rabbi.

Seized with an irresistible curiosity, she changed into the clothes of a servant, slipped from the back gate, and joined the throngs. At this early hour clouds hung low in the east like scarlet banners. The water of the lake reflected red. Beneath her veil and in the homespun robe of a peasant and in plain leather sandals, Claudia became merely another commoner melting into the crowd that hoped to take away some fragment of truth.

Smoke from cook fires drifted up from small homes. The smell of fresh bread made her hungry. Purchasing a loaf and an apple from an old woman by the road, she sat on a boulder and ate breakfast among the crowd that now gathered by the lakeshore.

A cool breeze from the water stirred her veil. She lifted her eyes toward the fishing vessels on the Galil as the sun beamed through and stood on tiptoe to see him. From this far distance, surrounded by his bodyguards, he seemed an ordinary-looking Jew—in his early thirties, with brown hair, tied back, and a thick dark beard—framed by the backdrop of boats and fishing nets. But instead of fish, a school of humanity swarmed toward him.

She watched as Jesus climbed into a fishing boat and his men shoved off from the shore. The crowd started to settle in, sitting on the bank that sloped up like an amphitheater.

Claudia found a shady spot and sat on the ground beside a family of farmers.

All fell silent as Jesus got to his feet, grasped the mast, and began to speak.

"A farmer went out to sow some seed. As he scattered the seed, some fell upon the path, and the birds came along and ate it up. Some fell on rocky places where there wasn't much soil. It sprang up quickly because the soil was shallow. But when the sun came up, the plants were scorched and withered because they had no root. Other seed fell among thorns, which grew up and choked the plants so they produced no crop. Still other seed fell on good soil. It sprouted, grew, and produced a crop, some multiplying thirty, some sixty, and some one hundred times."

The farmer at Claudia's elbow remarked, "This Jesus knows the perils of farming."

The voice of Jesus resounded over the water. "Whoever has ears to hear, let them hear."

Someone shouted, "Tell us what it means, Rabbi!"

Jesus laughed. "Don't you understand this parable? The sower sows the word. The ones by the wayside where the word is sown are those who, when they hear, Satan comes immediately and takes away the word that was sown in their hearts. The ones on stony ground are those who, when they hear the word, immediately receive it with gladness, but since they have no root in themselves, they only endure for a time. Afterward, when tribulation or persecution arises for the word's sake, immediately they stumble. The ones among thorns are the ones who hear the word, and the cares of this world, the deceitfulness of riches, and the desires for other things choke the word, and it becomes unfruitful. But the ones on good ground are those who hear the word, accept it, and bear fruit . . . some thirtyfold, some sixty, and some a hundred.

"The kingdom of God is like this—a man scatters seed on the ground, sleeps by night, and rises by day. When the seed sprouts and grows, he himself does not know how. For the earth yields crops by itself . . . first the blade, then the head, after that the full grain in the head. But when the grain ripens, immediately he puts in the sickle, because the harvest has come."[13]

After the teaching, Jesus and his close followers set the sail and caught the wind to skim eastward across the lake.

Along with the multitudes who wanted to hear more, Claudia arose, brushed bits of straw from her clothing, and headed home.

She longed to speak to Josephus the Elder about what she had heard.

It seemed to Claudia that in the simple metaphors of Jesus' teaching was truth. Inarguable and clear, she understood what he meant about life, hope, and disappointment and how goodness took root in the soil of a good person's heart and grew into something magnificent.

She asked herself, *What soil defines my heart?*

That evening, as a storm raged over the Sea of Galilee, she sat down to write Josephus the Elder.

Venerable friend, today I heard the teaching of the young rabbi named Jesus. In his words I feel as though I have waded ankle deep in the sea of truth for the first time in my life. I put a drop of truth upon my lips. I taste salt. Even one drop is the sea, but there is so much more I long to know. His truth is deep, so deep. I have no one with whom I may explore this new Kingdom. Please come here and join us in Galilee.

Claudia had no doubt that Josephus would come in response to her letter and that it would be as swiftly as possible. After their study together of the scriptures, she knew the elderly Jew would be as curious about the events surrounding the rabbi Jesus as she was.

Chapter 37

A s soon as Josephus was announced as drawing near
the front entrance of Pilate's Tiberias estate, she called
to one of the servants, "Quickly! Bring food, drink, and a
basin of water for our dusty traveler." Then she hastened
toward the door herself.

Stepping outside, she shaded her eyes against the late-
afternoon sun of Galilee. Josephus arrived in a cart pulled
by a donkey. As soon as he dismounted, he walked slowly
toward her, smiling, hands extended in greeting.

"Claudia, my dear . . ." He embraced her. "And where
is our boy, Philo?"

She laughed. "Where he would love to be all the time—
riding his pony out by the stables."

He took her hand. "So, tell me everything you have
heard, seen, discovered about this rabbi . . . and how you
and Philo are . . ."

They were just walking toward the house when the
rapid clattering of horse hooves surfaced and grew steadily
closer.

The instant Claudia saw Pavor, she knew. *Marcus.*

She tilted her head, puzzled. After his demotion, she hadn't seen much of him. Perhaps he was purposefully staying out of Pilate's sights. So why come by now? Because Pilate was away? Or because Marcus had something to report? Could it be about the healer?

As Marcus leaped off his horse, she moved toward him. When he turned toward her and she saw his eyes, she knew there was something different about him. Yes, he was still the sun-bronzed, battle-hardened soldier she had loved . . . and still loved, when she admitted it to herself. But now joy radiated from his being. Cockiness and anger toward her were gone, replaced with gentleness.

He halted a foot from her and extended one hand, as if beseeching her. "Claudia," he murmured. "I have found it—the truth we've been seeking. And hope . . . such hope! Carta was broken, near to death . . ." His voice choked.

"Carta?" She flung her hands to her mouth, covering it in dismay. The sorrow of a mother's heart overflowed. "Oh, Marcus, Carta was hurt? Is he—"

Marcus held up a hand. "I will explain all to you. But I must ask you to do something first—prepare for a journey. I have seen Jesus of Nazareth. Jono and I talked about him—"

"Jono? Where did you see Jono? How is—"

He held up his hand again. "He is all right. Fine, in fact. I will give you the answers you desire in due time. For now, you must trust me. We will have a journey ahead in which I can explain. Jono and I have agreed that Philo must be taken to the healer. Claudia, if Jesus could heal Carta, he could heal—"

"Our beloved boy," Josephus concluded. He had now arrived and stood behind Claudia like the immovable bulwark of an aging ship. He put a hand on her shoulder. "Yes," he said confidently, "Marcus is right. I have much to tell you too—of what I have heard. We must travel as soon as possible. I too want to meet this Jesus of Nazareth."

Hope stirred. Claudia made up her mind. Pilate was away. There was nothing to hold her here. "Then we will leave within the hour," she announced.

Claudia was already on her way, preceding the men to the house, when she suddenly swiveled. Fixing Marcus with an intense stare, she added, "And then, Centurion, you *will* tell me everything . . . until I am satisfied."

Marcus smirked. "At your service, Lady Claudia."

She gave a simple nod, then pivoted back toward the house.

Behind her, she heard a chuckle, quickly muffled. Another followed.

"Women," Marcus said in amused exasperation. "They think they have us wound around their fingers."

A full laugh bubbled from Josephus. "But they do, dear boy, they do."

Claudia swept on toward the house as if she hadn't heard a thing.

༺∽∾∿༻

The cart hauling Claudia, Josephus, and Philo rattled over stony ground. Pulled by a donkey, to keep from rattling the occupants to pieces it scarcely traveled as fast as a man could walk. Marcus, riding alongside on Pavor, had to rein him in to keep company with the wagon.

The trip up the tributary creek of the Sea of Galilee took much longer than expected. All night they traveled, unable to move faster and unwilling to stop for the night. A brilliant last-quarter moon hung in the eastern sky, illuminating the path. No one spoke. Philo dozed in his mother's arms.

Marcus drew to a halt and signaled Josephus to stop the cart as well. "I think I see their camp." Marcus pointed up the slope toward the deeper shadow cast by a grove of locust trees. "We should halt here, I think. Mustn't frighten them."

Peering ahead, Claudia spotted a faint orange glow that signaled a campfire. "I hope it's Jesus." Then she added in a hesitant whisper, "I hope he'll see us."

Josephus turned toward her and Marcus leaned over the horse's wither. "My dear child," the scholar said, "why would he not?"

"They say . . . ," Claudia began, then added, "what if it's true that he knows everything? What if he knows who I am—the wife of the Roman governor? What if he won't see us?"

Smiling gently, Josephus patted Philo's crooked leg and then touched Claudia's shoulder. "I will go first," he volunteered. "I will speak to him."

Marcus tied up his horse, then secured the reins of the donkey.

After clasping both of Claudia's hands in his, Josephus set off toward the glowing embers.

A few minutes later Josephus's words floated down to them. "Hello, the camp. May I come in?"

A trio of gruff Galilean accents challenged him. "Who are you? What do you want here? The master is asleep."

Another voice added a soothing quality to the mix. Claudia could not hear the words, but all argument ceased, and quiet returned to the mountainside.

Pressed against her, Philo stirred. Dreamily he stretched, yawned, and asked, "Where are we, Mama? Why have we come here?"

Firmly, investing her words with confidence she did not herself feel, she replied, "We've come to see a king."

A pair of forms loomed up out of the shadows into the silver light cast by the moon. One was the stooped form of the scholar.

The other became more defined as he walked closer. It was Jesus. There was no hesitation as he strode toward the cart. If he knew Claudia's identity, it did not seem to repel him. In fact, curiously, it did not matter at all. Coming directly to them, he nodded to Marcus and to Claudia.

But his first words were for Philo. "What is your name?" he said in a friendly manner.

"Philo. Are you a king? My mama says we've come to see a king. Are you him?"

Jesus simply smiled at the boy, then turned toward Claudia. When his face caught the moon's rays, his features leapt into startling focus. In that instant Claudia thought, *This is how I will remember this moment forever.*

The Nazarene asked, "Do you believe I can do this?"

Nodding, and then realizing the slight gesture was not adequate in the dim light, she said, "Lord, I do believe."

His smile beamed as fully as the tenderness that flowed from his eyes. Laying his hands on Philo's crooked leg, Jesus lifted his face toward heaven. His lips moved, but Claudia could not hear his prayers.

Claudia was also praying. *Oh, God of my ancestors, there is no reason for you to regard me or my prayers. But if this good man should ask on my son's behalf, please don't let anything I have done . . . or been . . . keep your mercy from flowing.*

"Philo," Jesus said, smiling even more broadly, "come with me. Let's walk awhile beside the river."

Philo leapt into Jesus' arms and was lifted above the head of his mother, up onto Jesus' shoulder. Together they moved toward the water, into the face of the rising sun. Boy and man were silhouetted against the blazing disk, as if their forms were outlined in gold.

Then Jesus put Philo down beside him—Philo on his own two feet.

Claudia held her breath. A cry was quickly stifled. Fear of hoping clashed with the fear of failing to believe. But the reality outstripped the fears.

Jesus and Philo walked together by the stream. Jesus pointed out where the penetrating rays of the sun gave the stream a crystalline quality as it bubbled over the rocks.

Covering her mouth with both hands, Claudia gasped to see her son . . . her only son . . . walking beside the

Nazarene. Relinquishing Jesus' hand, Philo ran ahead, skipped like a young lamb, and jumped up on a boulder by the river's edge.

Tears spilled down Claudia's cheeks. She did not sob. Her heart simply overflowed in streams of wonder and joy.

Beside her Josephus lifted both hands skyward, praying and thanking the God of miracles for allowing him to see this day.

And Marcus? Marcus wiped his eyes with the back of his hand.

When Jesus turned from the stream at last to walk back toward the cart, Philo ran—ran!—to catch up with him, tugging on Jesus' arm to take him back to Claudia.

Part Five

"What about you?" he asked. "Who do you say I am?"
Simon Peter answered, "You are the Messiah, the Son of the living God."

MATTHEW 16:15–16

Part Five

"What about you?" he asked. "Who do
you say I am?"
Simon Peter answered, "You are the
Messiah, the Son of the living God."
Matthew 16:15–16

Chapter 38

The closer Claudia, Philo, and Josephus drew near to the palace in Jerusalem, the more she dreaded the scene that would surely follow. The message from Pilate had been terse. *You and the boy will return to Jerusalem with all haste.*

There was no question that she would obey his authority. It was a command.

Had it been anyone else, Claudia would have thought with great joy, *So he has heard of Philo's healing and wants to see it for himself. Wants to rejoice with us.*

But this was Pilate, who had wanted Philo dead at birth and who had, other than that, ignored him for much of his life.

Then a tiny spark of hope entered. *Still, how could any man not rejoice at a child's healing?*

She shook her head. *No, more likely he wants us back within his control.* She shivered involuntarily.

Josephus, his expression knowing and compassionate, clasped Claudia's hand between his two wrinkled ones. "I will petition God on your behalf," he murmured to her. Then he smiled at the now sleeping Philo beside him.

Marcus had stood quietly watching. It was all he could do, she knew, to let them go.

As they were transported from the palace in Tiberias and toward Jerusalem, with one of the legionaries following in Josephus's donkey cart, Claudia sighed. Once again, the machinations of Rome and Imperial power had asserted control over their lives, and she and her son were being drawn inexorably in a direction she did not want to go.

The only choice she had was whether or not to look back at Marcus . . . and all she had been forced to leave behind. At Tiberias, the air had been fresh and the winds of Pilate's whims had not blown.

She chose not to glance behind. Thinking of the losses was too painful. Instead she set her mind firmly toward Jerusalem and what was to come.

∽∾∾

The campfire flickered, offering small competition to the myriad of brilliant stars wheeling overhead in the region of Caesarea Philippi. Fat from the quail spitted on sticks sizzled as it dripped into the coals.

James, the son of Zebedee, withdrew a roasting bird, studied it, then returned to holding it over the low flame. "More and more of John's followers are finding their way to us," he observed to no one in particular.

Judas, his heavy black beard and dark olive skin merging his face with the shadows, added, "And welcome to them, I say, as long as they bring their swords."

The man who spoke next had gold flecks in his brown eyes and gold lights in his brown hair. "Judas," Jesus said, "those who live by the sword will die by the sword."[14]

Judas would not be silenced yet. "We will have to fight them someday. Just as the Maccabees fought the Greek tyrants and won."

Breaking off a piece of barley bread, Jesus passed the loaf to Shim'on bar Jonah.

"And who do men say that I am?" Jesus inquired.

James spoke quickly. "Some say you are the prophet Elijah returned from the whirlwind."

Brushing crumbs from his beard, Shim'on rumbled, "Some say you are a prophet."

John, the younger of the two Zebedee brothers, offered, "Healer."

"Magician," Thomas suggested.

Nathaniel said, "In Jerusalem the high priest says you are a blasphemer because you heal on the Sabbath."

Judas cleared his throat before speaking again. "Herod says you are a liar and an impostor."

Matthew, the former tax collector, noted, "In the villages I hear men talk. They all hope you are a general, like Judah Maccabee, who will lead us in battle and overthrow both Herod and Rome."

John and James exchanged a knowing look and a wry smile. James passed the spit to his brother, who tore off a chunk.

John juggled the hot food, blew on his burned fingers, then said, "Everyone wants something from you. You cannot be everything. The truth is, nobody is sure who . . . or what . . . you are."

Jesus persisted. "But who do you say that I am?"

Blurting in a manner that suggested he surprised even himself, Shim'on asserted, "You are the Messiah, Redeemer. You are the Son of the living God!"

There was a stunned silence around the campfire. Everyone stared at the big fisherman.

Jesus offered Shim'on a gentle smile. "Blessed are you, Shim'on, son of Jonah. Flesh and blood did not reveal this to you, but the Holy Spirit. Your name was Shim'on, but from now on you will be called Peter . . . Rock. And this is the rock on which I will build my church."[15]

∽∾

A message arrived, summoning Marcus also to the palace in Jerusalem. Marcus shook his head at the timing.

Then reality struck. Pilate could have ordered Marcus to accompany Claudia and Philo back to Jerusalem. However, the summons had arrived mere hours after his wife and the boy, as well as Josephus, had left—but with no possibility of encountering them on the road.

So, Pilate was still jealous. Marcus would have to watch every word he said.

Chapter 39

Marcus had spurred Pavor on to travel as swiftly as he could to Jerusalem. When he arrived, Cassius stood at the entrance to the palace.

"Pilate is in a foul mood," Cassius warned.

With Philo now no longer crippled, why wasn't Pilate overjoyed?

"Worse than usual?" Marcus quipped.

Cassius nodded. "Ordered a legionary crucified for failing to salute him properly. I barely saved the man's life . . . thirty-nine lashes instead."

"Even after Jesus . . ." Marcus stopped himself. If the governor was already in such a temper, best not make Jesus his target. "Any reason?"

"I heard it just now from a wine merchant newly returned from Rome. Lucius Sejanus is dead. Executed for treason."

"Sejanus? Pilate's patron?"

"The same. Got too big for himself, even for a Praetorian . . . or so the man said. With Caesar in Capri, guess he didn't like Sejanus replacing the Praetorian Guard with those loyal to him instead of Caesar. Or that he pushed

so hard to marry into the royals and become Caesar's heir."
Cassius mimicked a man being garroted with a cord. "Just
think. The last words Sejanus heard when the silk noose
went round his throat were the ones he himself often used
when he executed any rivals. 'You are no friend of Caesar.'
I'll wager the news made our dear governor look over his
shoulder."

"I'll tread softly," Marcus agreed.

❧

Claudia had often suffered from her husband's arrogance
and haughty disdain, in addition to his physical beatings.
But she had never before felt such icy hatred emanating
from him.

Pilate, seated in his chair of office, pointed at Marcus.
"You risked the lives of my wife and child!" The governor's
words trembled with angry accusation.

The centurion, in his best dress armor, plumed helmet
tucked under his arm, remained coolly unmoved.

Claudia, struck with amazement and disbelief, blurted,
"Your child? Do you not see the good? Philo is healed!"

"Silence, woman," Pilate thundered. "You could just as
easily have been killed!"

"I won't be silent!" Claudia shot back. "It is a miracle.
My son can walk!"

"Longinus," Pilate said, ignoring Claudia completely,
"be grateful I do not order you crucified. Long ago, I trusted
you with the safety of my wife and son. You not only failed

in that trust, you willingly took them into danger. This is your doing."

With the slightest bow of his head, Marcus acknowledged Pilate's statement.

Even though neither man was looking at her, Claudia protested, "But he did not fail. Besides, I asked him . . . no." She lifted her chin. "I commanded him."

"So," Pilate remarked to Marcus, "what kind of soldier lets his good sense and his obedience be overruled by the whim of a foolish woman?"

Claudia opened her mouth but was silenced by an imperious gesture from her husband. Pilate's earlier threat finally hit home. The governor could order a centurion to be arrested and crucified and would have to answer to Caesar alone for his actions.

Now she merely stood, trembling with fury.

Pilate was not through flaying Marcus. "This is the second time since we arrived in Judea I had to demote you . . . and the last. Be glad you aren't imprisoned or worse. I am not convinced this Jewish sorcerer is no threat to Rome. So, your new posting? Keep your eye on this Jewish fanatic and your mind off my wife."

Claudia stormed out of the room, slamming the door behind her. Fleeing to her chamber, she did not stop moving until she reached the balcony. A weight on her chest crushed the life and breath out of her.

In sight, in the courtyard, Marcus drove away the grooms and sentries who came forward to assist and prepared to mount Pavor.

"Marcus," Claudia whispered.

When someone touched her shoulder from behind, she whirled, backing up until only the iron railing prevented her fall to the paving stones below.

"What I did was for your own good." Pilate placed one of his hands on her shoulder.

Claudia flinched at his touch, her whole body growing rigid.

"You are mine," Pilate asserted. "Just like my horse is mine. Like my sword is mine. Like Jerusalem and the Galil are mine."

"I never loved you," Claudia said, her reply devoid of emotion. If her words had been inscribed on parchment, they could not have been more detached and impassive.

"Do you think that matters?" Pilate crushed her to him and kissed her with such force that her lips bruised.

Claudia slapped him.

Pilate slapped her back, hard. He grabbed her wrists, laughed at her cries, and dragged her into the room.

Chapter 40

Another year had passed in the Roman province of Judea. Another year from Passover to Rosh Hashanah and Yom Kippur . . . from Tabernacles to Passover again. A time of turmoil and fear, hope and hesitancy.

Awakened from a sound sleep, Claudia heard Philo's feet pattering on the palace floor and the sound of his voice calling, "Mama! Mama!"

It was the urgency of excitement, not of fear.

Dashing into her room, he flung himself up onto the bed. "Mama!" he said again.

"Good morning. And what—"

"Today is the day! I heard the servants talking. Jesus is coming today. He may be here anytime. To Jerusalem, I mean. Today," he announced without taking a breath.

Warm sunlight crept over the window ledge, suffusing the chamber with a golden glow.

"We have to go meet him—we have to! Everyone's going. Is he coming as the king, Mama? Is today that day?"

Placing her finger against Philo's lips, Claudia shushed

him. When she added a nod, her raised brows also expressed, *This is our secret for now.*

～～

Dressed in the homespun garb of servants, Claudia and Philo slipped out through the gates of the governor's palace and merged into the teeming Passover crowds.

Philo held her hand and looked up. "I hope we will see him today, Mother. I hope we can speak to him. Thank him again."

"He will be surrounded by people, Philo. But maybe we can hear him if he teaches in the Temple courts."

They met Josephus near the Jerusalem gate that opened eastward. Lifting her eyes, Claudia traced the sweep of the road as it ascended the Mount of Olives and disappeared in the direction of the village of Bethany.

Today not one bit of the actual dusty, stony track could be seen. Instead the way was carpeted with thousands of pilgrims. On both sides of the route, the verdant hills of spring blossomed with all the colors of dyed wool and many shades of humanity as well.

"Almost Passover," Josephus explained. "Jews from every part of the world where our people have been scattered have returned to the Holy City. From Alexandria, they come. From Ethiopia. From Babylon. From Cyprus and Crete and Cyrene. From Rome and Gaul. Even from the Pillars of Hercules. All have come to worship the Almighty at the place on which he says his eye ever rests."

A ripple of elation ran through the crowds. This was more than the excitement of being in Jerusalem for the holiday. It was an enthusiasm born of anticipation.

There was a surge of movement at the top of the mount. A new upwelling of arriving travelers, like the seventh wave on a shore, broke over the crest and foamed downward toward the city.

"He's coming," was on every lip, pronounced by every mouth, ringing in every ear. "The Nazarene!"

And then there he was . . . Jesus, riding a donkey, making his way down the slope.

Chaos ensued. As if a dam had suddenly broken, a corresponding swell of onlookers swarmed out of the gates and down toward Jesus. Everyone in the whole world, it seemed, wanted to see Jesus.

For an instant, when the crowd opened, Claudia thought she saw Jono among the common folk. Then the mass of humanity closed again, and their friend and protector was gone.

"Blessed is he who comes in the name of the Lord," someone shouted.

"From the house of the Lord, we bless you." The throng around Claudia roared the antiphon to the psalm.

"Has there ever been such a day?" Claudia marveled aloud.

Lifting his hands skyward, Josephus fervently intoned, "Praise the God of Israel, who has let me live to see this day!"

It was like watching the most elaborate magician's trick ever. One moment the road was lined with nodding palm trees. The next instant their branches had been stripped and were placed in the clamoring hands of the audience.

Philo raised his hands and shouted, "Me! Me! I need a branch." As if signaling a ship a great way out to sea, the boy waved the frond with enormous energy, jumping up and down as he did so.

"Hosanna to the Son of David!" everyone shouted, stripping off their cloaks and lining the road with them.

And Jesus was there, a half smile below brows furrowed with compassion.

Then, almost right behind her, Claudia spotted Marcus. It had been nearly a year since Philo's healing. She hadn't seen Marcus since the day Pilate had ordered her back to Jerusalem and then confronted Marcus with his terse order, "Keep your eye on this Jewish fanatic and your mind off my wife."

Marcus had stayed away. She hadn't sought him. But now, suddenly, she saw him, dressed as a commoner—no uniform, no sword, his beard full and bushy. But he was not smiling, nor was he shouting joyfully. His expression was troubled, serious. Following the direction of his gaze, Claudia scanned the city walls above the gate.

There, red-faced and scowling, was High Priest Caiaphas, surrounded by his henchmen. He was talking incessantly and gesticulating wildly. He was not praying or thanking God for this day.

"Marcus! Marcus!" Claudia called.

By yet another miracle, he turned toward her. They saw each other for just a moment, reached out as if they would touch . . . and then the flow of the mob swept them apart. Claudia tightly grasped Philo's collar, and Josephus clung to them both, but there was no moving against the current to contact Marcus.

When the trio had reached the relative calm and safety of a side street, there was no sign of Marcus and no way to know where he had gone.

"I think he is concerned with Jesus' safety," Josephus said. "He acts like he is guarding Rabbi Jesus, as well he might."

As they walked back toward the palace, the scholar rehearsed over and over again all the signs of the Messiah that had their fulfillment in Jesus of Nazareth. "Including this day," he instructed. "Listen to what the prophet Zechariah wrote. 'Rejoice greatly, O daughter of Zion! Shout, O daughter of Jerusalem! Behold, your King is coming to you; He is just and having salvation, lowly and riding on a donkey.'"[16]

"Daughter of Zion! That's you, Mama," Philo said.

At the servants' entry to the palace, Josephus parted from them. "I also saw what the centurion saw," he murmured.

Claudia blinked. "Oh, my friend," was all she could say with Philo nearby.

"It is Passover," the scholar returned. "Perhaps, for good-will, Pilate may permit the daughter of a Jewish woman to celebrate seder in the home of her rabbi."

"Perhaps," she said aloud. But she knew it was highly doubtful her husband would agree.

She peered toward the tables of the moneychangers. They were thronged with poor pilgrims who waited in line to change common currency for Temple money . . . for a high fee.

The bawling of sacrificial animals blended into the voices of the people.

Claudia squinted upward. High Priest Caiaphas and the head of the Temple guard observed the transactions from the stone railing of a balcony. They pointed at Jesus moving through the pilgrims.

Philo tugged Claudia's hand, and they moved closer to Jesus.

A poor family stood at the head of the line at a money-changing table.

The pilgrim said, "A thirty percent commission to change my money into Temple currency? How will I pay my Temple tax and feed my children?"

The moneychanger replied, "Give me your coin." He snatched the money from the poor man as Jesus looked on. "See this?" the collector sneered. "The face of Caesar is on your coin. Idolatry. A Roman coin, see? Not allowed in the Temple. Only holy money allowed. That's the way it works."

The poor man glanced helplessly at his wife, then back at the collector. "But a thirty percent commission . . . Last year it was only twenty percent."

The moneychanger replied, "Last year John the Baptizer was alive. This year there is none left to criticize."

Jesus sat on the base of a stone pillar and began braiding a whip.

Claudia said, "This way." They worked their way closer to the high priest to hear his words.

Caiaphas chuckled derisively. "It is a good day. The Baptizer's followers have already forgotten him. And Jesus is all about peace."

The Temple guard laughed. "Sheep."

Caiaphas continued, "John is gone like a whirlwind in the desert."

The face of Jesus clouded with anger. He shook out the whip, testing it.

The Temple guard inclined his head toward Jesus. "He calls himself the good shepherd. What's he doing now?"

Caiaphas growled, "Leading his sheep to slaughter. He disregards our Sabbath laws. Calls himself the Son of God. A blasphemer. Liar. Lunatic."

"Yet look how all the people flock to him."

Caiaphas replied, "We have witnessed enough violations of Torah to indict Jesus and stone him in the street if he becomes troublesome."

The anger of Jesus built.

Caiaphas chuckled again. "Let the shepherd preach to the sheep. Blessed are the poor. We will make certain Israel's poor do not lose the blessing of poverty."

Suddenly, the voice of Jesus roared above the clamor. "Get out! You have made my Father's house a den of thieves!"

Total pandemonium erupted in the Temple marketplace as Jesus overturned the tables, whipped the moneychangers, and threw open the gates of the sheep pens. He waded in among the animals and drove them out.

Loose animals stampeded through the marketplace. Caiaphas and the Temple guard quickly retreated indoors.

The chaos continued as pilgrims scrambled after spilled coins and the followers of Jesus grabbed his arms and hurried him away.[17]

Suddenly at Claudia's elbow stood Josephus the Elder. His expression was greatly troubled. "Let us go to my home, my dear. It is not safe for you and the boy here, and the palace is too far. The spirit of violence is in the air."

Claudia nodded, scooped Philo up, and fought with Josephus against the crowds to reach his modest home.

ᵔᵔᵔ

It was hours after Jesus overturned the tables of the moneychangers, and there was still unrest in the streets. Claudia sat close to the fire in the scholar's home as he studied a scroll. Philo, exhausted, had fallen asleep.

Claudia was miserably afraid. The sound of a pot smashing outside and the harsh words that followed made her suddenly tense to the point of trembling. This time, there was no Marcus to defend her. She listened, fearful of what would follow, until the noises of drunken laughter moved away.

Jesus, the gentle healer, now faced the highest degree of opposition yet. By denouncing Temple corruption in such a public manner, he unified all the religious authorities against him. Preaching way up in Galilee was one thing, but turning over tables and whipping merchants here in the heart of Jerusalem? The wicked, cheating moneychangers probably felt the sting of public laughter and humiliation even more than the leather cords of Jesus' lash . . . and they would never forgive him.

What would they do to him if they caught him?

Josephus tapped the third line down from the top of a scroll. "Here it is written . . . written of the Messiah in the psalm of David, 'Those who would destroy me are powerful, being wrongfully my enemies . . . for zeal for Your house has consumed me.'[18] This is a true picture, eh?"

"No doubt the high priest wants Jesus to be consumed," Claudia replied. "By death. Stones or fire from heaven. Doesn't matter how."

The old man replied, "He has touched the raw nerve in the broken tooth of religion—he has disrupted their business. Condemned their crooked economy. Money is, after all, the one true god of man's idolatry."

Claudia blurted out the deep anxiety that gripped her heart. "If they find him, they will kill him."

"Yes, I fear they will." Josephus's expression was greatly troubled. "Corrupt leaders fear truth."

Wringing her hands together Claudia said, "They would have Truth dead and buried!"

"Truth," Josephus corrected, "may be buried . . . but it will never die."

aiaphas paced up and down in front of Pilate's desk. He clasped his hands behind his back, then across his front, then behind him again. Pilate stared at him sourly, angry that his evening was spoiled with this temper tantrum. Why couldn't the local authorities do what they were supposed to do? Pilate was frustrated that an issue involving a nobody like the Nazarene had to come before him at all.

"Arrest him!" Caiaphas demanded for the tenth time.

"Religion is your jurisdiction," Pilate responded in exact measure.

Caiaphas waved an admonishing finger, much to Pilate's displeasure, and his voice screeched. "This . . . matter . . . has nothing to do . . . with religion!"

Blandly, Pilate observed, "Then the issue is commerce."

"The Temple revenues collected for Rome," Caiaphas said with assurance he had the supreme argument.

"He disrupted your business dealings in the Temple. The bribes you pay Caesar to keep your power . . . are more important than your religion?"

"He is a threat to the Empire of Rome!"

Deliberately needling now, because he enjoyed tormenting this pompous, arrogant windbag, Pilate added, "Jesus claims he is the son of God."

"Blasphemy!" Caiaphas looked as if he might have apoplexy.

"Caesar also calls himself the son of a god. Perhaps Caesar and Jesus are brothers?"

Clenching his jaw and regaining a measure of self-control, the high priest stated, "You mock me, but you will see. The people love him. They will follow him."

"Will the people die for him?" Pilate inquired.

Ignoring the questions, Caiaphas stuck out his lower lip. "Better he should die for them!"

"You fear they will make Jesus high priest in your place," Pilate asserted, twisting the knife a bit further.

"You—" Caiaphas returned with deliberate coldness. "You should fear they will make him king in Caesar's place. Whose jurisdiction will it be then?"

❧

The close followers of Jesus spread their bedrolls out around the campfire. In the shadows just beyond the flickering firelight, Jono stood guard over the little band. Across the valley the torches gleamed on the Temple walls.

"That is some sight," Andrew said quietly as he sat between his brother, who now went by the name of Peter, and Jesus. "Lord, what did you mean today, when we were leaving the Temple and you said all the buildings would be destroyed?"

Peter jumped in. "And not only destroyed, but completely demolished. Not one stone left on another. When will all this happen, Lord, and what will be the sign of your return and the end of the world?"[19]

Jesus gestured toward the thousands of pilgrim fires, glistening like stars across the valley. He said to them, "Take heed that no one deceives you. For many will come in My name, saying, 'I am the Christ,' and will deceive many. And you will hear of wars and rumors of wars. See that you are not troubled; for all these things must come to pass, but the end is not yet.

"Then they will deliver you up to tribulation and kill you, and you will be hated by all nations for My name's sake. And this gospel of the kingdom will be preached in all the world as a witness to all the nations, and then the end will come.

"When you see the 'abomination of desolation,' spoken of by Daniel the prophet, standing in the holy place, then let those who are in Judea flee to the mountains. For then there will be great tribulation, such as has not been since the beginning of the world until this time, no, nor ever shall be. And unless those days were shortened, no flesh would be saved; but for the elect's sake those days will be shortened.

"Immediately after the tribulation of those days the sun will be darkened, and the moon will not give its light; the stars will fall from heaven, and the powers of the heavens will be shaken. Then the sign of the Son of Man will appear in heaven, and then all the tribes of the earth will mourn, and they will see the Son of Man coming on the clouds of heaven with power and great glory. And He will send His angels with a great sound of a trumpet, and they will gather together His elect from the four winds, from one end of heaven to the other.

"But of that day and hour no one knows, not even the angels of heaven, but My Father only. Watch therefore, for you do not know what hour your Lord is coming."[20]

Jono considered the teaching of Jesus. In spite of the danger, Jesus had come to Jerusalem. And now he spoke of the End of Days as though it was on the very doorstep.

"When the Son of Man comes in His glory," Jesus continued, "and all the holy angels with Him, then He will sit on the throne of His glory. All the nations will be gathered before Him, and He will separate them one from another, as a shepherd divides his sheep from the goats. And He will set the sheep on His right hand, but the goats on the left. Then the King will say to those on His right hand, 'Come, you blessed of My Father, inherit the kingdom prepared for you from the foundation of the world: for I was hungry and you gave Me food; I was thirsty and you gave Me drink; I was a stranger and you took Me in; I was naked and you clothed Me; I was sick and you visited Me; I was in prison and you came to Me.'

"Then the righteous will answer Him, saying, 'Lord, when did we see You hungry and feed You, or thirsty and give You drink? When did we see You a stranger and take

You in, or naked and clothe You? Or when did we see You sick, or in prison, and come to You?' And the King will answer and say to them, 'Assuredly, I say to you, inasmuch as you did it to one of the least of these My brethren, you did it to Me.'

"Then He will also say to those on the left hand, 'Depart from Me, you cursed, into the everlasting fire prepared for the devil and his angels: for I was hungry and you gave Me no food; I was thirsty and you gave Me no drink; I was a stranger and you did not take Me in, naked and you did not clothe Me, sick and in prison and you did not visit Me.'

"Then they also will answer Him, saying, 'Lord, when did we see You hungry or thirsty or a stranger or naked or sick or in prison, and did not minister to You?' Then He will answer them, saying, 'Assuredly, I say to you, inasmuch as you did not do it to one of the least of these, you did not do it to Me.' And these will go away into everlasting punishment, but the righteous into eternal life."[21]

He finished his teaching. "As you know, Passover begins in two days. Then the Son of Man will be handed over to be crucified."[22]

There was an unhappy whispering among the men, but no one dared to argue with Jesus. Surely he did not mean it, they reasoned. Surely Jesus was speaking of other men—rebels who would be captured and executed by the Roman tyrants. But Jesus could not be speaking of himself!

Judas skulked away from the campfire, then slipped into the night, Jono noticed. By and by the other disciples drifted off to sleep.

Jono leaned his back against a tree and studied the profile of the master. While his disciples slept, Jesus gazed into the flame as though he could see what trials lay before him.

∽◦∾

On the Temple Mount, in an assembly hall known as the Chamber of Hewn Stone, High Priest Caiaphas convened a secret meeting. He had called an emergency session of the Sanhedrin, the Jewish high council, but several of its members were deliberately not invited.

High-placed Temple authorities and wealthy Pharisees, normally rivals in religious dealings, were united by what they had recently witnessed when Jesus arrived in Jerusalem. The room buzzed with conversation—some anxious, some angry.

Caiaphas called the meeting to order with an imperious slap of his hands. "Jerusalem overflows with conspiracy," he announced. "The governor and Herod are concerned and have asked for our insight. We are fortunate to have an informant . . . a member of the inner circle of the charlatan, Jesus of Nazareth."

The noise of a hive of bees erupted again in the chamber.

At a snap of his fingers, Caiaphas summoned a guard. "Bring him," he ordered.

Looking around apprehensively, Judas was brought into the room. When the guard abandoned him in front of the high priest, Judas appeared to search for any friendly face. There was none.

Caiaphas pinned Judas in place by staring down his daggerlike nose. "Judas Iscariot. How long have you been a disciple of Jesus of Nazareth?"

"Three years."

"Three years among his closest followers . . . friends. You know him very well, yet you are willing to hand your master over to us? Why?"

Judas stammered. His face was sweaty, and he smelled foul. "This is . . . he is . . . not what I expected."

Caiaphas exchanged a pleased look with several of the other officials. "And what did you expect?"

"He was offered a crown and the swords of loyal men who would die for him. But he hasn't the courage to face our enemies. He will never fight to liberate Judea from—" Judas stared around as if suddenly fearful of condemning himself by association.

"From . . . Rome?" Caiaphas offered.

Judas licked dry lips and nodded. "From tyranny," he whispered.

"What, then, is his plan?"

"He claims . . . that is, he says . . . he is sent by God."

"Blasphemy!" Caiaphas spat.

The accusation, tinged with horror and satisfaction, was repeated all around the room.

"To establish a heavenly kingdom," Judas hastily added.

"Which will eventually overthrow the authority of Rome?" the high priest demanded. "Well?"

"To rule all peoples and all nations."

"Ha!" Caiaphas exulted. "Treason."

From being scarcely able to speak earlier, now Judas could not stop prattling. "He proclaims that if the Temple is destroyed . . ."

The recitation of Jesus' crimes was interrupted by renewed expressions of outrage.

Judas continued, "He will raise it up again in three days."

"Utterly ridiculous!" a Pharisee shouted.

"Blasphemy and treason," another shrilled.

"Makes himself a god."

"Inciter of rebellion!"

Motioning for quiet, Caiaphas waited for a measure of the noise to subside, then added, "So Jesus declares he will destroy our Temple and rebuild in three days what has taken more than forty years to build?"

Wiping his forehead with the sleeve of his robe, Judas held out imploring hands. "No, not like that. I don't . . . I don't know what he means. But I know this—love your enemies, he says. Pray for those who oppress us, he teaches. He believes God's love will conquer our enemies. His words pluck swords from the hands of loyal men . . . from the grasp of those of us who would fight to drive Rome from our land. Jesus declares he is the Son of God."

At this expression several of the Pharisees tore the lapels of their robes to show their abhorrence.

"The Son . . . of . . . God?" Caiaphas repeated. "You, a man of his inner circle, you will bear witness to his blasphemy?"

Judas looked everywhere but at the high priest, but there was no escape—nothing but hard stares. Finally, he nodded.

Caiaphas strutted around the room, hands clasped behind

his back and satisfaction imprinted on his face. "Then we have all the evidence we need." Turning again toward Judas he inquired, "When? Where?"

"Soon . . . by night . . . the Garden of Gethsemane."

At another snap of Caiaphas's fingers, a secretary tossed a small bag of coins at Judas's feet, forcing him to bend over to pick it up. The traitor hesitated, aware of every eye being on him. Finally he snatched it up and tucked it inside his robe.

When the same guard who had admitted him grabbed Judas's elbow, he flinched and looked stricken. The sentry merely escorted him out of the chamber and closed the door on him.

Caiaphas summoned the captain of the Temple Guard. "Alert Governor Pilate and Tetrarch Herod that we have proof of treason . . . and a plan to arrest the rebel leader."

Chapter 42

After tucking Philo into bed, Claudia heard the murmur of voices. There was a door leading from the private apartments of the palace directly to Pilate's audience chamber. It was behind this portal that Claudia crept to listen while two members of the Jewish High Council made their report to the governor.

"It is all arranged," she overheard one say.

"There will be no commotion," the other reassured. "When Jerusalem wakes tomorrow, it will already be done. No opportunity for trouble."

Pilate growled, "Tell your master that for his sake there had better not be!"

What was to be done? Claudia thought Jesus might be in Jerusalem, but it was said he returned every night to stay with friends in Bethany. How could she locate him? Warn him?

Josephus would know.

After a quick visit to her bedchamber to don a long cloak, Claudia headed for the palace grounds with her maid. Once outside, she swore her maid to secrecy. Then, disguised head to toe, she summoned two of the Jerusalem Sparrows and set out alone through the night.

The streets were deserted as the Passover celebration continued. Families gathered in homes; shops were closed and locked. Through shuttered windows Claudia glimpsed pilgrims and residents seated around meals of lamb and unleavened bread. Her heart beat faster as she neared Josephus's door.

∽∾

In Cassius's quarters in the Antonia, which had previously belonged to Marcus, Cassius shared his news with his former superior. "We've already called in troops from as far as Caesarea and Galilee for the holy days. Expecting riots, especially now that Jesus has come."

Marcus shook his head. "Nothing ever changes in Jerusalem."

"You've seen the man . . . heard him. What did you find?"

Taking a drink of wine from a clay mug, Marcus reported, "He is all you've heard . . . and more."

Cassius snorted. "Liar? Lunatic? Traitor? Blasphemer? A very busy fellow to manage all that."

Setting aside his cup, Marcus stared out the window at the enormous full moon rising over the Mount of Olives. "The truth will be revealed."

Laughing again, Cassius retorted, "Truth? No one wants truth. Too dangerous! Those who hold power have too much to lose if Jesus is . . . whatever it is Jews imagine their messiah to be."

Watching the moon's reflection dancing on the surface of the wine in the cup, Marcus corrected, "Not imagination, Cassius. No ordinary man. Not of this world. I've seen him. He heals the sick and feeds the hungry from nothing, and . . . he raises the dead. You've heard of Lazarus of Bethany, yes? Jesus . . . the perfect general. The perfect king. Everything Rome fears."

Incredulous, Cassius asked, "Is that what you'll tell Pilate? Herod? Caiaphas?"

"Yes," Marcus said forcefully. "If they ask me."

Putting a hand on his friend's shoulder, Cassius said quietly, "Then you'll be crucified alongside your Jewish king."

"I tell you, Cassius," Marcus replied with conviction. "He is a man worth dying for. It may come to that."

The sound of booted feet approaching the door was followed by a loud, hammering knock. "We are sent for! That Jesus character is being arrested tonight. Pilate wants us on alert to put down any trouble."

Marcus stood.

"You see?" Cassius also stood and rebuckled his sword belt. "It has come to this." Even more seriously than before, he advised, "Just follow orders. And if you want to survive the night, stay away from Jesus."

∽✻∽

Claudia reached Josephus's house. A hum of conversation came from within. After paying and dismissing the Sparrows, she knocked urgently on the door. The talk was instantly stilled, replaced a moment later by a babble of questions, and then by Josephus calling for calm. He answered the door and drew Claudia inside.

The small, rather plain dwelling was crowded with friends and relatives sharing the Passover meal together. Josephus did not introduce her but rather took Claudia immediately into his study.

Explaining why she had come, Claudia waited for the scholar's response.

"You're sure?" he inquired.

Claudia nodded vigorously. "The threat is now—real and immediate. We must get word to him. Warn him."

Stroking his beard, Josephus reviewed what she reported. "So Caiaphas called a council, excluding those of us who support Jesus?"

"Caiaphas, yes," she agreed. "A clever and violent man."

"And a frightened one," Josephus added. "And a frightened adder may be even more dangerous. Now, you must get back before you're missed."

Before they reached the street entry, another knock sounded from outside. Josephus and Claudia exchanged startled, apprehensive glances.

"Were you followed?" Josephus asked.

Claudia shook her head. "I don't think so."

The rapping came again, more demanding this time. Josephus leaned toward the panel and called out, "Who is it?"

"Centurion Marcus Longinus, Rabbi. Open the door! I bring pressing news."

The scholar opened the door.

Marcus said, "I'm sorry to interrupt, but the matter—" Then he spotted Claudia behind the scholar's shoulder.

While the dinner guests stared wide-eyed at the latest arrival, Claudia and Marcus saw only each other.

Stepping aside, Josephus opened a lane instantly filled by Claudia and Marcus rushing into an embrace.

"Claudia?" Marcus said with wonder. "You? Here?"

"Oh, Marcus," Claudia sighed. "Tonight, of all nights." And she laid her head against his chest.

"How? Why?"

Recalling her mission, Claudia grasped Marcus's shoulders. She held him at arm's length to look into his eyes. "Marcus, they're going to arrest Jesus."

As if both Claudia and Marcus had been rudely awakened from a pleasant dream, the centurion also shook himself and addressed Josephus. "It's true. I came to ask your advice. I was at the Antonia when the order was given. Armed Herodian soldiers marched out."

"Armed?" Josephus repeated. "They're expecting a fight, then?"

"And Roman troops to back up Herod's men," Marcus confirmed. "If Jesus' disciples resist, they'll be slaughtered. If any survive the night, they'll be crucified by morning."

"But the accusations against Jesus are purely religious matters," Josephus protested.

"Pilate cannot condemn him unless treason against Rome is proven," Claudia concurred, seizing on Josephus's words.

Marcus disagreed. "They will trump something up . . . or, like the Baptizer, he'll just die while in their custody. No. If we can warn him, he must leave tonight. I'll arrange horses. He can get to the seacoast and then sail for Alexandria."

∾∾

It was late, the dead of night after the most memorable Passover seder ever. Jesus brushed the dust from his clothing as he stood. His disciples were asleep. Jono, hand on the hilt of his sword, followed him as he walked. When Jesus came to a solitary place in the garden, he knelt to pray. Jono waited respectfully nearby.

Moonlight fell on Jesus' upturned face and revealed such grief that Jono could hardly bear to look upon him. As Jesus prayed, Jono scanned the shadows of the garden for any enemy who might attack.

After the most recent events, what will tomorrow bring? Jono wondered.

Chapter 43

$\mathcal{J}$oachim, captain of the Temple Guard, advanced at the head of his men along the road that descended into the Kidron Valley from the Temple Mount. The Passover moon stood almost directly overhead, pinning the outlines of gnarled trees onto black pools beneath them. The soldiers all carried blazing torches so that the procession was a giant, flaming serpent that slithered down the slope and up the other side.

"You men keep back thirty paces," he directed. "But come running when I call. Malchus." He addressed the high priest's servant. "You accompany me and Iscariot."

Joachim and Malchus would see that Judas did not escape if he was leading them into a trap . . . or tried to change his mind about betraying Jesus. The entry to the site of the ancient olive-crushing location was just ahead.

Joachim repeated his instructions.

Judas, trapped between Joachim and Malchus, moved like a man made of wood. Walking stiffly, he stared straight ahead. The bag of coins tucked in the fold of his robe clinked with each step like a length of chain.

A figure loomed up from beside the low stone wall that marked the rim of the olive press. It was Jesus of Nazareth.

Judas stood frozen in place as if the weight of the chain around his heart would not allow one more pace forward.

Joachim nudged him and growled, "Get on with it."

"Who are you seeking?" Jesus asked.

"Jesus of Nazareth," Joachim called out. His troops, holding their torches but also clutching swords and clubs, crept nearer.

"I am he," Jesus answered.

The foremost rank of soldiers fell back as if struck. Joachim dropped his sword, then bent to retrieve it.

Once again Jesus inquired, "Who are you seeking?"

"Jesus," Joachim repeated through clenched teeth.

"I told you, I am he," Jesus agreed. "Let these others go."

In a barely audible voice, Judas greeted Jesus, "Hail, Rabbi," and leaned in to kiss Jesus on the cheek.

Immediately the quiet night shattered into a thousand fragments of sound and motion. As Joachim and Malchus advanced on either side of Judas, a burly figure waving a sword rose up in fury, slashing toward the traitor. "You!" Peter shouted.

Judas jumped sideways, colliding with Malchus, who fell into the sweep of the descending blade.

The high priest's servant screamed and clutched his ear. Joachim shouted for his men, but even now they advanced cautiously, a wall of smoking torches held in trembling hands.

"Peter!" Jesus rebuked sharply. "Put your sword away. Shall I not drink the cup that my Father has given me?"

With a last helpless look around, Peter flung the sword into the pit of the olive press. Then he and all of Jesus' friends fled into the night.

Jesus put out his hand and touched Malchus's arm. The servant shrank away, but Jesus persisted. Putting his hands on either side of Malchus's head, he spoke a prayer.

Both agony and bleeding stopped. Malchus, appearing both relieved and confused, touched the ear that had been cut off, now made whole again.

"Am I a rebel that you come to take me with swords and clubs?" Jesus said. "Every day I was with you in the Temple, and you did not lay a hand on me. But this is your hour . . . when darkness reigns."[23]

∽∾

Marcus, riding on Pavor in advance of Josephus on a chestnut mare, reached the head of the Bethany road and halted abruptly. There, strung out across the dark flank of Jerusalem, was the blazing snake of torches—reclimbing the hill toward the Temple.

Josephus drew rein alongside and voiced the conclusion Marcus had already reached. "We're too late."

∽∾

Claudia sat at a dressing table, brushing her hair, when Pilate entered and stood behind her. Dismissing her maid, he regarded her reflection in the mirror.

The intensity of his gaze troubled her. She colored and lowered her eyes. When he touched the back of her neck, she stiffened.

"Where were you this morning?" he inquired. His tone, intended to sound casual, still had an edge of accusation.

Claudia was instantly on her guard. "This morning?" she repeated.

"You and . . . Philo?" Pilate placed his hands on either side of her neck as he awaited her reply.

"The garden," she said.

"Ah, the garden. And out through the servants' gate . . . and into the streets . . . off to greet the new king of the Jews." He squeezed her shoulders, making her wince with pain.

"You're hurting me," she protested, trying to writhe out of his grasp and rise from the chair.

Pilate pressed her down forcefully and held her there. Bending nearer, he hissed in her ear, "Do you know the penalty for treason?"

"Jesus . . . healed . . . your son," she returned.

Instead of releasing his hold at this reminder, Pilate pressed harder. When she tried to get away, he forced her to her knees, then grasped her hair. "If you follow this man, you bare your neck to the ax. Tiberius will execute us both for treason and laugh when he throws Philo to the lions!" Suddenly releasing his grip, he threw her to the floor but continued standing over her.

"Jesus' kingdom is not of this world!" Claudia argued.

"And am I supposed to kneel before him in gratitude?" Pilate demanded. "For the sake of my son, do you expect me to swear allegiance to this king of the Jews?"

"Yes! Yes, Pilate. And for the sake of your soul!"

Mocking her, Pilate offered a bow. "The blood of Jews courses through your veins, not mine," he said with derision.

"And I am no longer ashamed," Claudia fired back.

Pilate stared at her, as if amazed she was not begging to be forgiven. With studied calculation he said, "Jewish blood will flow . . . flow through the streets of Jerusalem . . . before this matter ends. Your blood will mingle with the blood of this Jesus whom you serve."

Dragging her by the arm, a furious Pilate opened the door to the room where Philo lay sleeping. Slinging her around him like tossing rubbish on the dung heap, he flung Claudia onto the floor, then closed the door on her quiet sobs.

Claudia heard the door being locked and Pilate issuing orders to a guard to keep her imprisoned no matter what she said.

Burying her face in both her hands, Claudia remained for a long time on the cold of the stone floor. At last she rose and went to her son, who had somehow miraculously remained asleep through it all. Sitting beside him, Claudia stroked Philo's hair while silent tears streamed down her cheeks.

At last exhaustion overtook her. She lay down next to her son, curling herself protectively around him, and soon fell asleep herself. As she tumbled down the slope of slumber, the darkness of the Jerusalem night receded . . .

Once again she saw the starlit night in the north giving way to the brilliant sunrise of Philo's healing. She witnessed again Jesus carrying Philo on his shoulder. She dreamed of her son running . . . running! . . . for the first time ever, because of the man from Galilee. She heard Philo laugh with pure glee and saw Jesus' approving expression of joy.

Then the scene changed. Pilate appeared on the bank of the stream. Philo dashed toward his father, lifting his arms for an embrace.

But Pilate shoved the child aside. From a coil at his waist Pilate unwrapped a whip and shook its sinister length free of tangles. Shouting a protest, Philo seized his father's legs as Pilate began to strike Jesus across the face with the lash.

Pilate kicked his son away from him so that Philo fell to the ground. Then Pilate alternated striking first Jesus, then Philo, then Jesus again.

At last, tired from the exertion, Pilate flung the whip away and picked up a hammer and a sharp iron spike.

Claudia saw Jesus stretched out on the dirt next to her son. She saw Jesus' hand held out flat on a beam of wood.

She saw Pilate grasp the spike, then raise the hammer to strike. "Nooo," she cried out. She awoke, gasping and racked with sobs that shook her whole frame.

Philo stirred. "Mama?" He reached to embrace her, trying to comfort her.

Hugging her son fiercely, Claudia could not speak. So the two rocked in silence inside the locked bedchamber.

Chapter 44

*T*he night had been infinitely long and exhausting. Now a blood-red dawn pried back the latticework over Philo's windows.

Claudia tapped again on the door and called out to the guard. Her voice was hoarse and feeble sounding from all her attempts. "Please! Please let me out!"

The sentry sounded uneasy as he replied once more, "Sorry, ma'am. Orders."

"But you must! I have to warn my husband. Something terrible is going to happen!"

"What is it, Mama?" Philo piped.

"I must see him. Get word to him. Listen," she said, stooping to the boy's eye level, "Jesus is in danger."

Scanning the room, Philo dashed toward the writing table. He held aloft a quill pen and a stoppered horn of ink.

"Yes! Brilliant boy!" Claudia praised.

Seating herself at Philo's table and pushing aside scraps of parchment lettered in Latin, Greek, and Hebrew alphabets, she wrote, *I have been tormented all night with dreams of Jesus. Have nothing to do with that just man.*

Hurriedly returning to the door, she pounded on it again. This time the guard spoke at once. "I'm sorry, ma'am. Orders are—"

"Yes, I know," Claudia responded impatiently. "Call your officer. I'm pushing a note under the door. See that it is taken to Governor Pilate at once! At once, do you hear?"

∽◡◠∽

Dressed in the purple-bordered toga of office, Pilate paced around the curule throne in his audience chamber as if suspecting the chair of harboring rebellion.

Cassius arrived and saluted.

"Well?" Pilate demanded.

"It's been going on all night," the officer reported. "First the high priest, then Caiaphas's father-in-law, the old high priest, then Lord Caiaphas again. Now the high priest and the other Jews have brought the prisoner to you."

"What do they want me to do with him?" Pilate mused aloud. "Never mind. Show them in."

"Pardon, sir," Cassius responded. "They say they won't come in, meaning they can't. It's a holy day and all, and they're terrified they'll be defiled."

With a frustrated sigh, Pilate nodded his assent. "Tell my servants to bring the chair." He pointed at the X-shaped frame.

The outside air in the courtyard was chilly. A thin film of ice frosted the cobblestones. Pilate ascended the platform, waited for his chair of state to be properly placed, then seated himself.

He was confronted by High Priest Caiaphas and a mob of his henchmen—Herodian guards and Pharisees, numbering about a hundred. In front of them, his face bloody, one eye swollen shut, and his hands bound behind his back, was the man Pilate knew was called Jesus of Nazareth. He looked neither majestic nor threatening.

"Greetings, Governor," Caiaphas said formally.

Pilate frowned. "It's the wrong time for a social visit. What do you want?"

Caiaphas indicated Jesus, as if Pilate might not have noticed him. "We brought a prisoner. A rebel. A traitor against Rome."

And then the whole crowd began to accuse Jesus, saying, "We found this fellow subverting the nation, and forbidding paying taxes to Caesar, and saying that he himself is Christ, a king."

Then Pilate asked him, "Are you the King of the Jews?" Jesus said, "It is as you say."[24]

Laughing at the pitiful spectacle in front of him, Pilate said to the chief priests and the crowd, "I find no fault in this man."

But the mob grew even fiercer, saying, "He stirs up the people, teaching throughout all Judea, beginning in Galilee."

Pilate's face lit up with relief as an idea struck him. When he heard the word *Galilee*, he asked if the man was a Galilean. As soon as he remembered that Jesus belonged to Herod's jurisdiction, he sent Jesus to Herod, who was also in Jerusalem at that time.

It took only five minutes for Caiaphas and his entourage to tramp with Jesus of Nazareth across the frosty stones to Herod's palace. Now when Herod saw Jesus, he was glad, for he had desired for a long time to see this man from Nazareth. Herod had heard many things about the country rabbi and hoped to see some miracle done by him.

Herod questioned Jesus with many words, but Jesus would not answer. The chief priests and scribes vehemently accused him. Then Herod, with his soldiers, treated Jesus with contempt and mockery before they sent him back to Pilate.

Once more, wrapped in a robe thrown over his toga against the cold, Pilate sat on the platform in the courtyard. He had not been able to pass the responsibility onto Herod after all.

Summoning the guards to bring Jesus forward and up to the dais, Pilate rose and faced him. Jesus was taller than the governor by a few inches. The governor studied Jesus closely with a mixture of curiosity and apprehension.

Pilate's trance was finally broken when a soldier arrived bearing a note from Claudia. After hearing its source, Pilate received it coldly, read it, then crumpled it in his fist.

Speaking again to Caiaphas, he demanded, "What accusation do you bring against this man?"

The high priest, exasperated at having to repeat what he'd already recited, said, "If he was not a rebel, we would not have delivered him up to you."

Pilate pulled the robe closer around his shoulders. "I still say he's your problem. Take him and judge him according to your law."

"But," Caiaphas shot back, waving his accusatory index finger, "it is not lawful for us to put anyone to death."

Pilate stared at Caiaphas and then at Jesus. Recollections of the fiasco with the images of Caesar played out in his memory. There had been other complaints about his governing to Caesar as well. How could this problem be played out without causing more damage to Pilate's shaky reputation?

Pointing to the high priest, he said, "You wait here." Gesturing toward Cassius, he said of Jesus, "Bring him inside."

Once back in the audience chamber, Pilate leaned back against his desk, leaving Jesus standing in the center of the floor.

"Are you the king of the Jews?" he said again.

"Are you asking this for yourself? Or has someone else told you this concerning me?"

Pilate was indignant at being queried by a prisoner and a common Jew at that. "Am I a Jew?" Pilate spat. "Your own people . . . the chief priest . . . brought you to me. Why? What have you done?"

Peering past battered eyelids and speaking through cracked and split lips, Jesus said, "My kingdom is not of this world. If my kingdom were of this world, my servants would fight . . . but my kingdom is not from here."

Pilate was dumbfounded. Memories of healings—his own son and reports of hundreds of others, including bringing a dead man back to life—and his wife's dream assaulted Pilate's thoughts from every side. To give him time to clear his mind, he repeated, "Are you a king, then?"

Lifting his chin, Jesus responded, "You speak rightly that I am a king. For this cause I was born, and for this cause I came into the world; that I should bear witness to the truth. Everyone who is of the truth hears my voice."

Pushing himself up from the desk, Pilate walked over to the window and stared out at the morning. Tiberius was no more the son of a god than Augustus was a deity. Yet they ruled the Roman world with absolute authority, the godlike power of life and death. What if this man— the beaten, bloody, much-maligned Galilean—really did have the power of life and death?

Unable to resolve the dilemma, Pilate mused aloud, "What is truth?"

When Jesus did not reply, Pilate summoned Cassius and the guards and prepared to return to the courtyard.

❧

The courtyard below Pilate's raised platform was full of onlookers. Marcus, still dressed as a commoner, stood with Josephus at the back of the throng, near the gate. Marcus tried to gauge the temper of the crowd.

Nearest the platform were the high priest and his devoted followers, the elite of the Jerusalem Sanhedrin, and the wealthiest merchants. Closely ringing those were folk in poorer dress. Marcus judged them to be paid supporters of the high priest, since they didn't speak or make any gestures without first looking at Caiaphas's minions for instructions. And, Marcus noted, many of them possessed a freshly minted shiny silver coin. This was evident because several took the payment out of their clothing to admire it.

There were precious few supporters of Jesus. Marcus saw none of the inner circle of twelve and not many others he recognized. Since Jesus was charged not only with blasphemy but also with treason, punishable by crucifixion, they were probably all in hiding.

Among those closest to the stage were stirring. Some pointed toward the curtain that draped the entry to the palace. Something was happening.

Pilate emerged first, followed by Jesus. Jesus, still bound, was led out with a soldier on either side. Clearing his throat before speaking, Pilate addressed the crowd. "I have questioned him, examining him thoroughly. Here is my conclusion—I find no fault in him at all."

Rumblings of discontent started with Caiaphas and then, encouraged by his subordinates, spread throughout the audience.

"And!" Pilate said, then repeated himself more loudly in order to be heard over the crowd. "You have a custom, and as a gesture of my goodwill, that I release someone to you at Passover." Flipping the tail of his toga across his arm so that the purple hem pointed at Jesus like the image of a darkly crimson lance, Pilate asked, "Do you want me to release the King of the Jews?"

When Caiaphas shouted his reply, spittle flew through the air. "Not this man! Give us . . . bar Abba!"

Speaking when he had not intended, Marcus cried out,

"No!" He had spent years chasing the worst of the rebels, the notorious bar Abba. How could this be happening?

No one heard his lone objection. "Bar Abba!" was the chant, encouraged by Joachim. "Give us bar Abba. Not this man. Free bar Abba!"

Marcus was stunned. Josephus grabbed the centurion's arm, expressing his distress as well. Would the mad hatred and envy of the high priest extend to letting a murderer go free rather than Jesus, the healer?

Turning toward Jesus, Pilate regarded the silent man with consternation and confusion.

Marcus willed Pilate to stand up to the mob. Surely the governor could see this was a huge miscarriage of justice. Surely even ambitious, arrogant Pilate could read the true motives behind the lies and the false witnesses. This demand to release bar Abba proved what an insane turn this affair had taken.

Whispering in Josephus's ear, Marcus said urgently, "This may be a good thing. They may have pushed too far, asking Pilate to release a man who has not only killed Romans and mercenaries but slit Jewish throats too. They've given him reason to resist them."

Josephus did not speak. The scholar's tear-filled eyes regarded Marcus with worry and apprehension. "This man has no sense of justice . . . of right or wrong," Josephus said, indicating Pilate. "He will be swayed by whichever wind blows the tale from here to Caesar's ear."

His face imprinted with frustration and annoyance, as

if he had bitten into a sour apple, Pilate announced, "I will take him and scourge him."

"He's delaying passing sentence. He still hasn't decided," Marcus said. "There's still hope."

Chapter 45

Claudia heard the key grating in the lock of the bed-room door. Before she could approach it, the panel was flung wide with a crash. Pilate stood framed in the entry. He clutched the crumpled piece of parchment.

Slamming the door shut, he strode across the room and threw the writing in Claudia's face. "What is this? A trick to save your precious rabbi? Do you think you can frighten me with ghost stories? Do you?!"

Terrified of his father, Philo ran and crouched behind the writing desk.

A warm tear trickled down Claudia's cheek. She wiped it away. "Listen to me, Pilate. Have nothing to do with this. You know it's wrong!"

Stiffening his back and tightening his jaw, Pilate declared, "This is no matter for me, not at all. I wash my hands of his fate."

"Don't let this happen, then," Claudia begged. "Escort him to the seacoast and send him to safety. Send him to Alexandria . . . anywhere! Jesus is the Messiah, the Son of the living God."

Despite his protest against Claudia's dream, Pilate's face drained of color. He rubbed first his hair and then his jaw with his left hand, a gesture Claudia had seen when he was still very young and was in distress.

When he left without further argument, he did not close the door. Neither did he give the sentry any orders requiring Claudia to stay imprisoned, so she and Philo followed him downstairs.

∽◌∾

Marcus dug his fingernails into his palms and bit his lip until it bled. His stomach was tied in knots.

He had just witnessed Jesus returned to the stage beside Pilate, and the sight sickened him.

Jesus' face was beaten so as to be unrecognizable. His nose was broken and smashed. His tunic hung in rags about his waist, and blood ran so freely down his legs that he left scarlet footprints when he staggered. When the soldiers turned Jesus for Pilate's inspection and approval, the extent of the flogging was revealed. The flesh of Jesus' back was all tattered shreds.

On his head was crammed a crown made of thorns. A corona of acacia branches possessing two-inch-long spikes had been braided together. It was then forced down so it pierced his forehead in multiple places. His hair and beard were matted with gore.

Pulling up his sleeve to avoid the blood flicking into the air whenever Jesus took a breath, Pilate gestured like a conjuror. "Behold the man," he said and waited for the mob's response.

Someone near Marcus vomited, and several turned away from the scene.

Then, beginning with those nearest the high priest, came the chant, "Crucify him! Crucify him!"

"You take him and crucify him," Pilate said. "I find no fault in him."

Sternly, Caiaphas addressed Pilate as he would an erring trainee priest. "We have a law, and by that law he ought to die, because he made himself the Son of God."

Marcus witnessed the effect on Pilate of these words. Something about that phrase gave the governor great concern. Even though there was no possibility of overhearing what was said, Marcus read Pilate's lips.

Addressing Jesus, Pilate demanded, "Where are you from?"

There was no reply from the man who had nearly been beaten to death.

Pilate's next words were so angry they were audible to all. "Are you refusing to speak to me? Don't you know I have the power to crucify you and the power to release you?"

The crowd noise dropped instantly. The governor was angry. In that state he could be dangerous to many more Jews than just the man from Galilee.

From where Jesus summoned any reserve of strength Marcus did not know, but his reply could be heard by those in the courtyard. "You . . . would have no power . . . at all against me . . . unless it had . . . been given to you . . . from above. So those who . . . delivered me to you . . . have the greater sin."

Waving for silence, Pilate spoke again to the mob. "This is an innocent man. I find no fault."

It was then that Caiaphas used his most powerful weapon. Quoting exactly the last words Pilate's mentor Sejanus had heard as he was garroted for treason, Caiaphas shouted, "If you let this man go, you are *no friend of Caesar*! Whoever makes himself a king speaks against Caesar."

"We have no king but Caesar," the mob chanted. "Anyone who says otherwise is no friend of Caesar."

Marcus knew the struggle for Pilate's soul had been lost, even before the governor drew his toga more closely around him. Marcus saw Pilate give up any attempt to free Jesus, any show of resisting the mob, when he seated himself in the Chair of Judgment.

Flicking his hand toward the bloody prisoner in a gesture of dismissal, Pilate said spitefully, "Behold . . . your . . . king."

"Away with him!" Caiaphas demanded.

"Away with him! Crucify him! We have no king but Caesar!"

"Shall I crucify your king?" Pilate asked, even though he already knew what the response would be. The official letter about this event would reflect that Pilate had tried several times to satisfy the high priest with a lesser punishment. It wasn't really Pilate's fault, his posture said. This course of action was forced on him.

"No!" Marcus shouted to those around him. "Spare

him!" he cried to onlookers who moved away from him as they would from a madman or a leper.

"We have no king but Caesar," chanted the mob. "Crucify him! Crucify him!"

∾∽

It was the worst of Claudia's dream . . . and more. On the hill called Golgotha, Jesus of Nazareth was crucified between two thieves.[25] Claudia stood with Marcus, Josephus, and Philo in a cleft in the rock. The edge of the precipice on which they stood was only a short distance from the crosses. The skull-like knoll was just west of Jerusalem. Curious passersby noticed the activity. Some inquired the name of the condemned. Most made the sign against the evil eye and rushed on about their business.

The site was in full view from Pilate's palace and from the Temple Mount. Politics and religion, ego and greed, fear and arrogance had conspired to kill an innocent man.

Claudia could not bear to watch, yet could not look away. "Let me take you and the boy away," Marcus suggested. "Or at least Philo. He doesn't need to witness this."

"No," Claudia replied. "I won't leave him alone back there with Pilate, and I must . . . be here."

Nearer the foot of the cross stood Jesus' mother. Sheltering her, his face a mask of grief, was John, the son of Zebedee.

The sun was still shining, but something was wrong with the light. Even though it was a cloudless midday, everything seemed dimmed, as though the air were full of smoke.

A knot of soldiers skirmished over Jesus' clothes. "Pitiful stuff!" one remarked. "Tear 'em all into rags and be done, I say."

"Hold," another retorted. "Not his tunic. I'll toss you for it."

"They divided my garments among them," Josephus murmured. "And for my clothing they cast lots."

"A prophet?" Claudia asked.

"King David."

"So all this"—Claudia fluttered a despairing hand like a wounded bird—"was known."

Sighing heavily, Josephus agreed. "Recorded in the psalms and the prophets both."

High Priest Caiaphas trudged up the hill from the caravan route to make certain the execution was properly carried out. Surrounded by his minions, Caiaphas could not help gloating even in victory. "If you are the Son of God," he said with a sneer, "come down! Show us your power. Even now we can be convinced."

With an elaborate shrug, the priest communicated that there was no reaction to his request. "Just what I expected," he intoned.

Appreciative laughter came from his underlings.

The others in his band took turns jeering. "No fire from heaven. No rescuing legion of angels. No danger to the Temple today."

The bleeding, broken figure of Jesus struggled upright for breath, cried out in agony, and slumped down again. Each of Caiaphas's supporters strove to outdo the rest in wittiness. "You claim you saved others. Can't you save yourself?"

The day grew darker and the breeze rose.

"The sun . . . looks gray," Marcus observed.

A *khamseen* wind out of the desert tossed handfuls of gravel at the soldiers and the priests and tore at their clothing, but Claudia and those next to her were sheltered by the rock.

Overhead the most enormous cloud of starlings Claudia had ever witnessed circled aimlessly. The precision of their formations broke into ragged fragments—disordered, like all of creation appeared to be.

In the distance something rumbled like thunder, though no clouds were gathering over the mountains. "Will you stay here with Josephus?" Marcus said, his voice hoarse with emotion. "I won't be long. There's something I have to do."

Pavor was tied to a tree in a garden at the bottom of the hill. Claudia watched Marcus open a saddlebag. From it he took the bronzed circlet of his *corona obsidionalis*.

The unexplained darkness and the gale had unnerved the priests, who hurried away. The soldiers squatted on the ground, sheltering themselves as best they could.

So Marcus was almost alone when he approached the foot of the cross. Kneeling beside where blood trickled down the wooden upright, Marcus deposited the corona upon the ground. He was choking back a sob, but Claudia still heard him declare, "Hail, *Aluf Ha'Alufim*, champion of champions. I tried to give you this once before, after you healed Carta, but you would not take it. Even so, it has always properly been yours."

"For this . . . I was kept." Jesus gasped for enough

breath to utter those few words. And then, summoning his remaining strength, Jesus forced himself up on the agony of the nails to shout, "IT IS FINISHED!"

The gigantic cloud of starlings launched themselves skyward. An inverted funnel, they spiraled upward, tighter and tighter, as if they would pierce the heavens. When they disappeared from view, so did the last of the light.

Day was swallowed up in night. A continuous peal of thunder boomed, smacked against the palace and the Temple Mount, and returned as a reverberating echo.

The ground began to roll like a ship at sea, pitching men headlong.

Where had the clouds come from? Suddenly a torrent of rain was falling from the sky, sluicing down as if to blot out any trace of the scene.

Blood and water flowed down and over the corona.

Standing, Marcus shouted at the soldiers, "Truly this was the Son of God!"

Chapter 46

Marcus was in the group that accompanied the wealthy Joseph of Arimathea, who had become a disciple of Jesus, to Governor Pilate, asking permission to bury Jesus' body.

"It's a new tomb I had built for my father," Joseph said. "Just at the bottom of the hill, not far from—"

"Yes, yes." Pilate waved a hand dismissively. "Take the corpse and be done. I've already spent too much time on this insignificant matter."

So it was that Marcus was present when Jesus' body, bathed for the last time and wrapped in a linen shroud, was placed in the grave. Just before the heavy stone disk was rolled across the opening, Marcus stood beside the stone shelf where the body lay. Near Jesus' feet Marcus placed two crowns—the one of thorns from Jesus' brow and his own *corona obsidionalis*.[26]

"Jesus," Marcus whispered as he gazed upon the body, "you have won the true crown of victory . . . the highest honor, woven from the thorns of this broken world. You alone have saved us all in this final battle."

The tears of the centurion fell upon the crown of thorns and then on the bronze circlet of his own battlefield award. "Truly you are the Son of God."

∽∾∽

It was night in Jerusalem. The city was quiet, but whether from mourning or terror was not clear. Claudia and Pilate sat together in the governor's audience hall. Though nothing official was pending, Pilate absentmindedly seated himself on the judgment seat.

The city was full of wild tales—stones splitting apart, foundations of great buildings moved, the heavy brocade veil of the Temple mysteriously ripped in two from top to bottom, holy men who had died being raised to life and walking around the city.[27]

When Cassius and a squad of soldiers entered, Claudia stood to leave, but Pilate held up his hand in a command. "Stay. This will interest you."

Cassius reported, "He is buried. The tomb is sealed and the stamp of Rome is upon it, as you ordered."

"One more thing," Pilate commanded. "It seems Lord Caiaphas is still not satisfied. 'Guard the tomb,' he said, 'so that impostor's friends don't steal the body and then pretend he's alive again.' So do it. I want a day-and-night watch posted there."[28]

"Done." Cassius saluted before he exited with the legionaries.

All the smoking oil lamps and all the flickering candles

could not remove the tangible gloom that hung over the palace.

Philo peered out from behind a curtain, his expression entreating his mother. *Can this be? The kind and gentle man who healed me and countless others is now dead at the command of my father?*

Tears brimmed as Claudia's eyes met Philo's. There could be only one reason the kindness of Jesus toward the boy had not touched Pilate's heart.

How very much Philo looked like Marcus, Claudia thought in awe. Surely Pilate had seen the face of his rival in the boy. The courage and strength of Marcus was unmistakable in the set of Philo's mouth. The fierce goodness of Marcus was clear in Philo's eyes. In that instant the truth was clear to Claudia: All along Pilate had recognized that Marcus was Philo's father.

Claudia nodded at Philo. Her glance gave him permission to follow and keep watch. Her expression told him to be strong; the story was not finished yet.

Philo lifted his chin defiantly. Then, unseen by Pilate, he slipped away, pursuing the soldiers and seeking the disciples of Jesus.

At last Pilate turned toward Claudia. "Well?" he mocked. "This Jesus, son-of-God . . . your Jewish Messiah . . . is mortal, it seems. Dead. A piece of meat laid out on a stone slab. Your Jewish dreams are as worthless as dust. Where is your healer now? Your giver of life? This Jewish Savior of the world?"

She regained her confidence. "He did say it, you know.

Told us he would rise from death. Destroy this temple and he will raise it up again in three days, he said."

Pilate snorted. "The ravings of a madman! Rantings! The Temple of Herod? Forty years in the making."

"Jesus was not," Claudia corrected, "speaking of stone and mortar. He was speaking of his own body."

Pilate's complexion changed. In the dusky yellow light it became green. "He's dead and there's an end of it," he said petulantly.

But Claudia could tell that doubt and fear existed. He scanned the corners of the empty chamber.

She challenged him fiercely. "Yes, Pilate, friend of Caesar. Jesus of Nazareth is dead tonight, by your order. But he promised he will rise from death."

"The tomb is sealed with lead and stamped with the seal of Rome," he shot back.

She tilted her head. "Do you really think the mark of Rome can keep such power from breaking forth? The grave cannot hold Jesus captive. And then it is written that all men will bow and confess that Jesus, Messiah, is King of Kings and Lord of Lords. Even you, one day, will be on your knees before him."

His eyes took on a furtive, hunted expression. "Leave me!" Pilate shouted and hurled his cup of wine across the room.

Claudia rose from her chair with the dignity of a beloved daughter of a king . . . only she knew in her heart that her father was not Caesar, but truly the God of Abraham, Isaac, and Jacob. "I pity you," she said quietly.

Then she gathered the train of her gown and swept from the room.

She knew that Pilate's sleep from this night on would be haunted by nightmares of the rabbi from Nazareth.

Epilogue

THREE DAYS LATER

*T*he sun rose from behind the distant hills, casting a golden light over the stones of Jerusalem. Claudia sat alone on her balcony and gazed toward the hill of execution and the mound of boulders outside the city walls that marked the entrance to the garden location of Jesus' tomb.

Each day Philo had returned to report to Claudia the rumors in the city and the terror of Jesus' disciples. Marcus was among the followers of Jesus as a defender, Philo told her. The centurion slept across the threshold of their refuge with his sword drawn.

Now dawn was breaking on the very day Jesus had spoken of as the morning of his victory.

"Three days," Claudia whispered as she stood and scanned the streets beyond the governor's compound. "You promised us, Lord . . . three days."

As if in reply, a lone bird soared high above her, then

swooped to perch on the stone railing of the parapet. She knew at once it was Starling, returned somehow from wherever she had been. Claudia gasped as the tiny creature considered her with golden eyes, then sang sweetly. *Hope!* he cried. *Hope!*

The heavy city gates swung open as a beam of blinding sunlight topped the rise.

The city, still packed with tens of thousands of Passover pilgrims, was just waking. The shofar blew from the Temple pinnacle. The single note seemed to be joined by ten thousand others as the echo resounded across the land, announcing the beginning of a new day.

Philo suddenly appeared through the gates. Claudia spotted him dashing—skipping!—over the paving stones. The boy's eager face turned upward toward the parapet where Claudia watched.

Just behind him a troop of soldiers clambered along in broken formation. Even at this distance, Claudia could see something was terribly wrong with the troop. In spite of the shouts of their commander, they struggled to stand at attention. Instead of marching, they stumbled forward, turning to peer back over their shoulders in terror as though they had been routed by a fierce enemy.

Claudia straightened, clasped her hands, and gazed heavenward in joy as the last blast of the shofar died away. "So it is true. Oh, Lord, it is true!"

When she looked down, she again located Philo running ahead of the soldiers. He scattered a small flock of sheep being moved toward the meat market.

"Philo," she called, "it is three days!"

"Mother!" Philo shouted up to her as he rounded the corner. "It is all just as he promised. Jesus is not dead, but alive! I have seen him. Jesus is risen!"[29]

Notes

CHAPTER 13
1. Read the story and message of John the Baptizer in Luke 3:1–20

CHAPTER 20
2. Isaiah 7:14
3. Micah 5:2
4. Isaiah 9:6 KJV

CHAPTER 30
5. Isaiah 35:5–6 NASB
6. Isaiah 35:4
7. Isaiah 35:6

CHAPTER 32
8. Matthew 6:24–32
9. See Matthew 8:1–4
10. See Matthew 5:43–44; Luke 6:31, 45

CHAPTER 33
11. See Matthew 8:5–13

CHAPTER 35
12. Matthew 18:23–35 NKJV

CHAPTER 36
13. See Matthew 13:1–35; Mark 4:26-29

CHAPTER 38
14. See Matthew 26:52
15. See Matthew 16:13–20

CHAPTER 40
16. Zechariah 9:9 NKJV
17. See Matthew 21:12–13
18. Psalm 69:4, 9 NASB

CHAPTER 41
19. See Matthew 24
20. Matthew 24:4–6, 9, 14–16, 21–22, 29–31, 36, 42 NKJV
21. Matthew 25:31–46 NKJV
22. See Matthew 26:1–2

CHAPTER 43
23. See Luke 22:47–53

CHAPTER 44
24. See Luke 22:66–23:23

CHAPTER 45
25. See Matthew 27:33–56

CHAPTER 46
26. See Matthew 27:57–60
27. See Matthew 27:51–53
28. See Matthew 27:62–66.

EPILOGUE
29. See Matthew 28:1–15

AUTHORS' NOTE

Authors' Note

*J*ésus clearly believed in the power of stories. He told parables—stories—to stretch the minds and transform the hearts of his listeners. We too believe in the life-changing power of stories, and that's why we're passionate about writing fiction.

In every work of our fiction, there is truth, based on research, and there is imagination, based on our minds and perspectives. We weren't here, on this earth, as Jesus walked among the people, but through the verses of Scripture and our imagination, we have portrayed to the best of our ability what he might have said and the way in which he might have said it. *Behold the Man* is how we imagine the events might have happened for Claudia, for Philo, for Marcus, for Carta, for Josephus the Elder, and for all the other characters in this story whose lives, bodies, and hearts were transformed by Jesus. It also traces the path of Jesus' days on earth, including some of his miracles and words, as well as his arrest, trial, and crucifixion.

Can lives, bodies, and hearts truly be transformed today as they were in the days when Jesus walked the earth? With

Jesus, *anything* is possible! Through *Behold the Man*, may the Messiah come alive to you . . . in more brilliance than ever before. And may you look forward someday to the realm of heaven, where the desires of your heart will be met and your questions answered.

Bodie & Brock Thoene

Discussion Questions

1. In what ways is Claudia held captive by her circumstances? How does she choose to make the best of them?

2. Have you ever felt trapped by the parameters of your own life? If so, how did you handle that situation? If you are in the midst of difficulties right now, how does Claudia's story encourage you to have a long-term perspective?

3. Philo and Jono rescue a bird with a broken wing. "She may grieve so much for her family, who have all flown south by now, that her heart may break like her wing. There is no mending a broken heart," Jono says.

    But Philo insists, "Mother will fix her wing. I will tend her heart . . . feed her and sing to her."

    Do you believe it's possible to mend a broken heart? If so, how? How might you be part of that "mending" in someone's life today?

4. Jono had every reason to hate Marcus. Their hand-to-hand battle spelled the end of Jono's nation, and Marcus

enslaved Jono, later giving him as a gift to serve Philo and Claudia. Why then does Jono consider Marcus as a friend and say, "Yes. I owe him everything"?

How might the two friends' story impact your treatment of those you consider enemies?

5. It has been eight years since Claudia and Marcus pledged their love to each other, planned their escape, and were betrayed by Pilate—someone Marcus considered as a friend. Now, though Claudia and Marcus still love each other, they can only gaze at each other from afar.

Have you ever loved—and lost—someone? Or been betrayed by a friend? If so, how has that experience influenced how you relate to others?

6. Josephus says, "The choices made by ordinary men and women can profoundly alter the course of history. If true, then all words spoken and deeds, done or not done, may be important." Do you agree? Why or why not? When has a single choice or a few words altered your life?

7. Imagine you are one of the people hearing John the Baptist speak in the valley of the Jordan: "The time has come for you to change your hearts! Look inside. You know the truth about yourselves. Rend your hearts, and not your garments. The Almighty is giving you one last chance!" How would you respond to his challenge? Which of the people below would your response be more like, and why?

DISCUSSION QUESTIONS

- A Pharisee: "Watch how you speak. We are true sons of Abraham!"
- Quintus: "This fellow's more abusive than a nagging wife!"
- Marcus: "He is no one Rome or Herod Antipas need worry about. . . . Son of David. It's a myth. Nothing more."
- Carta: "Who is the Son of David?"

8. Pilate's first work as governor is to incite a riot by carrying foreign gods into Jerusalem. Pilate insists the people are rebels. Marcus counters, "They are simple folk. Simple folk who happened to be in the street when the Zealots struck."

    Pilate shouts back, "What was I to do? Insult Caesar? Hide his images as if we were frightened to enter Jerusalem? This city belongs to Rome, and Tiberius *is* Rome. This is his property, isn't it?"

    Marcus chose not to reply. If you had to reply, what would you have said?

9. When Cassius and Marcus encounter a father, mother, and crippled child on the way to the Sea of Galilee, the father tells them, "We hear a rabbi named Jesus of Nazareth is there. Teaching our people the ways of peace."

    The mother adds, "They say he heals many diseases by the power of God . . . we are taking our son there."

    If you were Marcus, would you have stayed to listen to Jesus, or ridden away, back to Jerusalem? Why?

10. At first Marcus didn't believe the claims of John the Baptist or the claims of Jesus. In chapter 23, what events changed Marcus's mind about both? And led him to ride with Kuza all night so Jesus could work his miracle on Boaz?

11. When Jesus says Boaz is healed, and tells Kuza to go home, Kuza believes him . . . and goes home. Miryam, who has seen the boy's healing with her own eyes, flees Kuza and Joanna's home. Marcus pleads with her: "Come with me, to see the power of this man. To hear him. Maybe he can help."

    But she spats back, "Go see this healer yourself! I'm not sick. You're the one, not me . . . I'm content with my life the way it is."

    Why do you think Kuza and Miryam responded so differently? Which character most accurately reflects what your response would be? Explain.

12. If you could ask Jesus for any miracle today, what would you ask for, and why?

About the Authors

*B*ODIE and BROCK THOENE (pronounced *Tay-nee*) have written over seventy works of historical fiction. That these bestsellers have sold more than thirty-five million copies and won eight ECPA Gold Medallion Awards affirms what millions of readers have already discovered— that the Thoenes are not only master stylists but experts at capturing readers' minds and hearts.

In their timeless classic series about Israel (The Zion Chronicles, The Zion Covenant, The Zion Legacy, The Zion Diaries), the Thoenes' love for both story and research shines. With The Shiloh Legacy and *Shiloh Autumn* (poignant portrayals of the American Depression), The Galway Chronicles (dramatic stories of the 1840s famine in Ireland), and the Legends of the West (gripping tales of adventure and danger in a land without law), the Thoenes have made their mark in modern history. In the A.D. Chronicles they stepped seamlessly into the world of Jerusalem and Rome, in the days when Yeshua walked the earth. Now, in the Jerusalem Chronicles, the Thoenes continue that journey through the most crucial events in the life of Yeshua on earth.

Bodie, who has degrees in journalism and communications, began her writing career as a teen journalist for her local newspaper. Eventually her byline appeared in prestigious periodicals such as *U.S. News & World Report*, *The American West*, and the *Saturday Evening Post*. She also worked for John Wayne's Batjac Productions and ABC Circle Films as a writer and researcher. John Wayne described her as "a writer with talent that captures the people and the times!"

Brock has often been described by Bodie as "an essential half of this writing team." With degrees in both history and education, Brock has, in his role of researcher and story-line consultant, added the vital dimension of historical accuracy. Due to such careful research, the Zion Covenant and Zion Chronicles series are recognized by the American Library Association, as well as Zionist libraries around the world, as classic historical novels and are used to teach history in college classrooms.

Bodie and Brock have four grown children—Rachel, Jake, Luke, and Ellie—and nine grandchildren. Their children are carrying on the Thoene family talent as the next generation of writers, and Luke produces the Thoene audio books. Bodie and Brock divide their time between Hawaii, London, and Nevada.

www.thoenebooks.com
www.familyaudiolibrary.com

THOENE FAMILY CLASSICS™
THOENE FAMILY CLASSIC HISTORICALS
BY BODIE AND BROCK THOENE
Gold Medallion Winners

The Zion Covenant

*Vienna Prelude**
Prague Counterpoint
Munich Signature
Jerusalem Interlude
Danzig Passage
*Warsaw Requiem**
London Refrain
Paris Encore
Dunkirk Crescendo

The Zion Chronicles

*The Gates of Zion**
A Daughter of Zion
The Return to Zion
A Light in Zion
*The Key to Zion**

The Shiloh Legacy

*In My Father's House**
A Thousand Shall Fall
Say to This Mountain
Shiloh Autumn

The Galway Chronicles

Only the River Runs Free*
Of Men and of Angels
Ashes of Remembrance*
All Rivers to the Sea

The Zion Legacy

Jerusalem Vigil
Thunder from Jerusalem
Jerusalem's Heart
Jerusalem Scrolls
Stones of Jerusalem
Jerusalem's Hope

A.D. Chronicles

First Light
Second Touch
Third Watch
Fourth Dawn
Fifth Seal
Sixth Covenant
Seventh Day
Eighth Shepherd
Ninth Witness
Tenth Stone
Eleventh Guest
Twelfth Prophecy

Zion Diaries

The Gathering Storm
Against the Wind

Jerusalem Chronicles

When Jesus Wept
Take This Cup
Behold the Man

THOENE FAMILY CLASSIC ROMANCE
BY BODIE THOENE

Love Finds You in Lahaina, Hawaii

THOENE FAMILY CLASSIC
AMERICAN LEGENDS
Legends of the West
BY BROCK AND BODIE THOENE

Legends of the West
VOLUME ONE

Sequoia Scout
The Year of the Grizzly
Shooting Star

Legends of the West
VOLUME TWO

Gold Rush Prodigal
Delta Passage
Hangtown Lawman

Legends of the West
VOLUME THREE

Hope Valley War
The Legend of Storey County
Cumberland Crossing

Legends of the West
VOLUME FOUR

The Man from Shadow Ridge
Cannons of the Comstock
Riders of the Silver Rim

Legends of Valor
BY JAKE THOENE AND LUKE THOENE

Sons of Valor
Brothers of Valor
Fathers of Valor

THOENE FAMILY CLASSIC CONTEMPORARY
BY BODIE, BROCK, AND LUKE THOENE

Icon

THOENE CLASSIC CONTEMPORARY
BY BODIE AND BROCK THOENE

Beyond the Farthest Star

THOENE CLASSIC NONFICTION
BY BODIE AND BROCK THOENE

Little Books of Why

Why a Manger?
Why a Shepherd?
Why a Star?
Why a Crown?

Writer-to-Writer

Making the Call
LANCE EASLEY, WITH BROCK THOENE

Face to Face with Jesus
SAMAA HABIB, WITH BODIE THOENE

THOENE FAMILY CLASSIC SUSPENSE
BY JAKE THOENE

Chapter 16 Series

Shaiton's Fire
Firefly Blue
Fuel the Fire

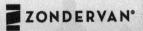